DRAWING

DRAWING

Daniel M. Mendelowitz

STANFORD UNIVERSITY

HOLT, RINEHART AND WINSTON, INC.

New York   Chicago   San Francisco   Toronto   London

2   3   4   5   6   7   8   9

Preface

Both connoisseurs and artists are rediscovering the rewards and pleasures of drawing, the activity which Cennino Cennini in the fourteenth century considered "both the necessary foundation of practice for all and a natural intellectual inclination of the talented." Only a generation ago drawing as it had been practiced in the past seemed about to disappear; artists, art lovers, and picture buyers, entranced with exciting new developments in the world of painting, appeared impervious to the charms of drawing. The enthusiastic response of the contemporary art world to this rediscovered realm of activity can be judged by studying some of the drawings in this volume produced in the last few years. Drawings are being more eagerly sought by collectors than ever before, more drawings or facsimiles are being hung on the walls of homes, and more exhibitions of drawings and books featuring drawings are available each year.

The revived interest is also evident in the classroom. Two decades ago drawing as it had been taught for generations almost ceased to exist as a significant part of the curricula of art schools and of college and university art departments. The procedures and recipes of the nineteenth century upon which most drawing instruction was based seemed incapable of satisfying the needs of the newer generation of artists and teachers. There was a period of bewilderment and a search for new methods. Today the desire to shake off the rigid and restrictive aspects of academic training remains, but certain of the traditional disciplines are again emerging as functional and necessary elements in the training of artists. Drawing has reappeared as one of the cornerstones of art training, although it is a new concept of drawing, one that incorporates the attitudes and concepts of the Bauhaus and the inner discipline of modern painting with the meaningful aspects of tradition. Now most colleges, universities, and professional art schools, like the academies of the past, again commence the artist's training with drawing, and while much latitude prevails as to the content and procedures in today's drawing classes, certain convictions seem widely shared. First it is generally agreed that, well taught, drawing establishes a habit that is fundamental to expression in the visual arts, the habit of looking, seeing, and expressing one's perceptions in graphic, painterly, or plastic form. Second, drawing familiarizes the beginner with certain elements of the artist's vocabulary—line, value, texture, form, space—and also color, for even when drawing is limited to black and white, an increased consciousness of color often accompanies the greater awareness of the external world that is experienced when individuals commence to draw. To illustrate the extent to which color has served the drawing artist, sixteen of the selected drawings in this book have been reproduced in full color. In the final analysis it is the more incisive awareness of the concrete, visual world that is the artist's most precious heritage, and it is stimulated more by drawing than by any other activity.

Many of the students now enrolled in drawing classes are challenged by the discipline of this old, yet always fresh, mode of artistic expression. They do not intend to become professional artists and consider their studio experience primarily a rich new dimension to a liberal education. To them it is a very practical and effective way of sharpening their perception of the arts, of honing their sensibilities to a finer awareness of the intellectual and sensual enjoyment available in the arts. The advantage of active involvement with materials and techniques, in creative collaboration with reading, listening, and observation, is that a much higher level of intensification can be achieved than when the art experience is communicated solely through words and pictures. Whether the reader is a professional artist, a student with professional ambitions, or an alert, uncommitted observer with a lively interest in the arts, it is the total engagement of mind with eyes, hands, body, and feelings that will make possible drawing as a genuinely creative act and bring about the taste and judgment essential to artistic growth and enlightened connoisseurship.

This book has, therefore, been planned to extend horizons by surveying the art of drawing from a variety of viewpoints, both internal and external: externally by first examining the scope of drawing (Chapter 1), and then surveying the history of drawing (Chapters 2 through 12); internally by analyzing the elements involved in the art of drawing. This analysis includes both a survey of the role of the art elements—line, value, form, and texture (Chapters 13 through 15), followed by an evaluation of the principal media used in drawing (Chapters 16 and 17). And because, in the ultimate analysis, the arts must always be seen as an extension of man's imagination and the creative spirit, the final chapter inquires into the role of imagination as a catalyzer to both appreciation and expression (Chapter 18). Since verbal understanding alone does not insure visual sensitivity, the text has been kept to a minimum to permit the 330 reproductions from the master works of artists of all ages to speak for themselves.

The author has wanted in preparing this book to provide a broad introduction to the art of drawing, both for those who are learning to draw and for those learning about drawing as an art. It is hoped that these pages will open vistas to beginners and enrich the technical and esthetic background of those who already know and love the art.

D.M.M.

Tours, Indre et Loire, France
May, 1966

Contents

List of Illustrations

COLOR PLATES

BLACK AND WHITE ILLUSTRATIONS

Chapter 1

part one

INTRODUCTION

1

WHAT IS DRAWING?

In studying the literature of art and artists, one cannot help noticing the frequency with which words that carry a special implication of affection appear in discussions of drawing. "Delightful," "intimate," "spontaneous," "direct," "unlabored" are used repeatedly, and they reveal the love that many critics and connoisseurs have for this particular form of artistic expression. In explaining this fondness for drawing, one is forced to the conclusion that it is based on the very informal and personal nature of the body of master drawings that form our legacy from the past. Unlike more elaborately finished works, these drawings provide an intimate contact with the act of creation and thereby permit the viewer to come closer to the kernel of the artist's being. Like notes in a diary or a notebook, drawings are frequently direct notations made by the artist for himself alone, free of artificial elaboration or the excess finish that often impresses the uninitiated who might value a work of art in terms of the amount of labor involved rather than in terms of its power of expression. Most paintings, prints, and sculptures of the past were thoughtfully planned and carefully finished; in fact, the word "finished" often implied a polished perfection of execution that obliterated all signs of the artist's hand at work. Achieving this high polish frequently represented a concession by the artist to the tastes of his patron or the conventions of the day, either or both of which might be to some degree in conflict with the artist's own sensibilities. To the perceptive observer these overrefinements of execution, when foreign to the temperament of the artist, stand like a barrier to prevent direct response to the

work. Drawings and sketches usually demand of the artist only that he satisfy himself.

Comparing Raphael's study for the "Alba Madonna" with the completed painting can be very revealing (Figures 1–1a, 1b). In such a drawing, one comes close to the impulses that formed the work: one can sense the process of gestation that accompanied its creation. An exciting sense of participation occurs as one feels the artist's enthusiasms, his sense of discovery, the lively interplay of hand, eye, mind, brush, pen or pencil, and paper; all the alive and intensely human aspects of the creative act.

Another factor also helps explain the appeal and power of drawing. The incomplete or fragmentary work, precisely because it does not provide a fully developed statement, may impel a greater play of the observer's imagination than does a more finished work. The increased appeal of the work of art which suggests rather than provides a complete statement has been sensitively explored in E. H. Gombrich's *Art and Illusion*. A certain level of ambiguity, he points out, demands imaginative involvement to complete the meaning of the work. The very act of imaginative involvement, operating in conjunction with the vague and undefined elements in the work, permits the viewer to interpret these undefined elements in terms most meaningful to himself. Thus ambiguity in art operates like the ink-blots in a Rorschach test, permitting the viewer to see what he wants to see. Our mind supplies the unspecified elements in a "Study for the Black Countess" (Figure 1–2) by Toulouse-Lautrec. The sketchy jottings evoke an image of elegant trappings, a haughty coachman, and the extravagance of fashionable late-nineteenth-century Paris. By contrast, a carefully finished drawing achieves a kind of closure through its finite forms that excludes such imaginative wanderings on the part of the viewer.

FIGURE 1–2

Henri de Toulouse-Lautrec (1864–1901; French). "Study for the Black Countess," *Sketch Book*, 1880–1881. Pencil, 6⅜" x 10". *Courtesy of The Art Institute of Chicago, Robert Alexander Waller Fund.*

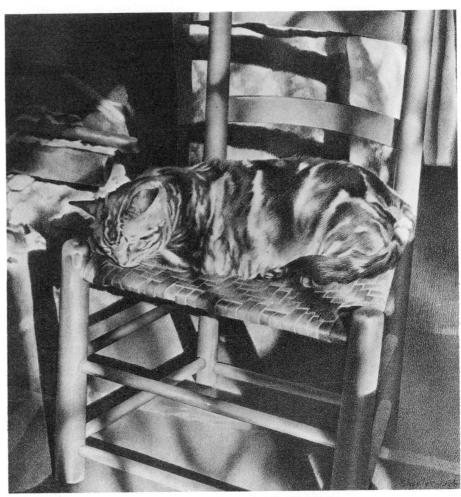

FIGURE 1–3

Charles Sheeler (1883–1965; American).
"Feline Felicity." Conté, 14⅛" x 13¼".
The Fogg Art Museum, Harvard University,
Cambridge, Massachusetts, Louise E. Bettens Fund.

If one observes the small sculptured models of Rodin or studies Michelangelo's unfinished slaves in the Gallery of the Academy in Florence, he discovers that the same magic that distinguishes the drawn study resides in the sculptor's visualizing sketch or unfinished work. Much modern painting recognizes and utilizes the expressive power of the evocative fragment; and in another respect, also, certain schools of modern painting retain elements of drawing to a greater degree than did painting in the past. Almost all modern painting which is "painterly" recognizes the power that comes when the gesture with which the medium is applied is evident in the finished work.

Excluding a few highly finished drawings such as Sheeler's "Feline Felicity" (Figure 1–3) that intrigue us by their virtuosity and polished perfection, most drawings appeal, as did the Toulouse-Lautrec "Study for the Black Countess" because of the immediacy of the artist's expression and the direct contact established between the viewer and the work. This sense of immediacy seems to relate both to the spontaneity of execution and the fragmentary nature of the work. Before discussing the art of drawing in more detail it may be wise to define drawing and survey the scope of activities included in this familiar but seldom-scrutinized world.

Definition of Drawing

Drawing has been defined in various ways. The *Oxford Universal Dictionary* defines it "delineation by pen, pencil or crayon," and then by way of clarification adds "delineation as distinct from painting." The *Encyclopedia of World Art* says, "The word drawing covers in general all those representations in which an image is obtained by marking, whether simply or elaborately, upon a surface which constitutes the background." Very sensibly the *Encyclopedia* continues, "In this sense drawing is the basis of every pictorial experience, particularly that of painting. In modern times drawing has become associated with a particular tradition and special artistic techniques: its methods comprise simple delineation to which may be added effects of light and shadow (produced by hatching or washes), highlights, and cursory color notes." Sheeler's "Feline Felicity" provides an excellent example of "added effects of light and shade." Even this broadened definition does not include all of what is now considered drawing, since "hatches and washes" comprise only a small portion of the techniques currently used to produce variations of light and dark. Furthermore, contemporary artists employ extremely varied techniques and materials for a wide variety of purposes beyond the creation of light and shadow effects. In the work of many contemporary artists light and dark patterns and textures are valued for their own esthetic character and expressive effects, quite independently of their effectiveness in conveying an impression of light and shade—as can be observed in a drawing by Jackson Pollock (Figure 1–4). Irrespective of medium or technique, drawing is frequently identified with the beginning or inventive steps in the creation of a work of art, but this does not preclude the possibility of a drawing being carried to an elaborate degree of finish and existing as a self-sufficient work of art in its own right. All of this suggests a very simple definition which might read: "Those forms of graphic notation in which an image is obtained by marking upon a background."

No definition, even though it is broad and all-inclusive, can give a sense of the range and variety of activities covered by the word *drawing*. A brief review of various broad categories of drawing will help extend our picture of this field. Three general divisions come to mind: (1) the drawing that is a record of what is seen, (2) the drawing that is a visualization of what is nonexistent (that is, the projection of imagined forms and relationships), and (3) the drawing that is a graphic symbol which can be read because the meaning is commonly understood. (An example of the latter is a graph or a floor plan.)

FIGURE 1–4. Jackson Pollock (1912–1956; American). "Birthday Card."

Ink and wash on paper, 16" x 20".
Collection of Clement Greenberg, New York City
(Photo: Myron S. Shepard).

FIGURE 1-5

Pieter Brueghel (1520?–1569; Flemish) or Hieronymus Bosch (1450?–1516; Dutch).
"The Cripples." Pen and brown ink, 11³⁄₁₆" x 10½".
Albertina, Vienna.

FIGURE 1–6

Hans Holbein the Younger (1497–1543; German).
"The Family of Sir Thomas Moore." 15⁷⁄₁₆" x 20¼".
Drawing Collection, Kunstmuseum, Basel.

FAMILIA THOMÆ MORI ANGL: CANCELL:

Thomas Morus Aº.50. Alicia Thomæ Mori uxor Aº.57. Iohannes Morus pater Aº.76. Iohannes Morus Thomæ filius Aº.19. Anna Grifacria Iohannis Mori Sponfa Aº.15. Margareta Ropera Thomæ Mori filia Aº.22. Elifabeta Damen Thomæ Mori filia Aº.21. Cæcilia Heroina Thomæ Mori filia Aº.20. Margareta Giga Clementis uxor Mori filiabus Coudiscipula et cognata Aº.22. Henricus Patenfonus Thomæ Mori morio Aº.40.

The most commonly held conception of drawing is that it is a way of recording what is seen—that it constitutes a kind of visual note-taking. For most people the words *a man drawing* conjure up a picture of a person, sketch pad in one hand, pencil or pen in the other, glancing at his subject and then jotting down what he sees. This kind of note-taking is typified by the sketch book, which is to the artist what a diary is to a writer—a collection of notes upon which the author can draw to reinforce memory. A page of drawings of "Cripples" (Figure 1–5), supposedly copied by Pieter Brueghel from the notebook of Hieronymous Bosch, provided a grim but fascinating storehouse of observations upon which both artists subsequently relied. However, drawing which functions as a record of what is seen can be much more than mere note-taking. Just as the written or spoken word, by fixing fragments of thought in logical sequences, makes possible the formulation of intellectual concepts of the greatest complexity, so drawing, by fixing visual impressions in static forms,

Drawing as a Record of Visual Facts

makes it possible to build knowledge step by step and eventually come to know the nature of forms that are too complex to be comprehended at a single glance. Our understanding of the visual character of the physical world around us was achieved largely by this patient accumulation of knowledge, and in this respect drawing constitutes a kind of visual exploration through which individuals and cultures become familiar with the various forms that make up the culture's artistic repertory. Such forms can be drawn with certainty, are accepted and understood by the cultivated populace and become part of the general cultural heritage.

One of the most familiar situations in which drawing provides the means for such exploration and discovery is in the life class. Here students gradually become aware of the full complexity of the human form through a long process of observing and recording various aspects of the body (Figure 16–19). Done as note-taking, drawing can with equal effectiveness record the precise details and characteristics of a subject, as in Holbein's drawing of the family of Thomas Moore (Figure 1–6), or suggest only broad movements and general relationships (Figure 1–7).

FIGURE 1–7

Jean Louis Forain (1852–1931; French). "Riot and Sketch of a Man." Black crayon, watercolor and brush with black ink, 11⅝" x 8½". *Courtesy of The Art Institute of Chicago (Gift of Frank B. Hubachek).*

Drawing as Preparation for Painting

From the Renaissance to modern times, a certain level of facility in drawing has been considered a prerequisite to painting. By drawing, the would-be painter learned to observe and record his observations so that he could communicate them to others. Training in drawing preceded painting, because the materials

FIGURE 1–9

Peter Blume (1900– ; Russian-American).
"Beggar Woman (Study for the Eternal City)" 1933. Pencil, 11¾" x 9⅜".
Collection Museum of Modern Art, New York
(Gift of Edgar Kaufmann, Jr.)

FIGURE 1–10. Jean-Auguste Dominique Ingres (1780–1867; French).

"Studies for the Dead Body of Acron."
Lead pencil on paper, 7¾″ x 14⅜″.
The Metropolitan Museum of Art (Rogers Fund, 1919.)

were easier to manipulate and the complications of color were eliminated. In the past, drawing remained an important tool for painters long after the learning stage for, traditionally, drawing constituted a preparatory step in planning a painting. Such preliminary studies included initial visualizations of compositional arrangements, such as Castiglione's "St. Bernard before Christ" (Figure 1–8), more developed compositional plans, as in Géricault's "The Bull Market" (Figure 7–3), notations concerning details of form, such as Blume's "Study for the Eternal City" (Figure 1–9), or visualizations of alternate arrangements of figures and groups, such as can be seen in a study in which Ingres probed the logic of various positions for the "Dead Body of Acron" (Figure 1–10). These drawings are but a few of the many thousands produced by the masters as part of the process of planning a painting, drawings which frequently achieve much of their distinction from the fact that they have been produced not for public consumption, but only to satisfy the painter's inquiring mind.

FIGURE 1–11a

Hugh Ferriss (1889–1962; American).
"First Presbyterian Church, Stamford, Connecticut." Charcoal.
Courtesy Harrison and Abramovitz, Architects.

Drawing as a Visualization of the Imagined

So far we have been concerned primarily with drawing what is seen, but drawing also functions to visualize the imagined. No matter how vivid an idea seems to its originator, it must remain a nebulous and undefined concept until it is given fixed form, and much drawing functions in this way. Such visualizing drawings usually develop from very general quick sketches to more exact and finished renderings of an idea. While drawing in an art class is most traditionally associated with the training of painters and the preparation of paintings, there is no area in the visual arts that is not to some degree dependent upon the effectiveness of drawing in visualizing the imagined. Raphael's sketch for the "Alba Madonna," seen in Figure 1–1b, represents an initial step in the translation into concrete form of an idea for a painting. An architect's initial renderings function in the same way, putting ideas that may be clear in the architect's mind or that may be only partially formed into a specific format, thereby giving the nonexistent building a definite form, often for the client's benefit (Figures

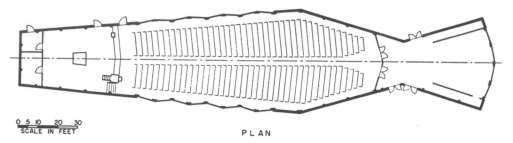

PLAN

FIGURE 1–11c

Wallace K. Harrison and Max Abramovitz, Architects (American).
"Floor Plan, First Presbyterian Church,
Stamford, Connecticut." Pen and ink.

FIGURE 1–11d

Harrison and Abramovitz, Architects (American).
First Presbyterian Church, Stamford, Connecticut.
Completed 1958. 227' x 48'. *Photograph courtesy
Joseph W. Molitor, Photographer.*

1–11a, b, c, d). A host of fine drawings from the present and the past by architects, sculptors, designers, and craftsmen provide vivid testimony to the important role played by drawing in giving graphic form to three-dimensional conceptions (Figure 1–12).

The first step in visualizing most contemporary industrial products is a sketch, although a piece of jewelry or a ceramic object might be modeled in some malleable material from its inception. Figure 1–13 illustrates the role of a drawing in visualizing an orthogenic device designed to exercise an arm impaired by accident or an operation. Such a drawing, by helping the designer visualize how his instrument will work, does away with the costly mistakes that might occur if the actual mechanism were built without such planning. The use of drawing to give definite form to an idea is not confined to the arts, for drawing is also helpful in making scientific notations, in engineering procedures, even in projecting certain mathematical concepts. Whenever one wants to translate

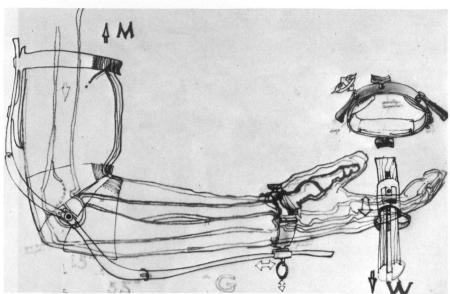

FIGURE 1–13

Michael Golden (1939– ; American).
"Orthogenic Device." Ink and pencil, c.
16" x 20". *Collection of the artist.*

relationships of space, shape, size, quantity, or movement into concrete visual images, drawing provides a ready instrument (Figure 1–14).

Visualizing the imagined need not always be a side production in the creation of a more elaborate project. Some of our most exciting drawings were only created to give form to the fantasies of an imaginative mind and in so doing to translate the nonexistent into pictorial reality. The grotesque imaginings of Dali (Figure 18–11) or the dreamlike images of Redon (Figure 1–15) provide a fascinating glimpse into the strange depths of the human mind.

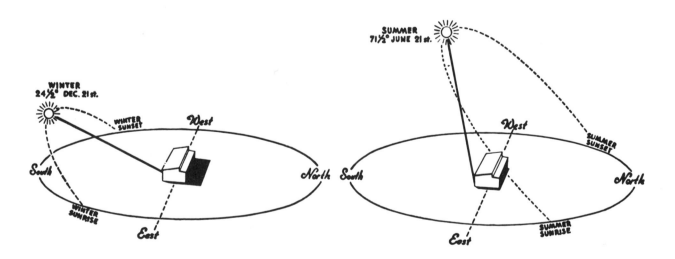

FIGURE 1–14

Winter and summer sun positions, noon, Chicago.
Courtesy Libbey-Owens-Ford Glass Company.

FIGURE 1–15

Odilon Redon (1840–1916; French).
"Human Rock (Idole)." Charcoal and red crayon,
20⁵⁄₁₆″ x 11¾″. *Courtesy of The Art Institute
of Chicago (The David Adler collection).*

FIGURE 1–16

Maggie Wesley (1918– ; American). "The Improper Use of Government Property Is Frowned Upon." Silk screen, 30″ x 40″. Designed for Lockheed Missiles and Space Co., Sunnyside, California. *Courtesy of the artist.*

Symbolic Drawing

A third general function of drawing is to symbolize, as distinct from describing appearances or visualizing. Throughout history the arts have played an important role in providing other than verbal symbols to communicate meanings. In fact, in early and nonliterate societies the artistic symbols provide the principal record by which we come to know their social institutions and value systems. Today a great host of picture-symbols is continuously used with commonly understood meanings which are read, as it were, by the initiate. We have already seen an architect's floor plan (Figure 1–11c). Such drawings, ruled to scale and elaborated with a complex of cryptic marks meaning electric outlets, plumbing fixtures, windows, doors, and so on, convey a concept of great complexity in very specific terms. Charts, graphs, advertisements, trademarks, comic books, cartoons, and a wide variety of forms of graphic expression are dependent upon similar systems of visual symbolism. Think of how readily and unconsciously an American youngster translates the imagery of the comic book into its intended meanings. Swirling lines and stars above a prostrate figure mean "knocked out"; wavy lines next to arms and legs mean shuddering with fear; sideburns and a mustache signify a villain. The humorous drawing "Improper Use of Government Properties Is Frowned Upon" depends upon public familiarity with patriotic symbols for its effectiveness (Figure 1–16).

Effective as symbolic drawing is for conveying specific ideas, it is equally potent in conveying subtleties of feeling. Many drawn symbols have the power to evoke the most complex train of associations, to unleash a myriad interrelated meanings which historically surround certain motifs. Thus the cross or swastika can awaken a torrent of ideas and feelings, the cross suggesting Christianity, spirituality, suffering and a wide range of ethical concepts, whereas the swastika recalls the ruthless cruelty of Nazi Germany or cryptic and mysterious Indian symbolism. The simplest arrow can suggest, among other things, direction, the hunting of primitive man, a weathervane, or the games of childhood.

Symbolic content alone does not determine the full range of meaning conveyed by a symbol—equally important is the way in which it is drawn. Every aspect of treatment colors the way a symbol affects the viewer. A heavy, clumsy cross conveys a very different meaning than does a thin elongated one, a wavering line creates a different reaction than does a ruled one. Much of the magic of "Village in the Storm" (Figure 1–17) by Varujan Bughosian is a result

FIGURE 1–17

Varujan Boghosian (1926–   ; American).
"Village in the Storm." Pen and ink on cardboard,
26″ x 23⅛″. *Collection, The Museum of Modern Art,*
New York. Blanchette Rockefeller Fund.

of the skill with which familiar symbols have been given an almost magic quality through the sensitive use of line. In using childlike perspective to reveal both ends of the village houses at the same time, a playful attitude is initiated. The delicacy of the lines, their slightly oblique lean, and the complex linear intertwinings of the rivulets reinforces the suggestion of a child's imaginative world. Small jewellike motifs are scattered throughout and they, too, take the observer outside the drama of a real storm and project him into some fantasy world of the imagination where the downpour of waters, like the horrors in a fairy tale, remain on a play level of fantasy without serious threat.

We have just classified drawing into three main categories: the drawing that reproduces what is seen, that which visualizes an imagined idea, person, or thing, and the drawing that symbolizes. The borderline between these broad categories is tenuous. Certainly sharp lines cannot be established between what is seen, what is imagined, and what is symbolized; many drawings function in all three ways. However, the very act of classifying can help extend and organize our thinking about the central role that drawing plays in the arts as well as in many other facets of our culture.

FIGURE 1–18
Black ink on white paper.

The Art Elements

What are the basic elements with which one draws? Faulkner, Ziegfeld, and Hill, in *Art Today*, answer this question by saying: "Poets and novelists use words to make known their verbal ideas. Musicians use varied sounds to convey their musical ideas. And artists, whether painters, sculptors, architects, designers, or craftsmen, use the plastic elements—*form, line, space, texture,* and *color* when they express their plastic or graphic ideas. Plastic means formed or molded and implies, but is not limited to, three-dimensional art objects. Graphic refers to drawing, painting, writing, and printing, which actually have only two dimensions but typically give some feeling of the third dimension." Even though many artists draw with colored chalks, crayons, or pencils, color is essentially a painter's concern and outside the draftsman's immediate province. But even when color as such is not considered, value (relationships of darkness and lightness), which is an aspect of surface coloration, still concerns the draftsman. This leaves *line, form, value,* and *texture* as the basic elements of drawing.

Later in this book an entire section will be devoted to analyzing the role of the art elements in drawing, but by way of introduction we shall explore briefly something of the nature of these elements. Let us commence with what might be considered the precursor of a line, the dot (Figure 1–18). Even a single dot placed upon a page instantly awakens conjecture. Is the dot accidental? If not, what is its meaning and purpose? Above and beyond the enigma of its why and wherefore, the single dot is an esthetic entity with its own dynamics. Its presence energizes the empty page by establishing relationships of size and tone—big empty space, little dot; white background, black dot. Two dots create a sense of distance between each other, establish space between one another and the remaining areas of the page, and create interrelationships of movement and direction. The simplest line suggests direction, divides space, has length, width, tone, texture, and may suggest contour. As soon as the line begins to change direction, to move in a curved or angular fashion, to fluctuate in width and to have rough or smooth edges, its active and descriptive power is increased many times. The beginning student, learning to draw, soon discovers he is assuming command of a most powerful tool. With it he can describe, suggest, evoke, and imply an endless variety of experiences, observations, conceptions, and intuitions. Every mark one makes, whether a thoughtful line or a careless scribble, will inevitably convey something of the maker to the sensitive observer. And every mark or blob has a certain line, tone, and texture potential.

A simple abstraction by Hans Hartung (Figure 1–19) provides a convenient vehicle for introducing the art elements, free of symbolic or representational complications.

FIGURE 1–19

Hans Hartung (1904–   ; German–French). "D. 42. 2." Charcoal and oil, 19″ x 25″. *San Francisco Museum of Art (permanent collection).*

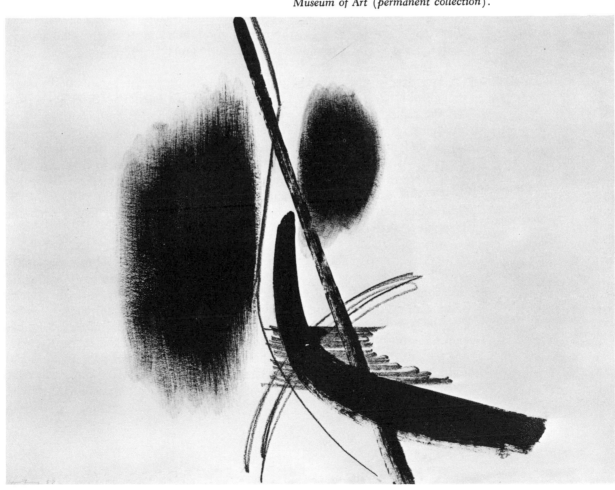

LINE .   Line is used here in three ways. (1) It functions to separate areas. In so doing, line defines boundaries. Notice how the two lines crossing the page from bottom to top, one thin and curved, one heavier and straight, divide the composition into two parts. (2) Line also establishes a sense of movement. Note the already mentioned diagonals, the freely scribbled curved lines, the rapidly drawn horizontal strokes, and the bold, heavy brush stroke that swings up from the lower right and flattens as it veers into the focal center of the composition. All establish different directional movements that give the composition its dynamic energy. (3) Line also creates a textured tone. Observe the way in which the rapidly drawn horizontal lines create a gray mass of a different textural quality than the other grays on the page. Each type of line has its own expressive character, depending on what one brings to the drawing in temperament, interest, and background. The heavy, thick lines can seem menacing, authoritative, or portentous; the scribbled ones lively, informal, or casual.

VALUE .   Value refers to the range of possible darkness and lightness that exists between black and white, black representing the greatest possible degree of darkness, white the maximum light. The Hartung achieves much of its effectiveness from its bold contrasts of black and white. At the edges of the black masses, intermediate values (grays) have been created by allowing the white paper to show through the dry-brushed black pigment. The areas of gray are small and appear almost exclusively as transitions from the black to white, but in other drawings, such as Sheeler's "Feline Felicity" (Figure 1–3), we see the artist using the grays as the most important element of the composition, with the blacks and whites used in more limited quantities.

TEXTURE .   The third element, texture, relates primarily to implications of rough and smooth. The *Oxford Universal Dictionary* describes texture as "the representation of the structure and minute molding of a surface." It is this sense of tactile quality, of surface roughness or smoothness, of coarse or fine pigmented graininess, of weave or relief pattern, that constitutes texture in drawing. As such, texture contributes a sensory amplification to dark and light. In the Hartung drawing the graininess of paint, the roughness of the paper which received the paint, the hardness of the charcoal, and the stiffness of the bristle brush by which the paint was applied were the factors that created the range of textures.

FORM .   The illusion of three-dimensional form (and its counterpart, space) exists to some degree in every drawing. Much of the early history of drawing, particularly in Renaissance times, reveals a concern with developing systems of perspective, foreshortening, and modeling that would create convincing illusions of volume and depth upon a flat surface. The Hartung drawing has purposely been kept flat with a minimal illusion of volume and space. Even so, suggestions of volume and depth appear in it. The large oval dark at the upper right seems to bulge, and the straight diagonal line that moves from lower right to upper left, being lighter on one side than on the other, appears rounded. The heavy upswinging brush stroke, almost too broad to properly be described as a line, narrows down as it moves between the two vertical lines in a way that suggests perspective and a form moving into space. The same bold upswinging black stands in front of the heavy straight diagonal, the freely drawn horizontals, and the parallel curved lines. The long straight diagonal, in turn, stands in front of some parts of the composition and behind others. Here the illusion of three-dimensional space is stronger than the sense of solid three-dimensional form. Line and tone can, when the artist so desires, be used to create an equally convincing sense of form.

Types of Graphic Expression

Today a much wider range of expression is accepted as drawing than in the past. This is a natural outgrowth of the increased variety of styles that exist in the contemporary art world where abstractions, such as the Hartung drawing we have just discussed, flourish side by side with the most disciplined realism (Figure 12–9) or with naïve primitivism (Figure 18–9). Our increased catholicity of taste is to an equal extent the result of psychological understandings as to the nature of man and learning with a consequent sympathy toward a broader range of expression. Children's artistic expression has come to be cherished for its childlike qualities, and it has been recognized that various types of artistic personalities exist.

Viktor Lowenfeld, one of the most systematic students of the development of pictorial expression, perceived that various types of personalities reacted to visual experience in different ways. Lowenfeld theorized that there are two main types of art expression which represent two extreme poles of artistic personality; these he designated as *visual* and *haptic*. The visual type of student concerns himself primarily with his visible environment. His eyes constitute his primary instrument for perception, and he reacts as a spectator to experience. The nonvisual type of student, whom Lowenfeld termed *haptic*, tends to relate his expression to his own bodily sensations and the subjective experiences in which he becomes emotionally involved; he is more dependent on touch, bodily feelings, muscular sensations, and on empathic responses to verbal descriptions or dramatic presentations. Lowenfeld discovered that pictorial creativity was quite unrelated to the degree of visual orientation and that with proper stimulus, either type could create art works of a high order. Using Lowenfeld's theory as a basis for classification, it becomes immediately evident that while Degas was essentially visual in his orientation, Van Gogh had a strong haptic bias—he imparted his strong bodily empathy through his art (Figures 8–9, 15–2). While this can be felt in his drawings and paintings, some sentences from one of his letters to his brother reinforce the visual evidence. He said, "The problem is —and I find this extremely difficult—to bring out the depth of color and the enormous strength and firmness of the soil. . . . I am affected and intrigued to see how strongly the trunks are rooted in the ground. . . . Therefore I pressed roots and trunks out of the tube and modeled them a little with my brush.

There, now they stand in it, grow out of it, and have firmly taken root." Many of the descriptive words relate to physical qualities which are essentially not visible but toward which Van Gogh had strong physical empathy: "strength," "firmness," "strongly rooted," "I pressed," "[I] modeled," "firmly taken root."

Lownfeld's theories and a general interest on the part of psychologists in the nature of perception stimulated a considerable body of research designed to relate visual perception, personality types, and artistic expression. It was discovered that individuals of the type Lowenfeld identified as haptic were less dependent upon vision in determining their own bodily orientation to surrounding space than they were upon muscular and postural clues. In the course of research carried on by the Air Force to determine how fliers orient themselves in space to determine true uprightedness, subjects were seated in chairs which could be tilted to the left or right by means of levers. The chair was located in a small room which could also be tilted in various directions independently of the chair. The subjects were placed in the upright chair, then blindfolded, and the chair and room were tilted by an independent operator into other than upright positions. The blindfolds were then removed, and the subject was ordered to place himself, by means of another set of levers, into a true upright position. The enclosing tilted room, of course, gave no clue as to what constituted uprightedness.

Some appeared able to assume an upright position readily, apparently judging their position by the pull of gravity on their bodies. These were termed *body-oriented*. Others tended to orient themselves according to the lines of the enclosing room, using the verticals of the walls as true verticals and therefore aligning themselves with the tilt of the room. Such individuals were termed *field-oriented*. Most individuals, of course, relied on both visual and postural clues. These experiences and subsequent experiments substantiated Lowenfeld's thesis that individuals differ in the way they perceive their environment and, consequently, in the manner in which they draw upon experience as a stimulus to pictorial expression. It follows that artistic standards which reject all expression except that which is dominantly visual in orientation reject the valid expression of many individuals.

The traditional academic approach to art training was confined to an analysis of visual phenomena. Students looked at the models, learned anatomy from the study of medical drawings, perspective from diagrammatic charts, and were trained to act as spectators to the visual scene. The Van Goghs, Delacroixs, Daumiers, and others whose work reveals a strong admixture of nonvisual elements matured as artists because they also had a sufficiently visual orientation to satisfy the academic demands of the day. How many great artists gave up or were discouraged because their talents were other than visual we will never know.

More than ever before in history, contemporary artists depend on senses and sources other than the eyes. Almost no one is completely visual or completely haptic. Thus, in drawing a figure, a contemporary artist might wisely assume the pose he wishes to depict, feel its tensions in the back, head, leg, and arm positions, be conscious of the lean, balance or unbalanced stress of the posture. In drawing an animal he might feel its soft fur, sharp nails, strong muscles, tapered tail, and so on. In this way, tactile experiences would supplement visual perceptions. Equally important to today's catholicity of esthetic standards is the habit of drawing from imagination and memory, of reacting to a wide variety of stimuli, such as reading, hearing music, seeing drama and sports events, and participating in the full gamut of communal activities. To the degree that artistic expression relates to a wide variety of stimuli, a rich and diverse culture develops.

Summary

This book has been designed to provide a survey of the extent and nature of drawing and to broaden the reader's appreciation, taste, and skills. Connoisseurs and art critics frequently display a particular fondness for drawing because drawings, since they are usually done for the artist's personal satisfactions rather than for a client or for public display, tend to provide an intimate contact with the artist and the creative act. Also, many drawings, because they are sketches or studies and are not elaborately finished, contain elements of ambiguity which encourage the viewer to interpret these drawings through his own imagination.

Drawing has been defined as ". . . those representations in which an image is obtained by marking upon a background surface." Drawings fall into three broad categories: (1) Drawings that are records of what is seen. (2) Drawings that are visualizations of what is imagined. (3) Drawings that provide graphic symbolizations of concepts and ideas. The basic art elements the artist employs in drawing are line, form, value, and texture. A broader variety of drawing forms are accepted as meaningful today than ever before in history, including drawings based primarily on physical empathy, as well as those derived from visual experience. The drawing enthusiast should be encouraged to respond to a wide variety of stimuli so that the many aspects of drawing are perceived and enjoyed.

part two

THE HISTORY
OF DRAWING

2

FROM CAVE DRAWINGS

TO THE

RENAISSANCE

15,000 B.C. – A.D. 1400

History begins with drawing: man's oldest records are on the walls and ceilings of certain caves in France and Spain. Here the hunters of the Paleolithic or Old Stone Age, between 10,000 and 20,000 years ago, drew, painted, and incised likenesses of the animals of the hunt, on which they were dependent for food. These were man's first attempts to imprison the ever-moving flux of reality into immobile forms, and basically this remained the role of the visual arts throughout history. As always, this desire to isolate certain elements from the cascade of images that continuously assault the eye and fix them into static forms was dictated by an urgent inner need. Paleolithic man was exclusively concerned with the animals that provided his livelihood, and the various animals were characterized by the identifying and differentiating features of each: the heavy hump and powerful body of the bison with its small eyes short sharp horns, and bony rump or the thin, long, and graceful legs and horns of the deer. By thus representing each animal, primitive man felt that he was achieving a certain magical control of that animal; the symbol on the walls of the cave remaining fixed was forever accessible for the magic-ritual activities that insured success in the hunt (Figure 2–1).

In these cave drawings (for convenience let us refer to all prehistoric pictorial art as drawings rather than trying to distinguish between drawings, paintings, and bas-relief), we dimly sense the perceptions of the innocent eye, the eye that saw for the first time without having vision predetermined to a degree by previously established conventions of representation. Forms are

FIGURE 2–1

Niaux (Ariége) Salon Noire, Magdalenian Era
(15,000–8000 B.C., France). Cave painting:
Part of a large composition with bison on
different levels. *Photo by Achille B. Weider, Zürich.*

depicted most frequently in profile, for the profile reveals the characteristic aspect of an object in its simplest terms. Certain shapes like the eye (the eye form is difficult to perceive in profile) were shown full face. An element of what might be termed *pertinent exaggeration* reveals man's freshness of vision in these early efforts to describe his world. The grace of a horn is seen rather than the intrinsic nature of the curve; the sharp boniness of leg and the hulking mass of body are almost caricatures. The innocent eye saw and felt and then, over the centuries of subsequent civilization, there followed a long and sometimes tedious quest for knowledge in which innocence of eye and strength of feeling were frequently lost. Today we are searching again for the fresh viewpoint that characterized many of these early forms of expression.

Thus drawing was born from the desire to gain some mastery over the mysterious and overwhelming forces of nature. This was a first step in that continued attempt to identify, then analyze, classify, systematize, and hypothesize about natural phenomena, that finally gave man his present control over his environment. These first magico-religious rituals later developed into more complex religious, ethical, and philosophic systems, and these in turn gave way to the scientific knowledge that has resulted in the elaborate technological, intellectual, and social systems that determine our modern way of life. The act and the art of drawing has at all times been one of the instruments by which modern man has achieved his conquest of reality.

At this point it might be wise to point out that implicit in every work of art, and therefore in every drawing, is a value judgment. What might be termed an esthetic will, either communal, personal, or both, always plays a part in determining what to draw and how to draw it. This decision as to what and how probably takes place more frequently and on a more conscious level today than at any previous period in history, since in very early civilizations the artist seemed to be acting out a socially or culturally predetermined role. Not until classic times did the artist emerge as a personality whose own will to a degree shaped his, and therefore the culture's, artistic expression. Paleolithic man drew and painted the animals of the hunt to achieve some power over them that would insure success in the chase. Fear and hunger and the unpredictable vagaries of the chase provided the set of values that determined how and what he depicted upon the ceilings and walls of his caves. As we survey the long vistas of history we see ever-changing beliefs and social institutions shaping the artist's concerns, or, we might say, providing the focus that determined what and how the artist saw.

Neolithic Drawing

The Neolithic Age that followed the Old Stone Age produced little art that would compete with that of the Old Stone Age in its realism. Neolithic means "new stone" age and the men of the New Stone Age made polished stone implements rather than using the chipped stone implements of Paleolithic man. The fresh, unformalized, and visually sensitive art of the Old Stone Age, as discovered in the caves of France and Spain, gave way to an art of geometric, formal, and at times abstract symbolism. This tendency to use geometric patterns or formal and standardized symbols to represent man, animals, or the deified forces of nature has characterized Neolithic cultures over most of the face of the earth, from ancient to relatively modern times. Certain socioesthetic philosophers have explained that, unlike the hunters of the Old Stone Age, Neolithic man lived in sedentary communities, raised his basic foodstuffs, and so ceased to be primarily dependent upon the uncertainties of the hunt. Unlike his hunting forebears, he cultivated a settled way of life and expended his inventive capacities upon developing his sources of food and perfecting the household crafts and the ceremonial arts most suited to a sedentary way of life. Men in the New Stone Age of culture have lived in Africa, Asia, the South Seas, and North and South America from ancient to relatively modern times, and they have all produced ceramics, weaving, finely polished tools and weapons as well as the ceremonial objects suited to their religious practices. All of these objects give evidence of the technological and practical concerns of Neolithic man. Much of

FIGURE 2-2

Pottery jar (c. 1875; Zuñi Pueblo, New Mexico). Slip decoration. *Smithsonian Institution, Washington, D. C.*

his art takes the form of making these useful things beautiful, frequently by adding surface decoration. Thus, on pottery, baskets, textiles, and in wood and stone carvings, certain symbols are repeated and endlessly interrelated and intertwined in the most ingenious manner (Figure 2–2). Technical perfection and virtuosity in the handling of familiar symbols appeared to be more highly valued than originality and novelty.

Neolithic man, like his Old Stone Age precursors, continued to practice his magico-religious rituals and to decorate his sanctuaries, but here also the tendency to abstract and formalize patterns that characterized his pottery, baskets, and weaving can be seen in the frescoes he drew, painted, and incised upon the walls and ceilings of his caves and canyons. A canyon wall decorated by the Indian cliff-dwellers of southern Utah around the thirteenth century A.D. (Figure 2–3) is covered with fascinating cryptic symbols, some easily identified as human figures, feet, and mountain goats, but the meaning of others cannot be unraveled. Unlike the cave paintings of the Old Stone Age, which seem uncomposed, the arrangement here appears systematic and orderly, as though some complex ritual were being recorded. A facsimile of a rock painting from Khargur Tahl, in the Libyan desert (Figure 2–4), picturing a fight for the possession of a bull, shows a further development of the tendency to settle on certain symbols and standardize them. Here the symbols used to represent the human figure, bows, and arrows are repeated with little variation, but the forms are carefully placed to insure narrative clarity. Thus, compositional habits develop even though the representational skills do not. From these conservative and highly formalized arts of Neolithic man were developed the major artistic cultures of ancient times.

FIGURE 2–3

Ritual Petroglyphs in Glenn
Canyon, Utah (c. A.D. 1100;
Anasazi Culture). 36″ x 60–72″.
*Photo by Gene Foster, courtesy
Museum of Northern Arizona.*

FIGURE 2 4

Facsimile of rock painting:
A fight, apparently for possession of a bull.
Khargur Tahl, Libyan Desert. *Collection
the Museum of Modern Art, New York.*

FIGURE 2–5

Tomb of Ptahneferher, Saqqara.
Fifth Dynasty (2480–2350 B.C.), Egyptian.
Ägyptische Staatssammlung, Munich.

Egypt and the Tigris–Euphrates Valley

The art of Ancient Egypt was first formed during the Neolithic Age and throughout the 4,000 years of Egyptian history certain traits of Neolithic art were sustained. Grand in scale, intellectually complex, and esthetically sophisticated, the art of Egypt frequently displays an astonishing technical virtuosity, and at the same time retains many rigid and naïve elements.

The artist of ancient Egypt probably made no personal decision as to what he drew or how. He worked for the priests and rulers in a rigid and unchanging society, decorating the walls of palaces, temples, and tombs according to long-established traditions and rules. (Figure 2–5.) Inasmuch as the adornment of tombs, palaces and temples grew from religious and courtly ritual and as this was a hierarchical society in which rigid conventions determined all ritual acts, depiction of the human figure remained the same throughout the long history of Egyptian art. As in other primitive societies, the early Egyptians fixed on the most easily characterized aspects of the human figure. Thus the head was usually shown in profile, the eye full face, the shoulders full face and the rest of the

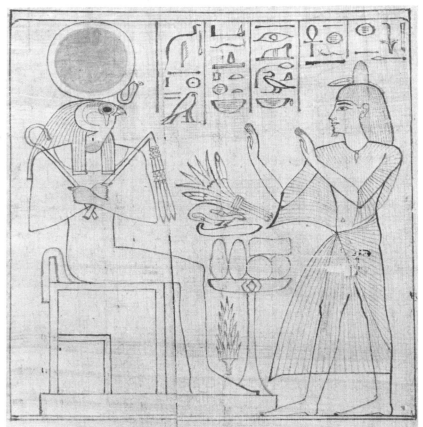

FIGURE 2–6

Painted papyrus with hieroglyphic inscription (detail) [c. 1000 B.C.; Egyptian, New Kingdom]. Ink on papyrus, 9⅝″ x 28¾″. *Allen Memorial Art Museum, Oberlin College, Ohio (R. T. Miller, Jr. Fund).*

body in profile, since such a rendering of form eliminates the complex problems of foreshortening (Figure 2–6). Egyptian art retained these conventions for almost four thousand years, during which time astonishing developments occurred in other areas of Egyptian culture, such as in the art of building. The artist remained an artisan, a tool of powerful conservative social elements, and the leaders of this rigid society, not the artist, provided the value judgments that determined the nature of artistic expression. While the arts became technically and esthetically more refined in execution, for the most part they did not break out of the boundaries of established convention.

Equally rigid conventions controlled the various aspects of representation. For instance, in depicting the Pharaoh, his family, armies, and servants, the relative sizes of the individuals was determined by their importance in the social scheme. A Pharaoh might well be shown ten times the size of a servant and twice the size of his Queen. Equally well understood and accepted conventions were used to suggest both intervals of time and the relative positions of figures and objects in space, perspective being implied by successive levels, the closest objects being placed on a base line at the bottom of a composition, the farthest away placed at the top.

The ancient civilizations of the Tigris-Euphrates valley showed less tendency to formalize their art than did the Egyptians, largely because their cultures were less static and enduring. Constantly engaged in warfare, their art reflects their warlike tendencies, their admiration of power and strength, and their

glorification of the hunt. A bas-relief of a "Dying Lioness" (Figure 2–7), from Nineveh in the seventh century B.C., depicts an incident of the hunt with knowledgable intensity. Though the form is still in profile, the details reveal acute observation of the animal, the face wrinkled in a howl of pain, the tense front claws and the broken dragging back. Freed from ritual restrictions, ancient man was capable of depicting his world with skill and power.

Drawing in Greece and Rome

In Greek art, for the first time, one can observe the rigid patterns of Neolithic drawing give way to pictorial naturalism. The human figure became the primary concern of artistic endeavor and an idealized realism became the dominant style. Subsequently, the arts of Greece and Rome played an important part in Renaissance culture and helped establish a noble realism of style as one of the chief aims of the Renaissance.

Little by way of drawing and painting has come down to us from the classic world except in the form of vase decorations. The painted plaster of walls and ceilings and the delicate mosaics have fallen away, but fortunately for us the painted vases reflected the major developments in the arts. The earliest style of drawing to appear in Greek art, to judge by vase decoration, retained a typically Neolithic formal and abstract character. The oldest Greek pottery to be discovered is decorated with purely geometric motifs: circles, squares, horizontal and vertical bands of straight lines, chevrons and similar motifs. Around 800 B.C. the vase decorations became more elaborate, and human and animal symbols are incorporated into the geometric framework. One of the grandest examples of the style of the eighth century B.C. is a great vase from the Dipylon cemetery in Athens (Figure 2–8). These large vases served as grave monuments and were less vases than funnel-like containers with holes in the bottom through which water or ceremonial wine could filter down to the body buried below. We see great technical finesse displayed in the precisely arranged bands of patterns, between

FIGURE 2–8

Dipylon vase (eighth century B.C. Attic). Height 42½″. *The Metropolitan Museum of Art, New York (Rogers Fund, 1914).*

which groups of figures, animals, chariots, and other forms appear treated almost as abstractly as the purely geometric motifs. However, the pictorial-narrative aim of the maker of this decoration is evident in the two main bands of the design in which we see the funeral bier, lines of mourners with their arms raised in a gesture of grief, and an impressive funeral procession of charioteers and warriors on foot. A detail reveals the deceased on his bier, the sacrificial animals and fowl, and the mourning family (Figure 2 9). Though highly formalized, this is drawing of great vitality. The artist was motivated to express complex ideas and feelings far beyond his pictorial skills, and his effort to convey these complex ideas initiated habits of resourceful inventiveness that were to affect the subsequent artistic expression of the entire Western world.

During the Archaic Age, which lasted from the seventh to the early fifth century B.C., the Greek vase painter continued to reflect the changing styles of Greek pictorial art in his decorations on vases. The geometric figures that served as human symbols in the eighth century B.C. gradually filled out, proportions became more naturalistic, details of muscles, hair, and feature enriched the

FIGURE 2–9

Dipylon vase, detail: Prothesis scene (eighth century B.C. Attic). Height 42½″. *The Metropolitan Museum of Art, New York (Rogers Fund, 1914).*

forms, and a wide variety of postures and actions were depicted, as can be seen in an Attic black-figured amphora from the sixth century B.C. (Figure 2–10). During the sixth century figures still tended to be in profile, but from the fifth century on foreshortened positions were delineated with great skill and the artists depicted a wide range of subjects drawn from mythology, legend, and everyday life. A lovely pyxis from mid-fifth century Athens reveals the pictorial ability that prevailed at that time (Figure 2–11). In this version of the "Judgment of Paris" narrative, realism and decorative charm are combined with refinement of taste. That the skill and artistry of the men who decorated the vases was recognized by the Greeks and was meaningful to them is evidenced by the fact that the finest vases were signed.

It is difficult to estimate the exact level of pictorial realism achieved in classic art. The painters who decorated Greek vases did not attempt to employ dark and light modeling to suggest roundness and solidity, nor did they use elaborate landscape or complex architectural backgrounds for the scenes depicted. No major piece of Greek painting has come down to us as evidence, but classic literature includes certain anecdotes which indicate the high regard in which visual realism was held. However, a fair number of Roman mosaics and paintings from Herculaneum and Pompeii, some copied after Greek master-pieces, are still extant, and from an example such as "Peirithoos, Hippodameia and the Centaur Eurytion" in monochrome on marble, supposedly copied from a painting by the Greek master Zeuxis, we can tell much concerning the pictorial skills of classic artists, Greek and Roman (Figure 2–12). Certainly the artist knew how to use gradations of dark and light to make forms look round and solid. A wide range of textures was depicted very successfully—flowing cloth, firm flesh, and soft hair.

Complex landscape and architectural subjects were also portrayed upon the walls of the villas of Pompeii and Herculaneum. Though in these decorations

FIGURE 2–11

Penthesileia painter. "Judgment of Paris." (Found at Cumae; c. 465–460 B.C.; Greek [Athenian]). Pyxis: white ground. Height (with cover) 5¾". *The Metropolitan Museum of Art, New York (Rogers Fund, 1907).*

FIGURE 2–12

Copy of a painting attributed to Zeuxis, from Herculaneum. "Peirithoos, Hippodameia and the Centaur Eurytion." Monochrome on marble, width 17¾". *Museo Nazionale, Naples (Anderson-Art Reference Bureau)*

FIGURE 2–13

Monogram page (folio 34 recto) from the *Book of Kells* (c. A.D. 800; Irish). Glair or tempera on vellum. *By permission the Board of Trinity College, Dublin.* (See Plate 2.)

the illusion of three-dimensional depth is striking, and individual forms are solid, the relationships of perspective often seem inconsistent, so that there is no evidence of a thoroughly understood, rigorously applied system of perspective from classic times, nor are the suggestions of deep space in the landscapes as convincing as the solidity of individual details. No major paintings from classical times are still extant. Consequently there is no way of determining whether these weaknesses were inadequacies of the individual artists who decorated these villas (these men were probably no more than average workmen who made their living by decorating the summer homes of the rich) or if the artists of classical times lacked a broad understanding of the principles of perspective. Because the chief area of classical concern was in the depiction of the human figure, the treatment of landscape and of architectural subjects may not have been so thoroughly developed.

The Middle Ages

In the centers where classic art had previously flourished little of prime significance to a study of drawing occurred during the long interval between the fall of the Roman Empire and the beginning of the Renaissance in fourteenth-century Italy. Early Christian and Byzantine art in Italy, Greece and the southeastern Mediterranean world ceased to concern itself with the illusionistic realism of the Greeks and the Romans and instead turned to an elaborate, symbolic, formal style which received its fullest expression in the decorations of churches, tombs, and ritual objects. In these areas drawing, as such, gave way to symbolic design.

In Northern Europe in the interval between the fall of Rome in the fourth century A.D. and the end of the Middle Ages, roughly A.D. 1400, a graphic tradition of book illumination of great vigor evolved in the monastic centers of learning. The monks, isolated from the secular world and devoting all of their energies to the greater glory of God and the church, developed the art of copying and illuminating manuscripts to high levels. In some of the Irish monastic communities, certain very unique and elaborate conventions were carried to an unusual level of development. Ireland, which had not been exposed to classical culture, maintained what has been termed the Barbarian style, a convoluted abstract decorative style which had developed in parts of Northern Europe independent of the classical pictorial traditions. In the seventh and eighth centuries Irish calligraphy reached unprecedented heights, and in the Book of Kells, from the early eighth century the Irish decorative genius received its most splendid expression. The extensive character of the original manuscript indicates that many artists must have worked on it; in fact, there is evidence that frequently more than one artist worked on a single page. A monogram page (Figure 2–13), one of a multitude of similar pages with elaborated initial letters, comes at the beginning of the eighteenth verse of the first chapter of Matthew. After citing fourteen generations of forebears, we find the announcement of the nativity of Christ heralded by this magnificent burst of linear decoration, decoration that is triumphantly northern, barbarian and abstract. The same

FIGURE 2–14

Illustration to Psalm XXVI from the *Utrecht Psalter* (c. 820–832 A.D.). Brown ink; page size 12⅞" x 9¾". *University Library, Utrecht. (Art Reference Bureau.)*

mystical and lyrical impulse appears here in graphic form that at a later date led to the sculptural elaborations that glorified the Romanesque churches of northern Europe and finally found expression in the lacy stone intricacies and stained glass of the Gothic cathedral.

With the passing of time the tradition of book illumination tended to become increasingly pictorial, particularly in those areas where remnants of classical culture still persisted. A fine example of the transition from book illumination to book illustration which provides a picture of the change that gradually occurred is from the Utrecht Psalter, which was produced in northern France in the ninth century (Figure 2–14). This entire book is illustrated with pen drawings, which in their vigor, freedom of execution and

FIGURE 2–15

Illustration for "The Original Sin" from the *Velislav Bible*
(Folio 4A, First Master) (c. 1340). Brown ink and color on parchment, 9″ x 8½″.
University Library, Prague.

imaginative translation of the imagery of the Psalms into pictorial language are without peer. In such works is forecast the vigorous realism of the Gothic and early Renaissance art of northern Europe.

In time the influence of the French practice of illuminating and illustrating manuscripts with pictorial narratives became widespread. An example of the way in which this practice developed in the late Middle Ages is provided by the Velislav Bible, from fourteenth-century Bohemia. A handsome page from the hand of the First Master illustrates the theme of Original Sin (Figure 2–15). In the top band Adam and Eve eat of the fruit and hide under a tree, and below, God questions Adam and Eve. Only a section of the original illustrated Bible remains, but the work of two artists can be discerned. The First Master, the better of the two, was probably the master of the workshop in which the manuscript was produced, the second master showing less firmness in his drawing and less imagination in the freedom with which he executed the rhythmic flutter of draperies and distributed the decorative motifs. The work of both men is sufficiently consistent so that a unified effect is produced. The drawings are executed in what is essentially a kind of pictorial calligraphy with fairly standardized motifs, ways of representing figures, draperies, and decorative embellishments, but sensitivity is displayed in the disposition of the decorative masses and the manuscript was executed on a high technical level. The drawings are in brown ink on parchment and are lightly colored. Objects are colored, almost by category: red used on lips and faces, green for landscape elements, yellow in the costumes but the decorative aspects of color are also effectively realized.

A page from the Göttingen manuscript from fifteenth-century Bohemia illustrates vividly the struggle experienced by the less facile medieval book illuminator when he was called upon to illustrate an idea for which he could find no precedent. "Apostles Sitting in Stocks" (Figure 14–5) is from one of a group of manuscripts created in the service of the Hussite idea, extolling Christ, picturing the suffering of Christ and the apostles, and condemning the vices of the clergy. Inasmuch as the draftsman had to originate his own composition, the drawing is vivid, energetic, and crude. Layered perspective, an absence of foreshortening of proportionate sizes between the parts of the composition, and other naïve features reveal the degree to which the ancient pictorial skills has ceased to be a common language.

Though the monasteries all over Europe were centers for the perpetuation of culture, France continued to be the hub of artistic activity during the late Middle Ages, and drawing proved to be a vital element in the expanding culture. Copy books were kept by artists, illuminators, designers, and architects, and in these books were recorded various decorative motifs, ways of rendering certain forms, traditional groupings of figures, recipes, and other elements of the craft. Thus drawing in the Middle Ages insured the continuity of certain traditional iconographic elements, yet at the same time sufficient freedom in rendering was permitted in these copy books to encourage the development of individual styles. One senses the vigor of the drawing tradition when one examines the notebooks of Villard de Honnecourt, a thirteenth-century French architect who filled his

FIGURE 2–16

De Honnecourt (thirteenth century; French). Page from an Album, Geometrics. Pen and ink, 9⅛" x 5⅞". *Bibliotèque Nationale. Art Reference Bureau.*

pages with sketches of architectural projects, systems for drawing the human figure, notations of animal, bird, and insect forms, and a wide variety of other subjects (Figure 2–16).

However, we can see in the beautiful books of this period a continuous development of pictorial realism. Small vignettes illustrating the text were embedded in the arabesques of line and pattern used to beautify the elaborate pages of manuscript that made up these magnificent volumes. These richly

PLATE 1
Raphael (Raffaello Santi, 1483–1520; Italian).
Study for "The Alba Madonna." Pen and red chalk, 15¾" x 10½".
Musées d'Art et d'Histoire, Lille, France (Ektachrome Gérondal).

PLATE 2

Monogram page (folio 34 recto) from the *Book of Kells* (c. A.D. 800; Irish). Glair or tempera on vellum, 13″ x 9½″. *By permission of the Board of Trinity College, Dublin.*

FIGURE 2–17

The Limbourg Brothers. "February"
from *Les très riches heures du duc de Berry* (1413–1416).
Tempera [?] on vellum, February 5⅜″ x 8¹³⁄₁₆″.
Musée Condé, Chantilly, France. Bulloz—Art Reference Bureau. (See Plate 3.)

colored illustrations might with equal logic be called paintings or colored draw-ings. Small, detailed, full of fascinating observations and imaginings, exquisite in craftsmanship, they provide a transition from the purely decorative embellish-ments of the earlier medieval style of book illumination to the full-blown painting tradition of the Renaissance. The miniatures from the fifteenth-century French *Trés riches heures du duc de Berry* by the Brothers Limbourg (Figure 2–17) represent the final and most impressive example of this style of book illustrations. Following this period painting left the pages of books to embellish the altars and walls of churches and palaces.

Summary

The earliest drawings to be discovered are from the caves of France and Spain. These Old Stone Age drawings of Paleolithic animals of the chase may date back as far as 20,000 B.C. Cave drawings and paintings were made as part of the ceremonial procedure which provided the caveman with the belief that he would be successful in the hunt. Old Stone Age drawings show sharp observation of animal forms and an ability to pick out and emphasize the characterizing aspect of each animal. Neolithic levels of culture first appeared in Mesopotamia and Egypt as far back as 4000 B.C., and Neolithic cultures have flourished in most parts of the world through the succeeding millenia. In the New Stone Age forms became standardized symbols and New Stone Age (Neolithic) man exerted his ingenuity in refining the symbolic forms for decorative purposes and in composing them for clarity of communication. Between 3000 and 300 B.C., first in Egypt and Mesopotamia and later in Greece and Rome, conventions were developed for the systematic representations of the human form and for placing objects in space. The artists of ancient Greece and Rome were particularly successful in creating idealized representations of the human figure in action. Although no original works by the great painters of classical times have been preserved, the drawings on Greek vases from the fourth and third centuries and the mosaics and wall paintings from first-century Pompeii and Herculanaeum reflect the high level of achievement in classical times.

In the Byzantine culture of eastern Europe and Asia Minor that followed the fall of the Roman Empire in the west, the science and art of realistic representation degenerated into decorative formalism. Parallel to reawakening of trade, commerce, and culture in western Europe during the early Middle Ages, the art of realistic representation was gradually redeveloped. From the ninth century on, in the monastic centers of Northern Europe, the illumination and illustration of books provided the vehicle for the revival and redevelopment of the arts of graphic decoration and representation.

3

THE RENAISSANCE IN ITALY
1300–1600

It was during the early Renaissance that drawing, as we practice it today, became established as the foundation of training in the arts. Like much else in our artistic heritage, many of our conceptions about the role of drawing in the arts comes to us from this period. The fourteenth-century Italian writer, Cennino Cennini, placed drawing as the cornerstone of art, for he considered that drawing gave the foundation of practice necessary for all and provided for the intellectual inclination of the talented. This conception of drawing as a mental exercise is most significant. It stresses the role of drawing as an intellectual tool in the formulation of an artistic idea as separate from the craft of execution, the latter being an essentially manipulative act. At the end of the fifteenth century Leonardo da Vinci considered drawing a recording instrument by which to investigate nature, thus making it a tool at the service of science as well as of the arts. In the sixteenth century this line of thought could be summarized in the theory that drawing was a metaphysical principle "which is found in all things created and uncreated, visible and invisible, spiritual and material," since it provided the means for making thought concrete by embodying an esthetic idea in visible form.

This intellectualizing about drawing was paralleled in the training of artists for, in the apprentice system through which artists were prepared for their profession, drawing from nature as well as the copying of drawings either executed by the master of the atelier or by older established masters became an established practice. A drawing by Michelangelo from a fresco by Giotto reveals

51

the role played by drawings in studying the earlier masters (Figure 3–1). In the early Renaissance, drawing escaped from the confines of the copy book and the illuminated manuscript to expand in size to large studies and full-scale cartoons designed to cover the walls of great buildings.

Accompanying this increase in size and variety of subject, there was an increase in the number of media used in drawing. Charcoal and chalk became standard materials for making large studies and cartoons, while metal point, pen with ink or wash, water color as well as charcoal and chalk, were used for the smaller, carefully executed drawings that were made both as studies for paintings, sculptures and other artistic projects, and also as works of art in their own right. Many drawings were executed on beautifully toned papers, frequently these were highlighted with chalk or tempera. From the mid-fifteenth century on, red and brown chalks as well as other color enrichments which added to the beauty of the drawings indicate the value in which they were held.

General Characteristics of Early Renaissance Drawing

Drawings from thirteenth and fourteenth-century Italy have firm contour lines supported by simple dark and light modeling to reinforce the suggestion of form. Two contradictory tendencies are evident at this time. The first retaining the simple grand forms of the older formalized Byzantine tradition used very simple rhythmically related contour lines. This style can be seen in "The Visitation" by Taddeo Gaddi (Figure 3–2).

The second and newer trend abandoned these simple forms for the involved and wavering lines of the International Gothic Style, which was prevalent in Italy and Northern Europe. This tendency is illustrated by Jacopo Bellini's "Christ in Limbo" (Figure 3–3).

"The Visitation" by Taddeo Gaddi was executed in pen, bistre, and wash on parchment. This study was done in preparation for the life-sized fresco on the

FIGURE 3–2

Taddeo Gaddi (c.1300–1366; Italian) or fourteenth century, anonymous. "The Visitation." Pen, bistre, and wash on parchment, 8⅟₁₆" x 13⅟₁₆". *The Uffizi Gallery, Florence.*

FIGURE 3–3

Jacopo Bellini (c. 1400–1470; Italian).
"Christ in Limbo." Silver point on bluish prepared
vellum, 13¾″ x 9⅜″. *Musée du Louvre, Paris.*

ceiling of the lower chapel of St. Francis at Assisi. The style of drawing was strongly influenced by Giotto, who in turn drew on certain concepts of the early Christian tradition of monumental wall painting for his powerful narrative manner. Contour lines were kept simple and rhythmic, so that they harmonized with the architectural framework of which they were a part. This grand simplicity of contour contributed a grave nobility in keeping with the sacred character of the subject matter and insured that the forms read well from a distance. Major characters were usually portrayed in profile and the chief action was placed stage front in the composition to insure clarity of narrative. Outlines are precise, and when dark and light enrichment of the contour lines was used to reinforce the sense of three-dimensional form it was massed close to the contour line. This means of course that linear elements play the dominant roles in the drawing.

"Christ in Limbo" by Jacopo Bellini (Figure 3–3) was done in silverpoint on bluish prepared vellum as a study for a predella painting now in Padua. Here one can see the predeliction for elaborate linear arabesques which characterized the International Gothic style—the term used for the late stylistic development in picture-making that accompanied the final spread of the Gothic style all over Europe in the thirteenth and fourteenth centuries. As compared with the tradition represented by Taddeo Gaddi, the International Gothic style seems concerned with details of pattern and form. The involved interlacings of rock strata, the fluttering convolutions of draperies, even the graceful spiral of the devil's tail, all reveal the delight in refined elaborations and elegance of execution that the artist of the early Renaissance in Italy inherited from the late Gothic manner.

Before discussing individual artists and their drawings, an overview of the general stylistic developments that occurred during the Renaissance in Italy is valuable. The drawings and paintings of the early fifteenth century are tight and precise in their style of rendering. The emphasis upon the exact character of surface detail is often carried to a point that suggests a display of technical skill. The forms appear slender and have sharply delineated edges. By contrast the High Renaissance style of the late fifteenth and early sixteenth century employs more weighty and voluminous forms, and surface detail is suggested rather than rendered with the precision and exactitude that characterized the earlier period. As the style changed from the earlier precise linear manner to the grander emphasis on mass and volume, the actual manipulation of the drawing media became increasingly free.

A drawing of water buffaloes by Pisanello (Figure 3–4) provides a beautiful example of the early Renaissance manner. The medium, silverpoint reinforced with brushed wash, is well adapted to such a sustained rendering of surface detail. We see here the typically early Renaissance delight in rendering the complexity of surface appearances, an enthusiasm and love which reflects the artist's absorption in the physical world about him. The firm contour lines are

Selected Fifteenth-Century Draftsmen

FIGURE 3–4

Antonio Pisano Pisanello (1397–1455; Italian).
"Two Water Buffaloes." Silver point and brush
on vellum, 5¹¹⁄₁₆" x 8". *Musée du Louvre, Paris.*

stressed, making them sufficiently dominant elements in the drawing to contain
the detail—hence the drawing is not weak or confusing. Pisanello left us a
number of studies of animals and birds, as well as many drawings of people, all
of which reveal a delight in nature's picturesque variety. One of his most
fascinating pages of drawings pictures a number of studies of hanged men.

As one moves into the fifteenth century, the interest in describing the
surface gave way to a concern with the inner structure underlying surface detail.
The study of human and animal anatomy, of plant and geological structure, and
of the laws of perspective, commanded the serious attention of many artists and
this was part of a continuous, expanding intellectual concern about the nature of
the physical world that was not confined to the realm of art. The beginnings of
modern science, medicine, political theory and many other fields were initiated
at this time. Studies in anatomy were carried on in many fifteenth-century
Florentine studios, and both the Pollaiuolo brothers and Signorelli were
concerned particularly with this area of inquiry. A study of "Adam" by Antonio
Pollaiuolo (Figure 3–5) and "Two Figures" by Luca Signorelli (Figure 3–6)

FIGURE 3–5
Antonio Pollaiuolo (1429–1498; Italian).
"Adam." Pen over black chalk with bistre wash,
9¹⁵⁄₁₆" x 7". *The Uffizi Gallery, Florence.*

FIGURE 3–6

Luca Signorelli (1441–1523; Italian). "Two Figures." Black chalk, 16" x 10⅜". *Musée du Louvre, Paris.*

reveal the results of the research of the mid-fifteenth century anatomists. The drawings are less descriptions of surface appearances than they are diagrammatic statements of structure. An understanding of the forms of muscles, bones, and tendons as they interlock and combine below the surface to create the projections and hollows that meet the eye gives these drawings a power and force that is absent from the lovely but, in comparison, naïve drawings of the earlier men. In the Signorelli drawing one is aware of the artist's realization of the flexible character of the human form. The legs carrying the weight of the figure bend. The upper half of the body of the figure at the left twists in the act of conversing with the other man and Signorelli by this twisted pose not only establishes a sense of psychological interaction between the two men but

provides an opportunity to project the complex anatomical forms into a
foreshortened position. If one compares the figures by Signorelli and Pollaiuolo
with the figure in Bellini's "Christ in Limbo" the increased weightiness of the
forms is easy to discern.

In the last half of the fifteenth century the changes which distinguish the style of the High Renaissance from that of the fifteenth century early Renaissance style begin to be evident. The increased breadth of chiaroscuro (the Italian word used to describe broad areas of dark and light) gradually diminished the importance of the contour line. The edges of forms became softened and broken and a feeling for light, air, and space dissipated the linear emphasis of the earlier style. These changes are very evident when one compares "Profile of a Man" by Jacopo Bellini (Figure 3–7) with "Head of a Boy" by Botticelli (Figure 3–8). Botticelli's study of the head of a boy was executed in pen and bistre, a popular brown-colored ink, with opaque white highlights accentuating the form. The change in style from the early to the late fifteenth century is very evident when one compares these two lovely drawings. In the Botticelli the contour line appears and disappears; for instance, the line which defines the right-hand side of the boy's head disappears under the chin, where the form is sustained by the shadowy dark of the neck. The nose emerges from the space between the eyes as a form gradually defined by the pen hatchings; only at the base of the nose are the contour lines used to define and sharpen the projecting form. The head is surrounded by airy spaciousness. By contrast a deliberate precision characterizes the Bellini, the very fact that the head is in profile reveals the preference for a defining edge. And although the contour lines are reinforced by the sensitive modeling of the inner surfaces (most noticeably in the mouth), the contour remains inviolate and continuous with no sense of light, reflected light, or air modulating its precise delineation of edge.

The increased freedom of execution, the sense of light and air, and the fuller form which distinguishes the drawings of the last half of the century in Florence from those preceding are clearly evident in a lovely "Kneeling Angel with Child" (Figure 3–9) that has been attributed to both Botticelli and Filippino Lippi. In such drawings the increasingly sophisticated esthetic and human attitudes of the period begin to be felt. The sensuous charm of the angel is not entirely otherworldly, the Christ child is pudgy and playful, and the graceful convolutions of line that appear throughout the drawing are savored for their decorative charm.

After the thirteenth century the writings of ancient Greece and Rome played an increasingly important role in turning men's minds from religious speculation toward philosophy, political theory, scientific concepts, and ancient history. Remains from classical antiquity were still standing in many of the cities of Italy and architectural and sculptural fragments were repeatedly discovered in the course of excavating and building. These elements of classical tradition did much to shape the evolving style of the Renaissance. Mantegna, another fifteenth-century painter whose major works were carried out in Padua, not far from Venice, was one of the many early Renaissance painters who studied the artistic remains of antiquity as seriously as the learned humanists at the University of Padua studied its writings. His drawings and paintings frequently picture classical subjects, and stylistically his work reflects an archeological devotion to the venerated remains of ancient Rome. "Mars, Venus, and Diana" (Figure 3–10) is such a work. The mythological subject matter is composed in

FIGURE 3–9
Sandro Botticelli (1444?–1510; Italian) or Filippino Lippi (1457–1504; Italian).
"Kneeling Angel with Child." Silverpoint,
accentuated with pen, sepia, and red chalk,
heightened with Chinese white
on a prepared pink ground, 8⅛″ x 7¹³⁄₁₆″.
The Uffizi Gallery, Florence.

shallow space in imitation of classical bas-relief, with the three figures placed against a smooth background which resembles a marble plaque. The nude figures in both body proportions and pose are reminiscent of the sculptured gods of Greek and Roman antiquity, their very nudity is classical rather than medieval and Christian. Their costumes and props are authentically derived from the study of ancient works of art and the rhythmic flow of draperies conforms to classical rather than medieval esthetic canons. In addition, the smooth finish of the drawing suggests polished marble rather than the texture of flesh, textiles, or earth. However, the precise edges and detailed execution found in Mantegna's drawing conform to the general style which characterized the early Renaissance.

FIGURE 3-10

Andrea Mantegna (1431–1506; Italian). "Mars, Venus, and Diana." Pen, brown ink, and wash with touches of white and color, 12¼″ x 14¼″. *Courtesy, the Trustees of the British Museum, London.* (See Plate 4.)

The High Renaissance

Leonardo da Vinci has long been considered the Renaissance prototype of modern man. The range of his interests spanned the intellectual life of his time, covering the arts and sciences, invention, mechanics and philosophy. His notebooks, extensively illustrated and thoroughly annotated, provide a valuable insight into the way in which artistic and scientific activities moved together during the Renaissance to advance the frontiers of knowledge. His art reflected his role as an intellectual leader in late fifteenth and early sixteenth-century Italy, and many characteristics of the High Renaissance style were initiated by him. Three drawings by Leonardo provide some indication of the variety and scope of his interests: a "Nude Man Seen from in Back" (Figure 3–11) in red chalk, the oft-reproduced "Five Grotesque Heads" (Figure 3–12) in pen and ink, and a perspective detail from his study for the "Adoration of the Magi" (Figure 14–4) done on a toned ground in silverpoint, then reworked in pen and bistre, and heightened with white tempera.

The study of "Nude Man Seen from in Back" is one of the most beautiful of Leonardo's drawings. The strong virile body stands surrounded by light and air. Multiple contour lines reflect the searching quality of Leonardo's mind; no hard restrictive edge limits the sense of volume in the figure but instead one senses that the three-dimensional form moves away from the field of vision and continues to exist on the hidden front plane. Like Pollaiuolo and Signorelli, Leonardo also dissected corpses and made careful analytical diagrams of muscles, bones, and tendons, but this drawing, unlike Figures 3–5 and 3–6, is no diagrammatic statement of structure, but a supple and alive form in which the artist's knowledge supports and reinforces his visual analysis, in no way formalizing or restricting it. The drawing has been modeled with the diagonal line of a left-handed person, slanting from left to right typical of Leonardo, but there is nothing mechanical about the application. In many areas, such as under the left arm, the angle of the diagonal changes to create an intensified sense of the changing directions in the form.

Leonardo was interested in the relationship between spiritual and moral values and physical appearances. Like every artist who attempts to portray religious themes, be they Christian or otherwise, the spiritual nature of the personages pictured has to be established through their physical appearances, gestures, and interaction with others. His studies reflect this concern with appearances as a keynote to character, and no artist has left drawings of a greater variety of types, ranging from the sweet faces of angels and beautiful youths, through the characterful visages of aged men to hideous monstrosities that personify evil. The "Five Grotesque Heads" appear to be studies of worldliness, perhaps a visualization of the statement, "Render unto Caesar that which is Caesar's." The hard, knowing, leaf-crowned patrician in the front plane appears to symbolize the self-satisfaction of the successful; the power that comes to those who can shrewdly promote self-interest, who never give way to a generous but impractical impulse. The bald pate, the swollen wen, the sagging skin of the throat, all add to the ugly reality, for none is outside the realm of the reasonable

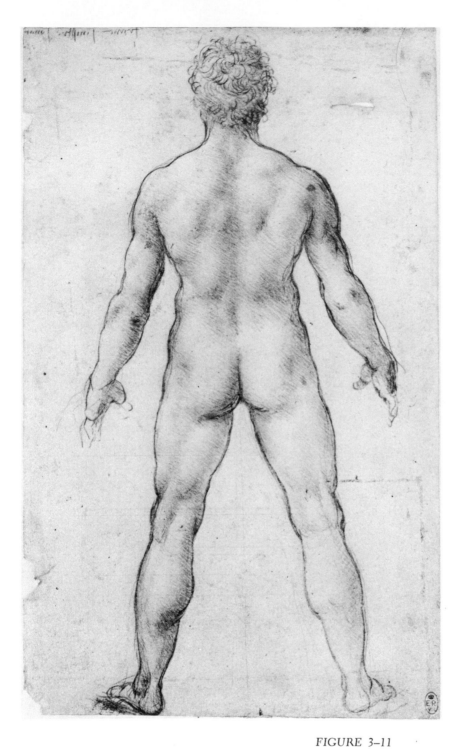

FIGURE 3–11

Leonardo da Vinci (1452–1519; Italian).
"Nude Man Seen from in Back." Red chalk, 27″ x 16″.
The Royal Library, Windsor Castle, England.
Reproduced by gracious permission of
Her Majesty Queen Elizabeth II.

FIGURE 3–13

Leonardo da Vinci (1452–1519; Italian)
or Cesare da Sesto (1480–1521).
"Tree." Pen and ink over black chalk,
on blue paper, 15″ x 10⅛″.
The Royal Library, Windsor Castle, England.
*Reproduced by gracious permission of
Her Majesty Queen Elizabeth II.*

and possible. To the left appears another aged and shrewd personage. The jutting chin and calculating eye project a frightening image of selfish determination, of unswerving connivance and ambition. The figure to the right is more gross. Greed and servility, aggression and hostility working hand in hand over the years have shaped the jutting lower lip, the weak chin, the sagging eyelids. The worldly mask is here less naked than in the other two figures, the evil more evident and therefore less sinister. In back, two more heads add an ugly embellishment to the theme that has been established with so much power in the front plane. In this drawing Leonardo has used pen, again with the typical left-to-right diagonal stroke, varying the stroke from fine to coarse according to the degree of emphasis and finish desired.

The perspective study (Figure 14–4) was done as a working drawing in preparation of the cartoon for the "Adoration of the Magi." A series of studies remains from this great project which reveal the steps by which Leonardo built up a concept and the precision with which he employed the science of perspective to build the space in which the action of his paintings was projected. Here too we realize that Leonardo's art was firmly entrenched in the science of his day. In his notebooks we find studies of the structure of flowers, plants, and the anatomy of animals which, like his perspective drawings, provided a firm foundation for the forms in his paintings.

Until very recently a lovely study, "Tree," was attributed to Leonardo (Figure 3–13). Certainly the firmness and vigor of the drawing and the way in which incisive detail and freedom of handling are combined suggest the hand of the master. However, the right-handed direction of the shading has been used as evidence to support the claim that it was done by Cesare da Cesto, a disciple of Leonardo. The drawing is in pen and ink on blue paper and, like many Renaissance examples, it proves that there is no basic conflict between esthetic values and objectivity. Though this drawing is accurate, there is no slavish copying of nature. Rather, one feels the selective eye of the artist noting the characterizing movements, bumps, angularity of branches and areas of shadow, stressing and then only suggesting the accompanying masses of foliage and minor branchings.

The drawings of Michelangelo and Raphael provide excellent illustrations of the previously mentioned development toward more grand and generalized forms in the High Renaissance period. "The Archers" (Figures 3–14), executed in red chalk, is one of the few drawings from the hand of Michelangelo which were not preparatory studies for sculptural or painting projects but appear to have been done as works of art in their own right. Presumably done as a gift for his beloved friend Tommaso Cavalieri, the drawing is unusually complex, containing nine major figures, some running and flying through the air, others kneeling or lying on the ground. They appear to be shooting arrows at a target suspended from the breast of a herma, that is, they assume the postures of shooting arrows although their hands are empty. Behind the animated archers a satyrlike figure holds a bow, while below two putti blow the flames of a fire and feed it with twigs. To the right of the main group of figures a cupid sleeps. The meaning of the composition is difficult to decipher but there can be no question

FIGURE 3–14

Michelangelo Buonarroti (1475–1564; Italian).
"Archers Shooting at Mark."
Red chalk, 8⅝" x 12⅛".
The Royal Library, Windsor Castle, England.
Reproduced by gracious permission of
Her Majesty Queen Elizabeth II.

but that its complex symbolism was meant to convey a subtle philosophic idea. Irwin Panofsky, in his "Studies in Iconology," relates the drawing to the neoplatonic movement and concludes that it might well be an illustration of a distinction made by Pico della Mirandola between sensual desire, love, and the desire for beauty. The putti and the satyr personify, as usual, natural sensual desire. Since cupid sleeps love is absent. The archers believe themselves to be shooting, whereas they themselves have become the darts, drawn to their target by some irresistible power. Through this elaborate symbolism Michelangelo conveys the idea that only the conscious desire for beauty lifts love above sensual desire and enables man to control the natural forces of his nature.

The complex symbolism of the drawing, the fact that it was done not as a

FIGURE 3–15
Michelangelo Buonarroti (1475–1564; Italian).
"Head of a Satyr." Pen and ink over chalk, 10⅝" x 7⅞".
Musée du Louvre, Paris (Alinari-Art Reference Bureau).

FIGURE 3–16

Raphael (Raffaello Santi, 1483–1520; Italian)
or Giulio Romano (1492–1546; Italian). "Three Graces,"
Study for "The Wedding Feast of Cupid and Psyche."
Red chalk, 8″ x 10¼″. The Royal Library,
Windsor Castle, England. *Reproduced by gracious permission
of Her Majesty Queen Elizabeth II.*

commission but in response to a personal attachment, the full development of
the drawing and its refined finish, all provide testimony as to Michelangelo's
serious intention in making the drawing. He employed the highly idealized
figure proportions which characterize his greatest works, in which small heads,
hands, and feet contribute a godlike grandeur to the great bodies which are
heavy without being clumsy. The figures were conceived as symbols of cosmic
forces rather than as anatomical studies such as the Pollaiuolo or Signorelli
drawings previously observed. As compared with the figures delineated by
Pollaiuolo and Signorelli, the anatomical structure is felt rather than explicitly indicated. This is particularly evident when one studies specific areas
such as the knees or the rippling muscles on the torso of the front archer.
Michelangelo, though fully cognizant of the nature and importance of the

FIGURE 3–17

Raphael (Raffaello Santi, 1483–1520; Italian). "Fighting Men." Brown chalk, 14¹³⁄₁₆″ x 11⅛″. *By courtesy of the Ashmolean Museum, Oxford.* (See Plate 5.)

anatomical forms, still seems most concerned with the sweep of the figures and their total volume and place in space.

The refinement of finish in "The Archers" hides the technique. In most of Michelangelo's drawings the method of execution is very evident and is frequently characterized by the use of bold cross-hatchings which emphasize the varying planes of the figure, thus avoiding the diagrammatic quality of the earlier anatomists but still providing a clear statement of structure. This style of cross-hatching can be best observed in the beautiful "Head of a Satyr" (Figure 3–15), where the clear pen lines and the larger scale of the reproduction reveals Michelangelo's brilliant use of this difficult technique.

Raphael, only a few years younger than Michelangelo, foreshadows more the developments of the urbane sixteenth-century mannerists. In the lovely though disputed "Three Graces" (Figure 3–16), done in chalk as a study for the "Wedding Feast of Cupid and Psyche," the ample figures are rounded and voluminous and the muscles, bones, and tendons ripple under the surface but do not project themselves into our consciousness. The tonal pattern is broad and simple, the major forms are modeled by generalized masses of light, shadow, reflected light, and cast shadow. Rather than use the complex cross-hatchings by which Michelangelo indicated the changes of plane within the mass, Raphael and his followers permitted a few directions of line to dominate shading and thereby established a more fluid continuous surface. Gracious and unforced, Raphael's amazing facility as a draftsman enabled him to employ the grand forms of the High Renaissance with an easy grace which pleases the eye and leaves the mind untroubled. It was this gracious sophistication of manner that made Raphael the ideal of certain of the middle sixteenth-century mannerists as well as of generations of later Baroque artists.

The apparently effortless ease with which Raphael drew can easily blind one to his power as a draftsman (Figures 3–17, 18–4). In "Combat" the lithe figures reveal the dynamic potentialities of the Renaissance concept of "contrapposto" when handled by this master. Contrapposto was a method of composing the human figure so that the major masses moved in different planes. Careful observation of the figures in "Combat" will show that no two major forms in any of the figures are parallel to one another but each moves powerfully in its own space trajectory. Thus each figure is charged with a powerful spiraling movement almost like a spring suddenly released from tension. Where any element of anatomical or spatial ambiguity might lessen the impact of the drawing, Raphael modeled the form with clearly defined cross-hatched lines, yet at no time does his insistence upon specific details inhibit the sweeping movement of the whole. Raphael was a nineteenth-century favorite because of his sweetness and idealism: the twentieth century, at first blinded by its anti-Victorian prejudices, is just becoming aware of his strength and power.

Two Venetian Draftsmen

A comparison between two drawings from Venice rounds out this brief discussion of the Renaissance in Italy. In Giorgione's paintings and drawings one sees for the first time a landscape with figures rather than figures in a landscape setting (Figure 3–18). This pen and bistre drawing reveals a sensitive response to the charm of the hilly landscape bordering the Adriatic. The rocky hillocks are softened by graceful trees and a small fortified village crowns the heights overlooking the sea. The towers, tiled roofs, chimneys and fortified walls are precisely rendered. Below, a small mill and house edge the water. The forms all through the drawing are carefully defined and modeled. The shading was achieved through the use of short clear lines, frequently applied in sets of straight or slightly curved parallels which were enriched in turn by cross-hatchings, stipplings, and other suggestions of surface texture. The result appears to be an objective description of fact in which sensitivity and accuracy, balanced by restraint, create a charming drawing.

Giorgione died in 1510, Titian in 1576. One sees vividly the rapid change which occurred during these years when one compares a study from Titian's mature years for the "Martyrdom of St. Peter" (Figure 3–19) with the carefully rendered Giorgione landscape. True, the Giorgione was a description of what was seen, the Titian a projection of an idea, and this to a degree can explain the

FIGURE 3–18
Giorgione (1478–1510; Italian).
"Landscape." Pen and ink, 6⁵⁄₁₆" x 9⁷⁄₁₆".
Musée du Louvre, Paris (Alinari-Art Reference Bureau).

factual and static nature of one as compared to the imaginative dynamic mood of the second. However, the essential differences arise from the contrast between the more precise factual manner of the earlier period and the grand manner of the High Renaissance. We see in this monumental composition of Titian's the way in which painterly techniques supplement and replace the more measured graphic manner of the earlier drawings. This is achieved by suggestion rather than delineation, by free sweeping methods of rendering and by a lack of surface detail. Movement and relationships became the primary subjects of such drawings rather than the picturing of objects, figures, and trees. These qualities not only characterize the end of the High Renaissance period but they set the stage for the bold and highly personal modes of drawing which distinguish the seventeenth and eighteenth centuries.

FIGURE 3–19

Titian (1488/90–1576; Italian).
Compositional study for "The Martyrdom of St. Peter."
33" x 15"? *Uffizi Gallery, Florence (Alinari-Art Reference Bureau).*

Summary

The revival of interest in ancient classical art and science which we term the Renaissance and which led to the modern age, first appeared in fourteenth-century Italy. It was during the early Renaissance that drawing became established as the foundation of training in the arts. Drawings were made as accurate notations of carefully observed forms or as preparatory studies for large murals or easel paintings and were most frequently executed in silverpoint, pen and bistre (a rich brown ink), chalk, or charcoal. Clearly defined contour lines and the careful and systematic rendering of precise details characterize the drawings in the late fourteenth and the fifteenth centuries. In this period human anatomy was systematically studied and the science of perspective was developed as part of the expanding fields of science and knowledge. The style of this early Renaissance period is clearly seen in the works of such artists as the Bellinis, Pollaiuolo, Botticelli, and Giorgione.

The High Renaissance style of the late fifteenth and first quarter of the sixteenth century represents the culmination of the Renaissance period. In the High Renaissance the forms become heavier, broadly massed tones of dark and light replace the earlier more linear manner, forms are composed so that they move freely in deep space, and drawings are executed in a free and bold style. The High Renaissance style received its fullest expression in such masters as Leonardo da Vinci, Michelangelo, Raphael, and Titian.

4

BAROQUE DRAWING IN ITALY

1600–1800

The profundity, opulence, and vigor of the High Renaissance masters seemed to throw a shadow over the generations that immediately followed them. The art of middle and late sixteenth-century Italy, generally termed *Mannerist*, tended to select and stress certain stylistic elements derived from the work of the High Renaissance masters, particularly Michelangelo and Raphael. An almost morbid taste for artifice and formality produced a certain cold elegance in the work of the Mannerists which contrasted sharply with the deep fervor that animated the High Renaissance. Although the innovations in the practice of drawing introduced by the Mannerists are of less importance in a short survey such as we are attempting here than those of the period which followed, these artists were the first to collect drawings and to do "master drawings" independent of preparatory sketches. With their doctrine of *disegno* or design equaling intention, the drawing became the most intimate part of their production. They started the academies, codified art rules, and even set up the types of drawings and academic drawing routines.

By the end of the sixteenth century a new spirit in art became evident. At first it grew from a desire on the part of the popes to make Rome the most

76

FIGURE 4–1

Attributed to Caravaggio
(1573–1610; Italian). "Study."
Pen, brown ink, 6½" x 7¹³⁄₁₆".
Achenbach Foundation for Graphic Arts,
California Palace of the Legion of Honor,
San Francisco.

beautiful city in the world. Termed the *Baroque*, the style that expressed the changing temper of the close of the sixteenth century expanded all through the Catholic world and became characteristic style of the seventeenth century. It provided a means of counteracting the Protestant Reformation and was widely adopted by the increasingly centralized European monarchies as a means of giving physical substance to the power and glory of the state. As an art form it

FIGURE 4–2

Simone Cantarini (1612–1648; Italian).
"Virgin and Child; Studies of Children." Red chalk, 10¾" x 8⅜".
The Royal Library, Windsor Castle, England.
*Reproduced by gracious permission of
Her Majesty Queen Elizabeth II.*

tended to emphasize great material splendor and dramatic impact. One of the first and most influential artists to give expression to this new mode was Caravaggio.

No artist in seventeenth-century Italy exerted a greater influence on subsequent artistic expression, both in Italy and the north of Europe, than Caravaggio. In his work there is a strong genre element which he achieved partly by using picturesque models which seem taken from the workaday world. His use of everyday types of people, naturalistic anatomical details such as wrinkles, hair, and veins, and of contemporary costumes and settings, were devices to make his biblical and mythological subject matter seem real by making it appear familiar. This was in opposition to tradition and the practice of his more academic contemporaries in whose work the human figure and other components were idealized and made remote from daily life in order to achieve a sense of nobility and grandeur. Caravaggio also initiated the use of intense dramatic lighting, so that the illuminated parts of his figures often stand out in startling brilliance against dark backgrounds. Caravaggio has left few drawings, but this may not mean that he did not make drawings, but rather that he did not value them highly enough to preserve them carefully, not too unlikely when we consider his tempestuous and impulsive nature.

A "Study" attributed to Caravaggio of brawling figures seated around a table, whether from his own hand or not, reveals the character of his work (Figure 4–1). A few broad tones of dark wash established the major areas of light and shadow and throw the illuminated parts of the figures into sharp focus. Particularly effective is the juxtaposition of the illuminated face at the left, with its startled expression of fear, and the threatening shadowed figure at the front lower right. A few speedy pen lines reinforce the washes to further define forms and suggest details of costume and expression. Subsequently the influence of Caravaggio became widespread; it appeared in the work of both Franz Hals and Rembrandt in Holland, Velásquez in Spain, La Tour in France, and in the work of a host of lesser men.

The breadth of handling, the freedom and vigor of execution shown in the Caravaggio drawing became increasingly characteristic of Baroque drawing in Italy. The major artists displayed a rich inventiveness in their unconstrained and expressive manner of drawing. The brilliance of their highly personal and often unique modes of working make the seventeenth and eighteenth centuries in Italy one of the most fertile and productive periods in the history of drawing. Drawing became highly valued as a form of artistic expression for its own sake rather than as a mere adjunct to painting, and many artists at this time preferred specializing in drawing and prints to a career as a painter.

Despite the general brilliance of performance that characterized drawing in Italy during these two centuries, many of the period's fine draftsmen are now virtually unknown except to a small group of scholars. Two factors have contributed to this lack of familiarity. First, taste during the first half of the twentieth century was not sympathetic to the florid and rhetorical nature of much of the painting of that day. Secondly, the work of a few great masters such as Tiepolo and Guardi, by its very virtuosity, blinded us to the general excellence

FIGURE 4–3

Pietro Testa (1611–1650; Italian).
"Compositional Study." Pen, brown ink, 11¹⁄₁₆″ x 16½″.
*Achenbach Foundation for Graphic Arts, California
Palace of the Legion of Honor, San Francisco.*

that prevailed. At present, this period is again being studied and the brilliant draftsmanship that characterized many minor painters is being recognized.

An example of a minor painter who preferred to draw and whose fine drawings are being rediscovered is Simone Cantarini, a seventeenth-century Bolognese who left us a beautiful "Virgin and Child; Studies of Children" (Figure 4–2), executed in red chalk. Cantarini was a deft and sensitive draftsman who died young leaving few paintings. His drawings are full of effortless grace and were much admired and collected by his contemporaries. The sketchy broken lines hardly seem to confine the forms but the certainty which permitted this freedom is felt throughout the drawing.

PLATE 3

Pol, Hermann, or Jan Limbourg (early fifteenth century; Belgian). "February," *Les trés riches heures du duc de Berry*, 1413–1416. Tempera: on vellum, 5⅜" x 8¹³⁄₁₆".
Musée Condé, Chantilly, France.

General Characteristics of Baroque Drawing

Regardless of the extreme variety, it is still possible to generalize about
Baroque drawing in Italy. In general, drawing became more painterly in
character, with flexibility and vivacity of handling creating an effect of
improvization (Diziani, Figure 4–9). Wash reinforced by pen or brush lines
(Castiglione, Figure 1–8) was frequently used for making studies and to a
considerable degree wash replaced the earlier "dry" media. The more restrained
and graphic types of rendering employed by fifteenth and sixteenth-century
draftsmen gave way to brilliant displays of technical prowess, as can be seen in a

FIGURE 4–5

Bernardino Gatti (1490/95–1576; Italian). "Study of an Apostle Standing." Brush and pen over black chalk heightened with opaque white and touches of color, 15¹³⁄₁₆" x 8¾". *By courtesy of the Ashmolean Museum, Oxford.*

drawing attributed to Pietro Testa (Figure 4–3). Here virtuosity of pen technique transforms a relatively undistinguished concept into a stunning performance. Another brilliant pen and ink technique applied to a very different subject can be seen in a landscape by Guercino (Figure 4–4). Media were combined freely, loosely applied tempera frequently being used to solidify the lights in free, richly sketched chalk studies (Figure 4–5). Often a drawing, commenced with charcoal or chalk, would subsequently be built up with washes, some of which were heightened with bits of color, and this in turn would be accented with flicks of dark pen accents (Dominica Mondo, Figure 15–18). The more systematic and regular use of parallel lines or cross-hatching to build up dark tones such as we have seen used by Leonardo, Michelangelo, and Raphael

FIGURE 4–6

Unknown Venetian (seventeenth century; Italian). "A Triumphant General Crowned by a Flying Figure." Quill pen and brown wash on white paper, 10¹¹⁄₁₆″ x 7¾″. *Courtesy of the Fogg Art Museum, Harvard University, Cambridge, Massachusetts (Meta and Paul J. Sachs Collection).*

gave way to much freer interlacings of curved, curled and tangled lines (Guercino, Figure 4–10). A pen and wash drawing from the hand of some unknown seventeenth-century Venetian artist reveals the brilliant freedom with which tangles of lines and splashes of deep-toned wash convey the impetuous excitement of the creative act (Figure 4–6).

*Selected Italian
Baroque Drawings*

Not all exhibitions of Baroque virtuosity were characterized by dynamic freedom of handling. In his "Self-Portrait" in the Uffizi (Figure 4–7), the seventeenth-century Florentine Carlo Dolci created a charming sober drawing in which each chalk mark was applied with a measure of control to equal that of an early fifteenth-century master. In like manner "The Drummer" by Piazetta reveals an almost caressing tenderness of touch in its carefully modulated tones and soft smudges of chalk. (Figure 16–16).

The Baroque was above all the style of the grand gesture. Artists delighted in drawing with a flourish, and a bold swirl of lines and tones provides an element of abandon that frequently obscures the firmness of structure beneath.

FIGURE 4–8
Gian Antonio Pellegrini (1675–1741; Italian).
"Venus Triumphant."
Red pencil, pen and sepia and sepia wash, 9¼" x 7" Museo Correr, Venice. Photo:
Smithsonian Institution, Washington, D. C.

Thus in the Castiglione, "St. Bernard before Christ Crucified," (Figure 1–8), the appearance of scribbled pen lines and splashes of wash might cause the novice to overlook the firm way the composition moves from the prone figure at the lower left diagonally over to the Cross, up through the bending body of Christ, to the upper right-hand corner. Playing against the diagonal of the body of Christ is the counter-diagonal line of the kneeling St. Bernard and the arm of the Cross. Against the dynamic lines of the diagonals is a stabilizing pyramidal form created by St. Bernard, the upper half of the body of Christ and the shadowy figure behind the Cross. The dark and light pattern is equally well thought out. A broad shadow on the strategically located head of Christ makes it the focal point of the study. Bold dark accents also direct our attention to St. Bernard, Christ, and the figure of an angel directly behind the Cross. Elsewhere the tones are less bold, thus avoiding distracting minor accents. A "Venus Triumphant" by Gian Antonio Pellegrini, one of the eighteenth-century Venetian masters, displays equal freedom and certainty and an even bolder juxtaposition of washes and free pen lines (Figure 4–8).

Both the pen drawing by Diziani of a "Flight into Egypt" (Figure 4–9) and the "Mars and Cupid" (Figure 4–10) by Guercino display the same combination of knowledge, clear purpose, and virtuosity of technique. Though many lines were used by Guercino to establish the contours of the figure, the form once found is modeled with sweeping diagonal shading that moves with increasing emphasis to culminate in the dark-shadowed head and plumed helmet. Using an astonishing tangle of lines, Diziani projects his forms and movements into clearly defined spaces. This drawing was done as a preparatory sketch for a large painting now hanging in the sacristy of St. Stephen's in Venice. Though executed in red chalk, pen and sepia ink with grey wash on yellowish paper, the pen lines provide the dominant element in the drawing, for they summarize the pictorial elements indicated tentatively by the less forceful media through which the composition was first explored. Diziani is considered by many students of eighteenth-century Italian art to be one of the most distinguished draftsmen of his age. In his early drawings he employed the more traditional linear hatchings, but his mature style, inventive in its free tangles of line, ranks with Tiepolo and Guardi. His paintings, oddly, lack the fire and distinction of his drawings.

As noted before, eighteenth-century Italian art was not all flourish and virtuoso performances. There were also masters, many of whom concerned themselves with genre subjects, who tempered the vigor of their statements with gentleness and charm. "The Drummer" by Piazetta has already been mentioned (Figure 16–16). Particularly notable is the sensitive use of tone in the Piazetta. The masterly handling of the white sleeve and the reflected light illuminating the face suggest both the warm radiance of the Venetian atmosphere and the urbanity of spirit that distinguished that time and place. Here an effortless grace rather than virtuosity of performance characterizes the drawing. Dominico Maggioto was another Venetian of this period who handled unpretentious subjects and preferred subtle tonality and a restrained rendering to the more prevalent flourish. His "Peasant Girl in Profile" (Figure 4–11) is a miracle of

FIGURE 4–9

Gaspare Diziani (1689–1767; Italian).
"The Flight into Egypt."
Black pencil and pen and sepia
on yellowish paper, 11⅝″ x 8½″. *Museo Correr, Venice. Photo:
Smithsonian Institution, Washington, D. C.*

FIGURE 4-10

Giovanni Guercino (1591–1666; Italian).
"Mars and Cupid." Pen and bistre, 10¹⁄₁₆″ x 7³⁄₁₆″.
Allen Memorial Art Museum, Oberlin College, Ohio
(R. T. Miller, Jr., Fund).

firm understatement. The sense of bony structure beneath forehead, check and chin is so subtle it seems felt rather than seen, and the use of the charcoal in the hair relates general tone and structural line beautifuly.

Bernardino Bison was another late eighteenth-century draftsman who preferred a modest and unforced style. Though he was widely recognized in his own day, his work has been obscured by the more brilliant stars of the Venetian firmament. A drawing of a "Seated woman" in pencil (Figure 4–12), reinforced with slight tones of wash, was probably done at the very end of the century, at which time there was a general turning away from the rococo flourish toward a more restrained style. Partly as a reflection of the increased dominance of French taste at the turn of the century, a preference for elegance and casual understatement replaced the earlier extravagance of manner.

The two star performers of eighteenth-century Venetian drawing and a few satellites remain to be considered. Giovanni Battista Tiepolo, perhaps the greatest painter-decorator of eighteenth-century Europe, was considered a master

FIGURE 4–11

Domenico Maggiotto (1713–1793; Italian). "A Peasant Girl in Profile." Black chalk heightened with white on blue-gray paper, 13⁹⁄₁₆″ x 10¹³⁄₁₆″. *Museo Correr, Venice. Photo: Smithsonian Institution, Washington, D. C.*

FIGURE 4–12

Guiseppe Bernardino Bi-
son (1762–1844; Italian).
"Seated Woman." Pencil,
6⅛" x 8¼". Collection of
Dr. Robert Prentice.

of his art at the age of nineteen. His fully developed style of painting is seen in his great ceiling and wall decorations and is distinguished by an endless inventiveness, a free painterly dexterity in the handling of paint, and a brilliant use of light clear color. These same qualities are revealed in the many sketches and studies he made, sometimes as preparation for his great decorative projects, though often Tiepolo's drawings appear to have been made for the pure pleasure he derived from sketching. The qualities that characterized his paintings and drawings are displayed with much brilliance in the beautiful "Hagar and Ishmael in the Wilderness" (Figure 4–13). Like most of Tiepolo's drawings, this

FIGURE 4–13

Giovanni Battista Tiepolo (1696–1770; Italian).
"Hagar and Ishmael in the Wilderness."
Pen, brush and brown ink and wash, over sketch in
black chalk, 16½" x 11⅛".
Courtesy of the Sterling and Francine Clark Art Institute,
Williamstown, Massachusetts. (See Plate 6)

FIGURE 4–14

Giovanni Domenico Tiepolo (1727–1804; Italian).
"Abraham Visited by the Angels." Sepia, wash drawing, 15¾″ x 11″.
The Metropolitan Museum of Art, New York (Rogers Fund, 1937).

FIGURE 4–15

Giovanni Domenico Tiepolo (1727–1804; Italian).
"Pucinello Hanged." Pen and wash, traces of black crayon, 11⅜" x 16".
Stanford Museum (Leventritt Collection).

was done in wash accented with pen lines. As is frequent in the Tiepolo drawings, only a small portion of the paper is covered and the reflected light from the white page seems to illuminate the entire scene with a dazzling luminosity. A dancing pen line suggests the contours; a few fluid touches of wash, accented with dark strokes of brushed ink, create sharp shadows. Occasional spotty squiggles of brushed black animate the pale washes and reinforce the sketchy contours. Yet, despite the fragmentary appearance, the forms are portrayed with certainty and power. A lifetime of knowledge enabled Tiepolo to project his figures into a blaze of light which, though it swallows the details of form and seems to consume even the shadows, leaves the forms and spaces vivid and convincing. Equally brilliant in execution is the more familiar "Rest on the Flight Into Egypt" (Figure 17–11). Both drawings radiate the sunny and untroubled sense of beauty that was the particular mark of that final phase of the Baroque style which came to be called the Rococo and which appeared in its most lustrous expression in Venice and the court of France.

To be the artist-son of a father like Giovanni Battista Tiepolo is both a challenge and a handicap. His son, Giovanni Domenico Tiepolo, continued in the stylistic vein of the father and produced an abundance of charming drawings. "Abraham Visited by the Angels" (Figure 4–14) was executed in sepia wash which has been reinforced with pen lines and the warm brown color permeates the darkest passages and makes them glow. The animated contour lines and splashes of wash which characterized the father's drawings are still used but are applied in a more pedestrian manner. Less is left to the imagination and the spirited certainty of execution is replaced by an amplitude of detail. In this more fully developed tonal study extensive areas of middle and middle-light values make focal points of the extremes of light and strong dark. Thus attention is directed most forcefully to the vivid head of Abraham and with slightly less emphasis to the group of angels. The unforced relationship, like a wedge in a cleft, between the pyramidal form in which Abraham is composed and the triangular grouping of the angels is admirable. The pen lines act as a linear counterpoint to the wash which, applied freely in broad areas, provides the cohesive element in the composition. Whether one observes the edges of the washes or the pen lines, the contours move rhythmically so that movement permeates the entire study.

FIGURE 4–16

Antonio Canaletto (Canale) (1697–1768; Italian).
"An Island in the Lagoon." Pen, brown ink and carbon ink wash
over ruled pencil lines, 7¹³⁄₁₆" x 10¹⁵⁄₁₆".
By courtesy of the Ashmolean Museum, Oxford. (See Plate 7.)

FIGURE 4–17

Francesco Guardi (1712–1793; Italian).
"Venetian Scene." Pen and sepia and sepia wash, 8½" x 11½".
Stanford Museum (Leventritt Collection).

His "Pucinello Hanged" (Figure 4–15)—pen and wash with traces of black crayon—is in the playful narrative vein of much Rococo painting. Real tragedy, like deep religious feeling, was too serious for the Rococo spirit. Instead, mock tragedy provided the motif for such whimsical narratives as this.

Venice was much beloved both by her visitors and her citizens, and in the eighteenth century a group of painters gave themselves over to celebrating the sensuous beauty of the city and the charm of her way of life. Canaletto, who made a wash and pen drawing of "An Island in the Lagoon" (Figure 4–16), left us many carefully executed views of the city in which deep vistas are projected into perspective with an orderly clarity that in no way minimizes their charm. In this drawing the brown ink and the contrasting blue-gray wash appear to have been superimposed on a carefully ruled preliminary pencil study. One feels that a comfortable balance has been achieved by using the solid pencil construction under the graceful pen lines. Many of Canaletto's drawings were made for sale and, as is the case with this particular drawing, he frequently repeated a composition many times.

FIGURE 4–18

Francesco Guardi (1712–1793; Italian). "The Visit."
Pen and sepia and sepia wash on yellowish paper, 5¹⁄₁₆" x 6⅞". *Museo Correr, Venice. Photo: Smithsonian Institution, Washington, D. C.*

Francisco Guardi was an assistant in the workshop of Canaletto and much of his earlier work is indistinguishable from that of Canaletto. However, in his later years he concerned himself less with panoramic views of the city and developed a preference for genre, depicted within the Venetian setting, with much emphasis upon the people and their ways. His style also changed from that of Canaletto, for he abandoned the rather precise manner of the older man for a free and sketchy rendering. A "Venetian Scene" (Figure 4–17) in pen and wash is typical in both style and subject matter. Pale in tone, the broken pen line reinforces the washes and at the same time suggests the constantly moving reflecting lights and the transparent shadows of the water-bound island city. The scribbled figures provide a delightful note of animation. Much of the charm of

"The Visit" (Figure 4–18) results from the way in which the handwriting on the back of the page works with the animated texture of the drawing to create a shimmering totality. Here again Guardi made an unlabored, delightful notation in which the architectural splendor of the city, the modes and manners of its citizens, and the ever-present movement of water are evoked with the most fragmentary means.

Before leaving Italy one more eighteenth-century artist must be mentioned. Although he was born in Venice, Piranesi left that city when he was a youth and spent his life in Rome. Though he considered himself an architect by profession, Piranesi received no important architectural commissions until he was forty-five years old, and until that time he supported himself by his imaginative drawings and etchings of architectural subjects. His work combined a feeling for the grandeur of ancient Rome, as revealed by the great ruins, with a taste for theatrical scale. Such a conception as the "Architectural Fantasy" reproduced here (Figure 18–1) is distinguished by the grandiose scale of the conceptions and the skill and knowledge with which architectural forms were projected into perspective. This drawing, done in pen and wash on top of a red chalk sketch, creates a sense of great height by using the dark accents of figure groups at the bottom of the composition.

The brilliant masterpieces of drawing produced by the eighteenth-century Venetian masters seemed like a last magnificent flowering of the Italian Renaissance promise. Long before, the dynamic center of European art had moved north, first to the Netherlands and later to Germany, France, and Spain. To continue our rapid survey of the history of drawing we must therefore turn back to the close of the Middle Ages in Northern Europe.

Summary

The High Renaissance masters seemed to overshadow the men who followed them in the last half of the sixteenth century. The artists of the last half of the sixteenth century, termed *Mannerists* because their work seems mannered and colored by High Renaissance precedent, initiated no important new tendencies in drawing. However, a new art style became evident at the end of the sixteenth century which reached its height in seventeenth-century Rome and later in Venice. This new art style has been termed the *Baroque,* and the Baroque style tended to emphasize material splendor and drama as a means of giving physical substance to the revived Catholic Church and to the emerging monarchies of Europe. The masters of the Baroque style were frequently brilliant draftsmen who drew rapidly, freely, and with great vivacity. They usually employed full, heavy figure proportions, boldly foreshortened poses, violent action and dramatic contrasts of dark and light. Styles were highly individualized and drawings were collected and valued for their own sake. In general, media were handled in a painterly fashion with wash and free combinations of media replacing the more linear means of the fifteenth and early sixteenth centuries. Rome and Bologna were important artistic centers in the seventeenth century, with Venice assuming leadership in eighteenth-century Italy. Guercino, G. B. Tiepolo and Francisco Guardi were among the most important Baroque draftsmen of Italy.

5

RENAISSANCE AND BAROQUE DRAWING IN GERMANY AND THE NETHERLANDS 1400–1700

The vigorous artistic developments of Northern Europe and Italy during the late Middle Ages were part of a common expansion of economic, political, and intellectual life and, despite the strong indigenous character of each nation's art, there was a constant interplay of influences. Early in the fourteenth century the book illuminators of France were already aware of what was happening in Italy and introduced into their work figure groups, architectural settings, and other stylistic details derived from the Italian masters. By mid-century, Italian painters were being imported by French kings to decorate their palaces. The transition from sharply observant and beautifully crafted book illumination to book illustration typified by the *Très riches heures du duc de Berry* (Figure 2–17) represents the final step before the pictorial art of Northern Europe, influenced by Italian example, broke from the confines of the book into full-blown easel painting.

Renaissance Drawing in Flanders

The vigor of the late Middle Ages received its most striking physical expression in the great Gothic cathedrals of Northern Europe, particularly in France. In the fifteenth century painting provided a medium through which both the physical and intellectual energies of the early Renaissance could find expression. Fundamental to the deep religious convictions of this age was a belief that the universe in all its beauty, variety, and ugliness was but a mirror of divine will and divine truth. Thus every aspect of the physical world demanded the full regard of the artist for each and every object, and every part of each object existed as expression of divine will. To those with the desire and power to understand, all creation had a symbolic meaning; thus space and light symbolized the all-pervasiveness of God. This philosophical concept led to the rapid flowering of an art of intense realism in the early fifteenth century, most strikingly expressed in that small area where Flanders bordered on eastern France. Every object in his world fell under the searching scrutiny of the artist, and this intense concern with his immediate environment resulted in an art distinguished by a microscopic sense of exactitude.

Much of the wealth of medieval Flanders grew from the excellence of such crafts as silversmithing, weaving, and the production of leather goods. The precise and exacting standards of a culture in which fine crafts were extolled were continued in the style of the painters, who demanded that the craft of painting contribute its share to the perfection of rendering required by the philosophic-religious convictions of the age. All of these factors aided in the development of a meticulously detailed style of drawing.

Because the artists of France and Flanders worked on a comparatively small scale as compared to the Italians, and both by temperament and tradition were guided by a taste for systematic procedures, their preference was for media which provided for control and precision. Thus silverpoint, pen and ink, or tempera applied with a fine brush, were preferred to charcoal and chalk, although a handsome sketch of a monk from the School of Gerhaert David appears to have been first sketched in chalk, and then the forms of the face and hands were developed with fine silverpoint hatchings (Figure 5-1). Silverpoint was the historic precursor of the pencil. A pointed rod of silver was used on a paper coated with a fine slightly abrasive material, and this produced a fine pale line similar to that produced by a hard pencil.

A careful examination of a detail of this portrait reveals the way in which the fine lines of silverpoint were used to build subtle and complex three-dimensional forms. The lines are generally parallel to one another, not rigidly so, but rather with a slightly arched or radiating relationship such as results from the natural sequence of movements made as the hand moves along the surface while the fingers holding the silverpoint make rapid small strokes. As these lines approach the contour they flatten out and become more parallel to the contour until they merge with it and thereby reinforce its strength. This creates an almost organic relationship between the deft, small lines producing the modeling and the contour lines, thus enabling the artist to describe the most subtle undulations of surface without overemphasis or exaggeration of tonal change.

FIGURE 5–2

Jan van Eyck (1390–1441; Flemish).
"Portrait of Cardinal Albergati." Silverpoint on
grayish-white prepared paper, 8¾₁₆" x 7".
Staatliche Kunstsammlungen, Dresden.

FIGURE 5–3

Jan van Eyck (1390–1441; Flemish).
"Saint Barbara." Brush on chalk ground
on wood, 7⅜″ x 13⅜″.
Musée Royal des Beaux-Arts, Antwerp. (See Plate 8.)

To the van Eyck brothers, Hubert and Jan, must be given much of the credit for the startling advances made in drawing and painting in Flanders in the early part of the fifteenth century. Through their activities the techniques for describing the physical world in the fullest detail without sacrificing either a sense of solid form or deep space were perfected. Their miniaturistic technique was a miracle of craftsmanship and through their exacting art they expressed a deep religious fervor, for their efforts were dedicated above all else to the glorification of a beneficent God. Only one drawing exists which is unquestionably from the hands of the van Eycks, the "Portrait of Cardinal Albergati" by Jan van Eyck (Figure 5–2). This silverpoint drawing, done on a greyish-white toned paper, was made as a preparatory study for a portrait which had to be completed without the presence of the sitter. It reveals the amazing ability to record the exact appearance of his sitter without any idealization and yet with complete sympathy. The firm and sensible character of Cardinal Albergati is projected with as much certainty as the physical forms.

The delicate modeling of the head was built up with diagonal shading such as we saw used in the "Head of a Monk." Where a heavier dark was needed, as in the accents under the chin, the diagonal lines were amplified with cross-hatching. The extreme delicacy of the silverpoint tones, applied with an intellectual certainty equal to the physical control, created a drawing of quiet distinction. To the left of the head one can see notations in the handwriting of the artist as to the color of the various parts of the painting, "the lips very white . . . ," "the nose sanguinous," and so on.

One of the loveliest sketches to come from Flanders in the first half of the fifteenth century is the drawing on panel by Jan van Eyck of "Saint Barbara" (Figure 5–3), executed in gray tempera, with a few slight indications of color. The paint is applied in tiny strokes, often hatched to build the forms which are firmed up by the exquisitely precise darker lines defining the edges. The sky alone shows a loose and airy application of paint. It might be argued that the Saint Barbara is less a drawing than an unfinished painting, but van Eyck's method of building the form through delicate small lines is sufficiently akin to the way in which he employed fine lines of silverpoint or pen strokes of pale ink to justify its inclusion here.

Christian thought in the fifteenth century constantly juxtaposed good and evil. God had, in his infinite wisdom, created the good and the beautiful, but the wicked and ugly were no less part of the total scheme whereby man tested his virtue and proved himself worthy of redemption. The good and beautiful and the evil and wicked existed both in the external world and in the unseen but no less real spiritual world. A counterpart to the reverence for the visible world, which led the Gothic artists to render it in all its detail, was their concern with picturing the heaven, purgatory, and hell of medieval Christian belief. The play of their imagination in giving form to this cosmos was no less impressive than their ability to describe the complexities of the physical world.

The art of Italy reflects the brilliance of the Mediterranean world, its blue seas, sunny skies and the Golden Ages of classic culture. A taste for the generalized, idealized and sensuously pleasing is everpresent, and the handsome pagan gods of ancient Greece and Rome seem to smile from behind the countenances painted by the Italians. The art of Northern Europe grew from a very different physical matrix: fog, grey skies, long cold winters, wind and rain, contributed to a certain morbidity of temperament. Equally important in determining its character was age-old folk mythology. Even though Christian belief is the theme of most of the early paintings, the fearsome creatures of pre-Christian legends still seemed to haunt the imagination of Northern artists. A world of gnomes, goblins, witches, and elves, suggestive of the craggy branches, tangled roots, and dark mystery of the Northern woods rather than the marble gods and goddesses of classic antiquity, provided the forms that symbolized evil and hell for the medieval artist.

This taste for the grotesque and the fantastic is constantly before us as we examine Northern art. "Devils in Hell," from the school of Rogier van der Weyden (Figure 5–4), employs the meticulous methods of the medieval craftsmen in building up a nightmare image of devils garroting a sinner in Hell. The precise renderings of the forms help to make convincing the imaginary monsters who inhabit Hell. As is so frequently the case in strictures on morality, the artists of Flanders seem able to picture the suffering of the damned with much more zest than the rewards of righteous living. Certain characteristics developed by Van der Weyden in the mid-fifteenth century influenced the entire subsequent character of Flemish art; in fact, the impact of Van der Weyden on Flemish painting is perhaps greater than that of any other single individual. Particularly influential was his use of graphic details of facial expression and gestures as a means of establishing psychological characterizations and dramatic narrative elements. As one studies the evil, tragic faces and the tense gestures of "Devils in Hell," there is an almost tactile awareness of the role of bone, tendon and muscle as the elements through which expression is achieved.

By the mid-fifteenth century the art of Flanders had absorbed many elements from the Renaissance style in Italy. Hugo Van der Goes had traveled in Italy and he incorporated some of the compositional concepts of the

FIGURE 5–4

School of Rogier van der Weyden (c.1400; Flemish). "Devils in Hell." Silverpoint, 3⅜" x 11". *Courtesy the Trustees of the British Museum, London.*

FIGURE 5–5

Hieronymus Bosch (1450–
1516; Dutch). "Man Being
Shaved." Pen and ink, 6⅞" x
8³/₁₆". *Courtesy the Trustees
of the British Museum, London.*

Renaissance into his work; the forms are larger, the relationships of forms more
spatially integrated. However, Van der Goes did not discard the singular
elements of his native style, and in many ways he continued Van der Weyden's
manner, particularly in his employment of familiar types of people to make his
Biblical subjects immediate and real. Like Van der Weyden, he also used
expressive gestures and vivid facial expressions to convey intense emotion. In a
copy of Van der Goes' "Lamentation" (Figure 15–7), one sees the same telling
use of detail to achieve a definite response on the part of the viewer that

FIGURE 5–6

Hieronymus Bosch (1450–1516; Dutch). "Tree Man in a Landscape." Pen and brown ink, 10$\frac{15}{16}$" x 8$\frac{3}{8}$". *Albertina, Vienna.*

FIGURE 5–7

Pieter Brueghel, the Elder (1525/
30–1569; Flemish). "The Painter
and the Connoisseur." Pen and
bistre, 10″ x 8⅜″. *Albertina, Vienna.*

FIGURE 5–8

Swabian master (end of fifteenth century).
"The Genealogical Tree of Jesus." Pen and ink, 11⅜" x 12¹³⁄₁₆".
Courtesy Staatsgalerie Stuttgart, Graphische Sammlung.

distinguished Van der Weyden's work. The spare forms are delineated with an almost harsh energy. Pen lines of brown ink were applied in short sharp strokes to create an intensely animated surface, in which clarity of form is equalled by strength of feeling. At times, as in the lower right-hand figure, the surface animation is intensified by adding sharp dots to the parallel and cross-hatch patterns. Although the authorship of this drawing is not certain, it has been attributed to Pieter Brueghel the Elder, and it is certainly very similar in technique to many Brueghel drawings.

Hieronymous Bosch and Pieter Brueghel the Elder were two Flemish painters of great originality and power. Although some of the late fifteenth and sixteenth-century artists of Flanders adopted the Italian manner to the point where the singular character of Flemish art was lost, both Bosch and later Brueghel remained close to the genre tradition of Northern Europe. Both men

FIGURE 5–9
Albrecht Dürer (1471–1528; German). "Ninety-Three-Year-Old Man." Brush, India ink and white body color on grayish-violet prepared paper, 16⅜" x 11⅛". *Albertina, Vienna.*

shared the already mentioned taste for the macabre and both were consummate craftsmen. A continuous delight in the immediate and the familiar is inherent in even the most fantastic imaginings of these richly productive geniuses. Bosch made innumerable studies of beggars and cripples, on which he drew for some of the grotesque details which characterize his more fanciful allegories. Two very similar pages of drawings of "Cripples" exist, one in the Albertina in Vienna (Figure 1–5) and another in the Royal Collection in Brussels. Whether one is from the hands of Bosch or both were copied from Bosch by Brueghel remains doubtful. In either case they reveal the influence which the older man had upon the younger. A study of a "Man Being Shaved" by Bosch (Figure 5–5), like the drawings of cripples, shows how interrelated were the real, the grotesque, and the supernatural in his art. In the midst of this earthy vignette of village life, a stick capped with a human head raises itself unnoticed, seemingly as much a part of the natural order of daily life as the act of shaving.

It was in his extremely involved and elaborate fantasies that the particular genius of Bosch received its fullest expression. Those great works from his later years reflect the imagery of medieval legendry and alchemy, in which the esoteric and allegorical meanings are expressed through complicated, obscure and mystical symbols, often nightmarish and strange, always vivid and fanciful. Not many of the drawings made as studies for these painted allegories exist, but a "Tree Man in a Landscape" (Figure 5–6), from the Albertina Museum in Vienna, attributed to Bosch despite the signature of Brueghel in the corner, introduces a motif which Bosch repeated with slight changes in at least two of his major paintings. Executed with pen in brown ink, the drawing shows the typical combination of realistic elements to create a strange and fantastic monster. Not a small part of the ominous effectiveness of the drawing results from the contrast between the unemotional style of rendering with its precise and controlled development of forms, and the unreal mood created by the presence of the dreamlike tree man, peering balefully from his station surrounded by a benign peaceful landscape.

Much of Brueghel's early work derives from Bosch (Figure 18–10). The meticulously rendered surfaces in which the forms were built by small sharp strokes of the pen, the imaginative combinations of human, animal, insect, bird, and vegetative elements in extremely complex and tightly interwoven details, the landscape setting filled with numberless small forms are barely distinguishable from the older master. But Brueghel matured to a more mellow mood, and his later works seem dominated by a more accepting and kindly temper. Both nature and man are felt to be ultimately good. The "Painter and the Connoisseur" (Figure 5–7) has humor moderating its sharpness. A careful study of details of rendering, particularly in the dour head of the artist, reveals the certainty with which this master draftsman directed his unerring pen to build forms and textures.

Renaissance Drawing in Germany

The important role played by the tradition of medieval book illumination in the development of pictorial realism in Northern Europe has already been mentioned. At the end of the fourteenth century the art of woodcut printing appeared, and, soon after, techniques were perfected for casting type in metal and for printing. Germany, particularly the Rhineland area, became one of the early centers for the production of illustrated books, and this proved a stimulus to the development of graphic arts.

FIGURE 5-10

Albrecht Dürer (1471–1528; German).
"The Great Piece of Turf."
Watercolor, 16¼″ x 12⅜″.
Albertina, Vienna. (See Plate 9.)

Much of the art of Germany reveals a strong kinship with that of Flanders. There is the same delight in fine craftsmanship and this tendency was nurtured by the demands of wood cutting and wood and metal engraving, crafts used in book illustration which demanded the utmost control and precision. The involved symbolic and allegorical elements of late medieval thinking also played a part in shaping the art of Germany. These various elements are all apparent in the fascinating "Genealogical Tree of Jesus," done around the end of the fifteenth century by a Swabian artist who has sometimes been identified as Martin Schon (Figure 5–8). The rather precisely placed sets of parallel lines and hatchings recall the techniques of wood engraving. The elaborate interlacing pattern of tree branches, scrolls and other symbolic motifs remind one of the meandering patterns with which medieval illuminators enriched their manuscripts, whereas the rich variety of facial types and gestures relate to the penchant for picturesque realism which we have seen in Flanders, France and medieval Bohemia.

Like all of Northern Europe, Germany was aware of the persuasive art of Italy. Albrecht Dürer holds a position of unique importance in the art of Germany for he introduced certain resources of the High Renaissance, at the same time giving the most complete expression to the graphic genius of Germany. Dürer traveled to Italy, observed and admired the art of the High Renaissance. In his drawings, paintings, and prints his genius achieved a fusion of the realism, the taste for the grotesque, and the technical brilliance that characterized the art of Northern Europe with the strength of composition and grandeur of concept that distinguished Italian painting. His "Portrait of a Ninety-Three-Year-Old Man" (Figure 5–9) is one of a series of five drawings still in existence which were executed by Dürer as studies for a painting of St. Jerome. Although the unidealized realism and the detailed manner of treatment of this drawing relate to the art of Northern Europe, the sense of physical vitality and solid, full-bodied form would not have been possible had not Dürer studied the Italian masters.

Like many of the artists of Italy, Dürer used a toned paper as a background for the drawing, in this case a warm brownish violet. The drawing was executed in India ink, applied in firm lines with a brush, and the form was heightened with white tempera. Dürer's technical skill as an engraver enabled him to lay in the brush lines with admirable certainty. The continuous changes in spacing, length, and degree of curvature reveal the unhesitating coordination which existed between the artist's eye moving across the surfaces and his hand as it recorded forms and surface textures. The smooth cap, the crinkled texture of aged skin, and the curly beard stand in vivid contrast to one another, without any sacrifice in unity of handling.

The miracle and wonder that can be achieved when the simplest and most familiar object is scrupulously observed and rendered with complete fidelity is nowhere more apparent than in Dürer's "The Great Piece of Turf" (Figure 5–10). The artist felt no need to be more than a faithful transmitting agent who revealed the facts about his subject and through this fidelity to nature created a work of art the beauty of which is to a large extent a reflection of the artist's humility and honesty. The medieval tradition of technical virtuosity fused with

FIGURE 5–13

Rembrandt van Rijn (1606–1669; Dutch).
"Winter Landscape." Reed pen and bistre, 2⅝" x 6⁵⁄₁₆".
Courtesy of the Fogg Art Museum,
Harvard University, Cambridge, Massachusetts (Charles A. Loeser Bequest).

FIGURE 5-14

Adrian van Ostade (1610–1685; Dutch).
"Scene in an Inn." Pen and bistre with bistre wash, 6⅞" x 10".
The Metropolitan Museum of Art,

FIGURE 5-15
Adriaen Brouwer (1601–1638; Flemish).
"Scene in a Tavern." Pen and bistre with bistre wash,
5½" x 7⅞". *Albertina, Vienna.*

the passionate interest in this world which characterized the Renaissance to create this beautiful drawing.

The Renaissance reached its height in Germany in the work of Dürer and Holbein. Hans Holbein the Yonger, like Dürer, commenced his career as a designer of woodcuts but his power as a portrait painter was revealed early in his career, and it is as a portrait painter that his fame persists. The conventions of the day regarding painting demanded a full rendering of detail and a carefully finished surface. Consummate artist that he was, Holbein probably enjoyed displaying his technical skill in rendering cloth, skin, hair, and jewelry with an enamel-like perfection of surface. Many of Holbein's finest portraits were executed while he was court painter to Henry VIII of England. Fortunately for us, his sitters were busy people and the artist formed the habit of making quick studies to which he could refer while executing the more time-consuming paintings. A felicitous example of one of these studies is his "Portrait of Cecelia Heron" (Figure 5–11), one of the daughters of his patron, Sir Thomas More, who commissioned the family portrait referred to in Chapter 1 (Figure 1–6). With Holbein the art of portrait drawing achieved a new power and graciousness. This was the result of what appears to be an effortless emphasis on the telling details of feature and facial structure to establish the sitter's appearance and personality. Rather than the all-inclusive realism of his precursors, who recorded every wrinkle and surface blemish, Holbein's discriminating gaze picked out the characterizing detail—the soft contour of a mouth, the firmness of bone beneath chin, the smooth roundness of high forehead, and it is these revealing elements which communicate the personality of the sitter through the facts of physical appearance. These descriptive details are recorded with equal assurance in easy wisps of charcoal line, soft crumbles of chalk, thin washes of color, light accents of pencil or pen, all of which work together to create an incisive record of appearances far beyond what appears to be the potential of the separate parts. Holbein's drawings exemplify the miracle of understatement, of power through restraint, of knowledge and skill leading to certainty (Figure 16–13).

Baroque Drawing in Holland

In the seventeenth century Holland became a major center of artistic developments. While certain Flemish painters, particularly Rubens and Van Dyck, adopted the more extravagant aspects of the Italian Baroque manner to create splendid decorations for the great palaces and churches, in Holland a more middle-class attitude prevailed.

The artists of Protestant Holland, lacking the patronage of the Catholic Church and of an artistocratic court, painted for an audience of affluent burghers with relatively unsophisticated tastes. Their preference was for Biblical scenes couched in a familiar setting, for country or city genre—preferably with a storytelling element, or for landscape and still-life. Whatever the subject, the Dutchman liked a skillfully rendered painting in which the surface qualities of objects were depicted in a convincing, detailed manner. During Rembrandt's formative years, this Dutch tradition was modified by the impact of seventeenth-century Italian painting, particularly as it was formulated by Caravaggio and his followers, but the more grandiose elements of this style were essentially unsuited

FIGURE 5–16

Adam Pynacker (1622–1673; Dutch).
"Landscape." Pencil and ink with wash, 10″ x 14¾″.
*Allen Memorial Art Museum, Oberlin
College, Ohio (F. F. Prentiss Fund).*

to the taste of Dutch patrons. Rembrandt was influenced by the new mode, and in his early period he showed a penchant for dramatic subjects, theatrical lighting, and picturesque types of personages. Unlike Rubens, he did not visit Italy in person, but absorbed the new Italian mode from the artists with whom he worked and studied.

Part of Rembrandt's genius lay in the way in which he reconciled the prosaic Dutch tradition and the theatrical manner of the followers of Caravaggio. As one studies the evolution of his mature style, it is evident that the elaborate, involved, and theatrically costumed compositions of his early years gave way to a simple, deeply emotional manner of drawing and painting. Many of the qualities that characterize his work were derived from the Baroque masters, but as time passed all artifice disappeared, transmuted by his sincerity. From the modish exaggerations of his early manner, the elements of his mature style emerged—his feeling for light, space, and the deeply emotive power of the shadow, the masterly

FIGURE 5–17

Alaert van Everdingen (1621–1675; Dutch).
"A Rocky Mountain Landscape." Brush drawing
and India ink on gray paper, 13¾″ x 16⅜″.
*Courtesy of the Fogg Art Museum, Harvard
University, Cambridge, Massachusetts (Charles A. Loeser Bequest).*

freedom with which he manipulates his media, and his amazing facility as a draftsman. These qualities are brilliantly displayed in the masterly "Holy Family in the Carpenter's Workshop" (Figure 5–12). The velvety but transparent darks were applied in great fluid washes. The shining lights illuminate the sacred presence. The linear elements which give form to the washes are at the same time vividly descriptive and magnificent as abstract calligraphy. Rembrandt's artistic genius and his warm human responses combine to create a master drawing. These same qualities are evident in the simple Study of "Rembrandt's Studio" (Figure 14–17). An airy tone, laid on in broad washes, establishes the pale indoor light and the transparent shadows. The tumble of objects on the table, the seated model, the artist's easel, and edge of the mantle, emerge softly from the dim interior, their outlines defined by rough, crisp lines. There is no hint of virtuoso performance; the vitality of the linear accents plays against the fluid washes and projects both the facts and the artist's feelings without sham or show.

Two other drawings reveal very different facets of Rembrandt's strength as a draftsman. "Winter Landscape" (Figure 5–13) presents a breathtaking ability to summarize the fundamental relationship of forms in the deep space of a colorless winter landscape. With only a few quickly brushed lines and a pale wash, Rembrandt recorded the all-encompassing whiteness, the sharp perspective of fence and road, the faint distant horizon, and the huddled cluster of trees and farm buildings. The brushed lines equal those of the masters of Oriental calligraphy in textural variety and the vigor with which they reveal the gesture of the drawing act. It is easy for the observer to overlook the role played by the few dark accents in the foreground in creating the sense of a blanket of snow. Without them we would have merely a pale drawing.

Of a completely different nature is a drawing of an "Elephant" (Figure 16–15). Rembrandt made a few other studies of animals, but the exotic character of this elephant must have enthralled him, for he made a number of sketches of it. Here the chalk is used vigorously to model the form and establish the rough-textured hide of the animal with its deep, loose folds. The imposing but clumsy movements of the feet have been evoked admirably with a few deft strokes. The rough, almost awkward handling of chalk derives from the very nature of the subject, just as the grace of rendering is intrinsic to the elegaic quiet of the previous "Winter Landscape."

A host of painters were at work in seventeenth-century Holland, many of whom specialized in particular subjects. Some men were primarily painters of farm animals and rural scenes, some painted the proprieties of bourgeoise life, some specialized in still-life or straight landscape. Adrian van Ostade, a student of Franz Hals, loved to depict the dark interiors of taverns enlivened by the rough carousing of peasants. His "Scene in an Inn" (Figure 5–14) and "Peasants Dancing" (Figure 14–20) provide superb examples of his vigorous illustrative style. Executed in pen and bistre reinforced by a bistre wash, these studies lack nothing as finished works of art for being quick sketches; in fact, they exude vitality and strength because of their direct unpremeditated execution. Van Ostade was a master of the art of massing simple tonal relationships. In his "Peasants Dancing," the main figure group is silhouetted against the central area of light, whereas in the "Scene in an Inn" the strong accenting lights and darks single out the chief figures from the more neutral-toned background. In both drawings the short jabbing pen strokes energize the fluid washes and at the same time define the forms and establish the textures of the various surfaces. The rich brown color of the bistre adds to the glowing warmth of these charming drawings.

Adrien Brouwer, like van Ostade and Hals, enjoyed portraying the lusty activities of brawling peasants, as can be seen in his pen and wash drawing of a "Scene in a Tavern" (Figure 5–15). His paintings and drawings are small in scale, animated in texture, and the characterizations approach caricature in their

FIGURE 5-18

Albert Cuyp (1620–1691; Dutch).
"River Scene with Cows." Chalk, 8¼" x 17¹⁵/₁₆".
Teyler Museum, Haarlem.

breadth and vigor. The chief concern of the artist was to paint an amusing anecdote in an animated painterly way and his drawings reflect this interest in humor and a casual, unlabored rendering.

In the seventeenth century the popularity of landscape painting became widespread, not as a background for mythological, religious and genre subjects as it had been previously, but as a full-fledged artistic subject. Rome, still the center toward which art students were drawn and from which new painting movements emanated, witnessed the development of a vigorous school of landscape painting. The seventeenth-century school of landscape painting in Rome reflected the continued presence of the monumental Italian High Renaissance and the ancient classical tradition. Venetian and Bolognese precedent was revealed by the taste for a grand panoramic landscape with carefully balanced masses of trees, hills and architectural forms receding into deep and spacious vistas. The classic past continued to make itself felt through the use of the impressive ancient ruins that were a feature of the Roman landscape. A number of Dutch artists came to Rome to study, and they reflected the popular mode in varying degrees. Many of them proved to be more successful as draftsmen or print-makers than as painters. Bartholomeus Breenbergh was one of these. A draftsman of vigor, many of his drawings dramatize the grandeur of the Roman ruins that dotted the *compagna*. "Roman Ruins" (Figure 15–17) has a largeness and simplicity of conception and breadth of execution. Broad washes were used to establish the main large areas of tone, and pen and brush lines describing the various structural details of buildings and the patterns of plants provide textural richness and surface vivacity.

Many of the Dutch artists who studied in Rome were too deeply imbued with the traditions of their homeland to abandon their taste for the unpretentious and familiar. They returned to Holland to paint the picturesque Dutch rural scene without idealization or classical overtones. Others never left their native homeland but absorbed their enthusiasm for landscape painting from their more traveled fellow artists. Adam Pynacker, Alaert van Everdingen, Albert Cuyp, and Meindart Hobbema were among the Dutch landscape painters of the mid-century who not only left us a handsome legacy of drawings and paintings but subsequently influenced English and French artists toward a similar natural and unpretentious type of landscape painting.

Adam Pynacker was one of many competent mid-seventeenth-century Dutch landscape painters who studied in Rome, but in his later years he abandoned the more obvious mannerisms of the Roman school. His pencil and wash drawing "Landscape" (Figure 5–16) reflects his sensitive observation of nature—of twisting tree trunks, sharp branches, rough-textured bark and leafy masses of foliage, seen through the luminous subdued light of the woods. The only Baroque element that remains evident in his work is the circular rhythmic movement that permeates the composition. Pynacker's sketch contrasts interestingly with the "Rural Landscape with Milkmaid" by Lievens (Figure 6–5), in which the more systematic use of hatchings and formalized leaf patterns favored by the followers of Rubens prevents so sensitive a recording of the landscape textures as distinguishes the work of the Dutch artist.

FIGURE 5–19

Meindert Hobbema (1638–1709; Dutch).
"The Mill." Black chalk and India ink, 7¹³⁄₁₆″ x 12⁵⁄₁₆″.
Teyler Museum, Haarlem.

"A Rocky Mountain Landscape" by Alaert van Everdingen (Figure 5–17) infused the wash techniques favored by the Roman school with an almost Oriental richness of line and texture. Though the drawing reveals a Baroque sense of dramatic movement and grandeur of scale, there is nothing melodramatic or foreign to the Dutch temperament in it. The increased esthetic maturity of the Dutch painters enabled artists like Van Everdingen to render the forms of nature with sophistication yet without artifice or falsification.

Albert Cuyp spent his entire life in his native city of Dordrecht. Although he portrayed an unusual variety of subjects he is now best known for his sympathetic renderings of the rustic scene, particularly its farms and farm animals (Figure 5–18). Of particular distinction is his feeling for the pale mist-diffused light of the Dutch lowlands, communicated in this drawing by the bland, unaccented tonality. Meindart Hobbema drew and painted the familiar rural countryside without idealization or drama. His direct and unmannered reporting, skilled, without affectation but warm and human, pleased the comfortable Dutch burghers who loved to surround themselves with pictures of familiar and pleasant sights. "The Mill" (Figure 5–19) like most of his drawings shows a preference for a richly massed, linear manner that is deft and capable in its objective rendering of picturesque rural motif.

Summary

The Renaissance in Italy was part of an awakening social, intellectual, and economic expansion that occurred all over Western Europe. The exchange of goods and ideas between countries was continuous and Italian Renaissance techniques and concepts rapidly became a part of fifteenth-century culture in France, Flanders, and Germany. During the Northern Renaissance the medieval religious concepts of Flanders began to be expressed in realistic pictorial forms. In the work of the Van Eyck brothers and a number of subsequent fifteenth and sixteenth-century artists the character of subsequent Flemish drawing was defined. Small-scale drawings were executed with amazing detail and silverpoint was the favored medium since it was well adapted to controlled precise effects. In the late fifteenth and early sixteenth centuries Bosch and Brueghel gave original and vivid expression to the north European predeliction for subjects of a grotesque and fantastic nature.

In Germany the Renaissance appeared in the late fifteenth and early sixteenth centuries and though it shared many common characteristics with the art of Flanders, German Renaissance drawing reflects the more fully developed manner of the Italian High Renaissance. Dürer and Holbein, two of the most distinguished German Renaissance artists, produced many fine drawings, among the most beautiful being the sketches Holbein made as studies for portraits.

In the seventeenth century Baroque influences dominated the art of Northern Europe. Holland became an important center of artistic development. Holland was a nation with a prosperous middle class and, rather than an aristocratic court, the wealthy burghers provided the chief patronage for artists. The Dutch burghers preferred subject matter drawn from Dutch daily life to the classical allegories which prevailed where aristocratic influences were dominant. Rembrandt, Holland's greatest painter, produced hundreds of superb drawings covering a wide range of subjects. He drew in pen and ink, wash, chalk, and free combinations of these media. In late seventeenth-century Holland, landscape and genre subjects which pictured a wide variety of commonplace subjects with warmth and fidelity were popular.

6

BAROQUE AND ROCOCO
DRAWING IN FLANDERS,
FRANCE, ENGLAND, AND
SPAIN

1600—1800

The stimulus of Baroque developments in Italy produced a brilliant flowering of the art of painting in seventeenth-century Catholic Flanders. Here the flamboyant style used in the great palaces and churches of Italy acted as a catalyzer on the older Flemish tradition to produce an ostentatious art which, while it was rhetorical and grand, was at the same time immediate and convincing because of its surface realism. Excellence in the craft of painting, which in Renaissance Flanders expressed itself in the skillful rendering of surfaces, in the seventeenth century took the form of a free and painterly handling of media.

FIGURE 6–1
Peter Paul Rubens (1577–1640; Flemish).
"Abraham and Melchisedeck."
Black chalk, 10⅞" x 15½".
Albertina, Vienna.

127

FIGURE 6–2

Peter Paul Rubens (1577–1640; Flemish).
"Study of a Bullock." Chalks and wash, 11¾₁₆″ x 17⁵⁄₁₆″.
Buckingham Palace, London (*Photo Albertina*).

The Baroque Tradition in Flanders

Rubens was the master of this grand manner, and his influence was great on subsequent painters and draftsmen in Flanders, France, England, and even Spain. In the drawings of Rubens and his followers, particularly Van Dyck, such typically Baroque qualities as freedom of execution, bold contrasts of value, and fluid and facile draftsmanship provided the vehicle for a supple and direct form of expression. Rubens produced a tremendous number of drawings, many as studies for paintings, but a goodly number were done purely for pleasure.

A black chalk drawing by Rubens made as a study for a painting (Figure 6–1) portrays in a striking fashion the rich vigor of his manner. The composition is typical, with its wedge-shaped, heavily massed groups of figures, almost bulging out of the picture plane in the foreground and subsequently receding into airy space. The figures are placed before a rich architectural background which provides a monumental setting for the action. Vivid facial expressions, bold gestures, fluttering draperies and a variety of stage props all add to the rhetorical effectiveness of this essentially decorative and grand style. Rubens' skill as a master draftsman is always evident—in the effortless manner in which the narrative elements are integrated with the compositional plan, in the supple,

FIGURE 6–3

Sir Anthony Van Dyck (1599–1641; Flemish) also attributed to Sir Peter Lely (1618–1680; Flemish). "Two Heralds," Study for the "Knights of the Garter." Black and white chalk, 20⅛" x 10¾". *Albertina, Vienna.*

FIGURE 6-4

Sir Anthony Van Dyck (1599–1641; Flemish).
Study for the portrait of "Caspar Gevartius." Chalk, 9½″ x 6³⁄₁₆″.
Courtesy, the Trustees of the British Museum, London.

FIGURE 6–5

Jan Lievens (1603–1644; Dutch).
"Rural Landscape with Milkmaid." Reed pen and brown ink on India paper, 8¹¹⁄₁₆″ x 14¹⁄₁₆″.
The Metropolitan Museum of Art, New York (Rogers Fund, 1961).

flowing forms of the heavily muscled bodies at the left, and in the range of tone and the bold juxtapositions of shining armor, luminous flesh, and airy soft distance. Nothing appears labored, but instead, the entire complex of forms seems to have been achieved without effort as the fortunate result of imagination and technical power.

A black chalk study of the figure of Christ for "The Raising of the Cross" (Figure 13–10) demonstrates with particular power Rubens' ability to create, without recourse to a labored or detailed manner of drawing, a magnificent body which is solid and full in its swelling anatomical forms. The contour lines seem barely to define the rich masses suggested by the sketchy application of black and white chalk, yet the dynamic form which emerges bursts with life and energy. The impact of the drawing is the result of a positive and unquestioning attitude that can only exist when knowledge is combined with certainty of purpose. The sketch of the thumb at the top of the page reveals Rubens' exactitude of work. The original thumb, not being sufficiently foreshortened, appears slightly disjointed and lacking in tension as compared to the subsequent notation.

A drawing of a bullock by Rubens (Figure 6–2) provides a clear illustration of his characteristic technique. The chalk lines are applied freely, in groups of almost parallel lines that follow the contour. Each undulation of the form is revealed and the interlacings of curved lines insure the continuity of surface so characteristic of organic forms. Again, much of the power of the drawing resides in the illusion of effortless execution. Rubens maintained a large atelier and employed and trained many artists, who continued to work in his style. Jacob Jordaens employed the manner of Rubens, but one feels the earthy realism of Flanders taking precedence over the grand tradition of Italy in both his preference for middle-class subjects and for less monumental compositions. Even though his study of "Two Bacchic Revelers" (Figure 16–14) relates to a mythological theme, the gross heavy flesh and unidealized faces reflect his tendency to bring even mythology down to earth. Though the touch is not as light as that of Rubens, the same system of flowing cross-hatched lines to build a sense of form is employed.

There is an air of masculine vigor about the work done by both Rubens and Jordaens that prevents their most artificial efforts from becoming effete. Anthony van Dyck retained the technical methods of Rubens but though his drawing is unlabored and free, the boldness and strength of the master gave way to grace and facility. A chalk study for a portrait of "Caspar Gevartius" (Figure 6–4) shows that when a sitter interested him, Van Dyck could produce a masterly record of appearances, although here the surge of energy and enthusiasm that one always senses beneath the efforts of Rubens is replaced by a somewhat tired worldliness. A concern with elegance of costume, with courtly distinction of manner seems to provide an enervating touch which later in the hands of his less talented followers deteriorated into a kind of stylish superficiality. A chalk drawing of "Two Heralds" (Figure 6–3) also attributed to Sir Peter Lely was done as a study for the Procession of Knights of the Garter. The details of costume are indicated with precision and clarity; the heads of the Heralds appear to have been of less concern to the artist. An impressive competence and sensitivity distinguishes the portraits of Van Dyck at their best, but the exuberance and power of the Baroque tradition appears to have spent itself, setting the stage for the charming but somewhat effete manner of the Rococo.

Like the Dutch seventeenth-century painters, Rubens and his followers painted a number of landscapes which usually included picturesque elements of farm life. One of these, Jan Lievens, was born in Holland, and worked there as well as in England and Flanders. Lievens was a master draftsman of both animal and landscape subjects, whose style reflects the clean lines and light tones that characterized the Rubens school. His "Rural Landscape with Milkmaid" shows the skill with which he treated both animal and landscape forms (Figure 6–5). Here, a series of light parallel lines function almost as a wash in providing the pale shadowy tones which encompass the farmhouse on the right and the cow and sheep at the left. Scribbled leaf shapes and bristling grass patterns enrich the hatchings with characterful details of texture.

FIGURE 6–6

François Clouet (1505–1572; French).
"Head of a Man" (probably M. Claude Gouffiée de Boisy).
Black and red crayon, 12⅝″ x 9¹⁄₁₆″.
Courtesy of the Fogg Art Museum, Harvard University,
Cambridge, Massachusetts (Meta and Paul J. Sachs Collection).

Renaissance and Baroque Drawing in France

The important role played by Italian painters and sculptors in providing splendid decorations for the palaces of the French aristocracy has already been noted. Throughout the sixteenth century the Italian modes were imported but certain French characteristics became increasingly apparent. A taste for restraint and logic and a discreet counterbalancing of decorative and realistic elements seemed essential to the French style. A portrait of a gentleman of the court by François Clouet (Figure 6–6) reveals this combination of sensitive realism, restraint, and elegance. François and his father Jean Clouet were portrait artists in the French court of the sixteenth century and each left behind a multitude of

FIGURE 6–7

Nicolas Poussin (1594–1665; French).
Study for "The Triumph of Bacchus." Pen and bistre on paper, 6¼" x 9".
Courtesy Nelson Gallery–Atkins Museum (Nelson Fund), Kansas City, Missouri.

FIGURE 6–9

Jean Antoine Watteau (1684–1721; French).
"Six Studies of Heads." Black, white, and two tones
of red chalk on gray-brown paper, 8½" x 8¾".
Courtesy of the Fogg Art Museum, Harvard University
(Meta and Paul J. Sachs Collection).

drawings. The father Jean, who came to France from Flanders, drew in a more direct manner, with less emphasis upon details of costume. The son's drawings, usually executed in red and black chalk, place the figures higher on the page, show a concern with niceties of costuming, and reflect a restraint on the part of the artist that reinforces the air of aloof dignity characteristic of his aristocratic subjects. These portrait drawings, firm and unequivocal in touch, seem typically

French in their orderly and sensible realism and their sensitive feeling for both the stylish elegance and human qualities of the sitters.

The dominant current in French seventeenth-century art was toward an aristocratic style that veered toward the more conservative trends in contemporary Roman practice. Poussin was the painter in whose work the characteristics of French court painting during this period are most effectively revealed. A pen and bistre study for "The Triumph of Bacchus" (Figure 6–7) reveals his preference for formal balance, the clear articulation of planes of actions, and his general adherence to traditional and conservative Italian precedent. French landscape painting (and landscape played an important part in Poussin's compositions), strongly influenced by current Roman practice and theory, tended to be formal and grand. The paintings were rendered with a smooth enamel-like finish and were usually composed with panoramic vistas in which masses of trees, classical ruins, distant hills and waterways were carefully balanced against one another.

The most distinguished of the French seventeenth-century landscape

FIGURE 6–10

Jean Antoine Watteau (1684–1721; French).
"Four Studies of Italian Actors." Red, black and white chalk, 10¼" x 15⅝".
Courtesy of the Art Institute of Chicago (Gift of Tiffany and Margaret Blake). (See Plate 10.)

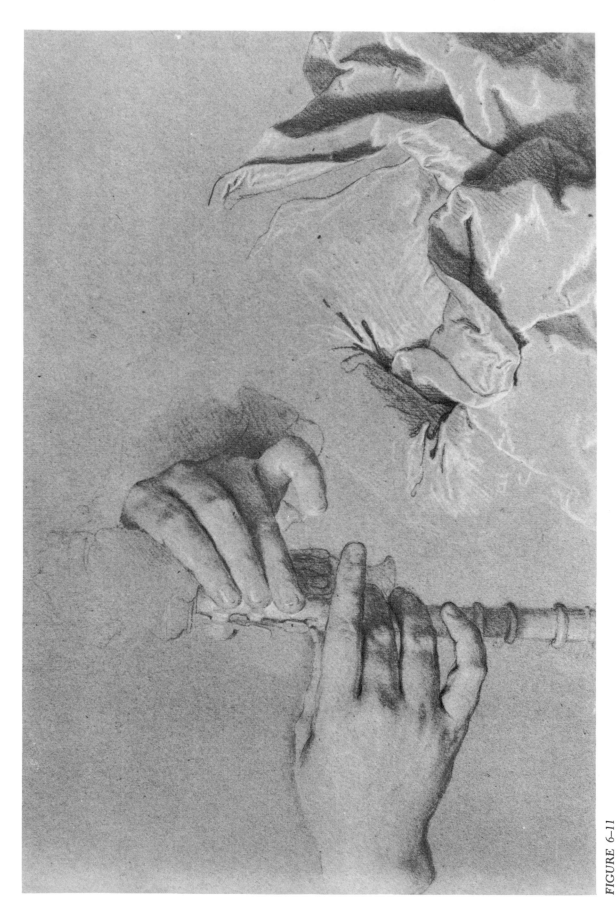

FIGURE 6-11

Hyacinthe Rigaud (1695–1743; French).
"Study of Hands and Drapery." Pencil on blue paper
heightened with white chalk, 11¾" x 17¾".
Achenbach Foundation for Graphic Arts, California
Palace of the Legion of Honor, San Francisco
(Gift of Mr. and Mrs. Sidney M. Ehrman).

FIGURE 6-12

William Hogarth (1697–1764; English).
"The Idle Apprentice Stealing from His Mother." Pen, brown ink, and gray wash.
8½" x 11⅝". Courtesy the Trustees of the British Museum, London.

painters were Hubert Robert and Claude Gellée. Hubert Robert specialized in imposing ruins. The paintings of Claude Gellée, usually called Claude Lorrain since Lorraine was the area of his birth, are large, imposing, and impersonal. By contrast his studies from nature, made both as a record on which he could draw when planning his grand compositions and in response to his genuine enthusiasm for the landscape, have none of the cold dignity and restrained formalism of his paintings. Two wash drawings by Lorrain reveal different facets of his genius for recording the beauty of the landscape. "A View of the Tiber Above Rome" (Color Plate 16) is one of the great landscape drawings of all time. The open sweep of the Roman *compagna*, receding to the distant hills, is recorded in freely brushed strokes of wash. In the middle distance a few towers, umbrella pines, and cypresses particularize the scene. In the foreground the gleaming surface of the Tiber reflects the heightened luminosity of the overhead twilight sky, contrasting with the velvety darks of the heavy tree masses, deep in the shadow of late day. The entire drawing is silent and reverent in tone, resonant with the awe of the artist before the grandeur of nature.

"A Study of Trees" (Figure 6–8) reveals a very different aspect of Lorrain's talents. Here the broken tones of bistre wash are reinforced with pen to suggest the textured vivacity of the out-of-doors. The splotchy application of wash creates the illusion of filtered light and shadow. And yet, as in his "Tiber above Rome," the richness of the darks and the large scale of the forms that spread across the page create a sense of nature's magnitude and nobility that is absent from the landscape drawings of the Dutch and Flemish and that, despite the illusory naturalism of these studies, relates them to the grand tradition of Italy with its emphasis on monumental forms.

A particularly imposing interpretation of the Baroque style, reflecting the authority and centralization of the regime of Louis XIV, characterized the arts in France in the last half of the seventeenth century. The creation of a centralized academy to supervise the production of works of art and insure a royal style brought architecture, sculpture, painting, and the minor arts under the control of a conservative group of men led by the painter Lebrun. Lebrun established systems of rules to insure the quality and character of the arts produced to enhance the court of France, rules based upon the most conservative tendencies of academic circles in Rome. The resulting style, grand and imposing but mannered, impersonal, and academic, acted as a virtual straitjacket that stifled initiative and the development of personal styles at variance with the official court style.

Rococo Drawing in France

The death of Louis XIV in 1715 initiated far-reaching changes in France which eventually led to the French Revolution and the end of the monarchy. The most immediate evidence of these changes was the increased informality and freedom of court life. This tendency toward informality and greater freedom was reflected in the arts by a shift toward a livelier, more graceful and feminine style termed *Rococo*. The painters who created the paintings and decorations to grace Rococo interiors found their inspiration in sources other than academic Italian precedent. Rubens in particular, with his freely brushed, painterly style

FIGURE 6–13

Thomas Rowlandson (1756–1827; English).
"At a Cottage Door." Gray and tan wash
with brown ink lines, 7″ x 5½″.
Collection of the author. (See Plate 11.)

and his dependence upon color and atmospheric elements, provided an artistic model for the antiacademic forces. The example of the eighteenth-century Venetians gave added impetus to the development of a lively and unlabored style. Antoine Watteau, who was born in Flanders but spent his mature life in France, became the first painter to express in painterly form the new social attitudes. His admittance to the academy sounded the death-knell of the grand Baroque manner of the seventeenth century. During the eighteenth century France became the chief center of artistic innovation, when the vigor of her intellectual and artistic life placed her in a position of world leadership in the arts, a role which was continued through the nineteenth and early twentieth centuries.

Watteau's style of drawing reveals less the influence of Rubens than his own inimitable gifts and their particular suitability to the Rococo spirit. The drawings of Watteau, like his paintings, have a light piquancy and delicate touch that are particularly expressive of the Rococo ideals of grace, charm, and courtly sophistication. The subjects that he chose were usually drawn from court life—its concern with amorous and playful activities—and these are artfully depicted with an idealized, sentimental feeling. A page with "Six Studies of Heads" (Figure 6–9) reveals the fresh easy execution that characterizes all of Watteau's work. Sensitive contour lines are reinforced with only enough modeling to make the forms firm and convincing. Watteau's own gentle spirit modulates all that he describes and imbues it with a sweet poetry that reflects the courtly ideals of the period, if not the actuality. A drawing of "Four Studies of Italian Actors" (Figure 6–10) is one of his largest studies. In it one can see the way in which Watteau departed from the academic formulas of the seventeenth-century Baroque draftsmen. The contour lines are more broken and the areas of tone are less solidly massed. This more fragmented way of working produces a light animation that seems to epitomize the Rococo ideal. The characters depicted in this study were undoubtedly drawn from one of the companies of touring actors who produced the entertainment for court fetes and similar occasions, and these particular studies provided the basis for subsequent paintings and engravings. Many of Watteau's drawings were executed on gray paper in red, black, and white chalk, the broken and fragile chalk lines creating an effect of vivacity and animation while the gray paper, by providing a unifying tone, contributed a cohesive effect.

The importance of order, control, refinement, and precision as elements of what might be termed the French style sense has been mentioned before. A study of "Hands and Draperies" (Figure 6–11) by Hyacinthe Rigaud in pencil on blue paper, heightened with chalk, reveals these typical French qualities. Rigaud was a minor painter, but the distinction and elegance of this drawing reveals how deeply these qualities were imbedded in French artistic culture. Particularly revealing is the systematic way in which the white chalk and dark pencil are used to convey both the form and the texture of velvet without producing a mechanical rendering.

The nude, particularly the female nude, was drawn beautifully by a number of Rococo painters, but certainly no one has surpassed Boucher in his ability to create lovely idealized bodies in which sensuous beauty is presented in solidly realized forms (Figure 14–19). The delicacy of tone can be misleading, for though the firm surfaces are modeled with a light touch there is nothing weak about the drawing; the firm rhythmic contour lines establish the sense of form with a certainty and vigor that recalls Rubens.

FIGURE 6–14

William Blake (1757–1827; English).
"Pity from Shakespeare's *Macbeth*." Color-printed drawing on paper, 16⅝" x 20⅞".
The Metropolitan Museum of Art, New York (*Gift of Mrs. Robert W. Goelet, 1958*).

Eighteenth-Century English Drawing

Though both aristocratic portraiture patterned after Flemish example and landscape painting in the Dutch tradition flourished in eighteenth-century England, English genius never found its primary outlet in the visual or plastic arts. Instead, the English national genius seemed to express itself in literary forms and it follows logically enough that English pictorial talent achieved its most original form in the painting, drawing, and print-making where social satire took the form of storytelling. Hogarth, the best known of the social satirists, produced many studies for his engravings which range from quick sketches to fully finished paintings.

"The Idle Apprentice Stealing from His Mother" (Figure 6–12) is one of a sequence of drawings prepared for a series of engravings entitled "Industry and Idleness," in which the careers of an industrious and an idle apprentice were contrasted. Needless to say, the industrious apprentice reaps all of the honors and the idle apprentice comes to ruin. It must be admitted, however, that Hogarth seems more fired with enthusiasm when picturing the evils of idleness than the rewards of virtue. "The Idle Apprentice Stealing from His Mother" was done with pen, brown ink and gray wash over pencil. Like many of Hogarth's drawings, it was executed with rather large flourishes of the pen and freely applied areas of wash that provide an animation which contributes to the general gusto of the drawing. Verging on caricature, the drawing proves a delightful contrast to many eighteenth-century works which, though frivolous in content, are serious and joyless in style. "The Idle Apprentice Steals from His Mother," like many drawings in this series, was never engraved.

No English artist has left more fascinating and varied drawings than Hogarth's successor, Thomas Rowlandson. Rowlandson caricatured the spectacle of London life, laughing at the pretensions of the world of fashion and the vulgarities and hypocrisies of all classes of English society. A man "At a Cottage Door" (Figure 6–13) reflects his affectionate yet scoffing view of mankind: the churlish smoker holding forth with his dog is depicted with warm humor. The characterizing elements of face and posture as well as the architectural details and other accessories are drawn with zestful exaggerations, the forms being established by a few quickly executed flourishes of the pen and subsequently reinforced with light washes of clear color: blue-grays, tans and browns. The same good-humored satire characterizes his delightful record of an eighteenth-century fashionable promenade, "In the Garden of the Tuilleries" (Figure 18–20). Rowlandson's remarkable ability to characterize is most evident here for though the individual figures are subordinate to the total scene, he has managed to establish a vivid personality in each of his characters no matter how sketchily they are indicated. There is a Rococo animation in the curlicues of line, the sketchy indications of form, and the light color used to tint his studies.

No two men seem farther apart in spirit than Rowlandson and his contemporary, William Blake. Both men were born and died in the same years, but while Rowlandson observed life with merry amusement and tossed off his telling sketches with casual zest, William Blake set himself the difficult task of

PLATE 6
Goivanni Battista Tiepolo (1696–1770; Italian). "Hagar and Ishmael in the Wilderness."
Pen, brush, and brown ink and wash over sketch in black chalk, 16½″ x 11⅛″.
Courtesy of the Sterling and Francine Clark Art Institute, Williamstown, Massachusetts.

FIGURE 6–15

Sir Thomas Lawrence (1769–1830; English).
"Prince Regent." Black, white, and red chalk on canvas, 30⅜" x 40⅞".
The Royal Library, Windsor Castle, England.
Reproduced by gracious permission of Her Majesty Queen Elizabeth II.

trying to probe into the endless enigma of existence. His drawings and paintings, filled with involved literary allusions and esoteric symbols, are religious and mystical in character and were designed to communicate moral concepts and values through idealized forms and carefully calculated compositional arrangements. The grave forms of his finished watercolor drawings, of which "Pity, from Shakespeare's *Macbeth*" (Figure 6–14) is an excellent example, were arrived at only after extended preliminary studies. Here, one can see both the literary-symbolic nature of Blake's fascinating works and also the carefully designed forms by which he communicates spiritual meanings rather than surface appearances. Rowlandson continued the Rococo delight in wit and the light-hearted acceptance of man as an amoral animal; the art of Blake seems shaped by the deep religious questionings and moral fervor of nineteenth-century Romanticism. The drawings of both men, because of their illustrational tendencies, relate to the English literary tradition.

The practice of portrait painting was established in the English court in the fifteenth century both by native English artists and distinguished painters from the continent. Hans Holbein in the sixteenth century and Anthony Van Dyck in the seventeenth produced some of their most noteworthy portraits in England. In the eighteenth century Reynolds, Gainsborough, Lawrence, and others followed the precedent of Van Dyck and recorded the faces and figures of the great and fashionable. Though these portraits are symbols of social position rather than penetrating psychological studies, they have delighted generations of art lovers because of their elegance, taste, and skill. Most of the famous English portrait painters worked directly on canvas; we thus have few drawings done as studies for portraits. However, a splendid example of this tradition as it was practiced in the early years of the nineteenth century can be seen in the unusual sketch Sir Thomas Lawrence has left of "The Prince Regent" (Figure 6–15) in black, white, and red chalk on canvas. The drawing was apparently made as the first step in planning a portrait and was discarded. It bears a striking similarity to a portrait of George IV exhibited in 1815 and is almost identical to a lithographic portrait published at a later date and signed by Lawrence. In it one sees the skill, knowledge, and artifice that constituted the great portrait tradition Lawrence inherited from the eighteenth-century masters. The head is modeled with delicate precision; the chalk applied with the certainty that comes with the unquestioning acceptance of a tradition of long standing.

Drawing in Spain

There has been little study made of drawings by Spanish masters, perhaps because there are no large collections of such drawings which would facilitate study in this field. We cannot say with certainty whether the habit of training artists in the practice of drawing was not developed in Spain to the same degree as in Italy, the Netherlands, and France, or whether drawings were not highly valued and therefore not collected. Not even a half-dozen drawings can be attributed to Velásquez with certainty, although a larger number are thought to be from his hand. Certainly the style of Velásquez, with its remarkable visual exactitude, would suggest both a long period of apprenticeship accompanied by a thorough discipline in drawing, as well as the continued practice of making

FIGURE 6–16

Francisco de Zurbarán (1598–1664; Spanish).
"A Monk." Charcoal, 10⅞" x 7⅜₁₆".
*Courtesy, the Trustees of
the British Museum, London.*

preliminary studies in drawing for his portraits. Unfortunately, logical though this may sound, no body of work exists to substantiate the theory. Authenticated drawings from the hands of El Greco, Ribera, Zurbarán, and Murillo are almost as rare but the British Museum does own a very fine "Head of a Monk" by Zurbarán (Figure 6–16) which reveals certain characteristics which Zurbarán shared with other Spaniards including his friend and fellow painter, Valásquez. Though influenced by the bold theatrical style of Caravaggio, the typically Spanish qualities of restraint, dignity, and realism are strongly felt. Almost harsh in his sobriety, Zurbarán like Velásquez was most concerned with recording the visual image before him with sensitive exactitude.

The Spanish temperament seems one of extremes: while other Spanish artists left hardly a sketch, Goya drew continuously. Like many eighteenth-century artists, he left a tremendous number of studies, some of which constitute a kind of visual note-taking; many were studies for prints. Over six hundred drawings have been attributed to Goya, and the largest single collection remains in the Prado. They cover a wide range of techniques and media, many reflecting his amazing ability to summarize the human drama with irony, humor, or compassion in a few telling lines and bold tonal contrasts. "Easy Victory" (Figure 6–17) has the peculiarly Goyaesque combination of sardonic humor and zestful execution. Drawn in black chalk, its sketchy freedom is misleading. Close study reveals the certainty with which the artist has placed the two figures to fill the entire space of the page with movement, to direct the observer's eye to the crucial points—the grinning brutal head of the victor, the ugly hand pressing down the head of the vanquished, and the energetic fist holding the knife. The rough burr and open texture of the chalk line suggests that Goya made this as a study for an etching. Goya remains one of the undisputed masters of value relationships. "Sainted Culottes" (Figure 14–22) displays the power with which Goya opposes black and white. The quickly brushed masses of black convey both a sense of dark fabrics, of harsh blinding sunshine, and bold shadows. A brilliant opposition of textures is created by contrasting the heavy brushed contours and the delicate crinkled linear surface of aged hands. Equally brilliant is the way in which sharp irony of idea is conveyed in purely visual terms. It is this amazing ability that makes Goya one of the great commentators on man as a social animal, an ability to evoke from the simplest graphic notations a complex of ideas and feelings that illuminate the conflicts between human beings and social, political, and religious institutions.

Summary   Seventeenth-century Flemish art, unlike the art of the same period in Holland, revealed a taste for aristocratic display. Rubens, the dominant figure, produced a multitude of drawings characterized by exuberance, strength and facility. Often done in red or brown chalk with black or white accents, Rubens' drawings were made both as studies for paintings or for the sheer joy of execution. Rubens' influence and manner was continued in the work of Jordaens, Van Dyck, and Watteau in Flanders, England, and France.

In seventeenth-century France a school of landscape painters who were trained in Rome developed a grand and formal manner, frequently featuring a

FIGURE 6–17

Francisco Goya (1746–1828; Spanish).
"Easy Victory." Chalk, 5⅝" x 8".
Museo del Prado, Madrid.

panoramic landscape punctuated with classical ruins. Claude Lorrain, one of the foremost exponents of this school, made many studies from nature which unlike his grand efforts were direct, fresh, and sensitive to outdoor atmospheric effects. Lorrain, like many seventeenth-century landscape painters, most frequently worked in pen and wash. In the Rococo style of the first half of the eighteenth century, French art reflected the increased informality, even frivolity, that characterized French court life after the demise of Louis XIV. The drawings of Watteau and Boucher are typical of French Rococo drawing in their light, evocative charm, their facile grace, and sketchy depiction of amusing scenes of court life.

Except for the aristocratic portrait tradition which flourished in eighteenth-century England, English painting and drawing reveals a literary and illustrational emphasis. This illustrational tendency received its most original expression in the satiric drawings whereby Hogarth and Rowlandson commented on the hypocrisies and foibles of English social life. The mystical drawings of William Blake reveal another facet of English expression.

Few drawings remain from any Spanish master except Goya, who left a multitude of works, executed for the most part in chalk or wash. Bold in handling and biting in their irony, these drawings clearly portray Goya's authority as a unique and powerful representative of the Spanish pictorial genius.

7

NEO-CLASSICISM,
ROMANTICISM, AND REALISM
1800—1860

France, and more specifically, Paris, was the undisputed center of the nineteenth-century art world; to it students from all countries gravitated. During this century a series of artistic movements were initiated as a revolt against the classicism which dominated the official French academy: first the romantic movement, then the mid-century realism exemplified by the Barbizon School, and in the last half, impressionism and postimpressionism. Students returning to their homelands carried the new movements with them. It is, therefore, to France that we first turn our attention, but before studying the individual artists, an overview of the ideologies that animated the art world may establish the milieu from which the men and the changing styles emerged.

At the end of the eighteenth century the conflict between the increasingly powerful middle class and an extravagant and autocratic court culminated in the French Revolution. The republics of ancient Greece and Rome provided both inspiration and the prototypes for the emerging republican government, and so played a considerable role in shaping the ideas of the revolutionary forces. In the mid-eighteenth century the ancient city of Pompeii came to light, and the excavations at Pompeii, coinciding as they did with the political events of the day, reinforced the general reawakened interest in the philosophies and arts of

*The Classic
Revival*

FIGURE 7–1

Jean-Auguste Dominique Ingres (1780–1867; French).
Two Nudes, Study for "The Golden Age." Pencil, 15⅜" x 11".
Courtesy of the Fogg Museum of Art, Harvard University, Cambridge.
Massachusetts (Grenville Lindall Winthrop Collection).

the ancient world. Thus neo-classicism in the arts was initiated, and the demise of the old regime signaled the end of the Rococo style. In contrast to the Rococo affection for the whimsical, the charming, and the sensuously pleasing the Classicists held rationalism as an ideal. The Classicists thus proceeded to create a style which would summarize and combine the finest elements from the past. The sculptural forms of Greece and Rome, the lucid compositional devices of the High Renaissance, particularly of Raphael and the Venetian masters, and the idealized figure proportions of the same masters, provided the principal stylistic sources. Compositions were stable. Strong vertical, horizontal, and pyramidal elements were introduced to replace the sinuous curves of the Rococo. Line and form were given preference over color, and spontaneity of execution and variety of brushwork were abandoned for an enamel-like smoothness of finish. These neo-classical elements became formulated into academic practice, and drawing of a highly disciplined character again assumed an unprecedented importance in the training of artists. Most of the dynamic movements of the nineteenth century grew from revolt against the cold and formal nature of academic practice. Inasmuch as the academy dominated the awarding of government commissions, and controlled entrance into the great salon exhibitions and the awarding of prizes at those exhibitions, its power was great and its influence as a restrictive and reactionary force was equal to its power. Thus the romanticism of the early nineteenth century, the naturalism and realism of the midcentury, and the Impressionist and Postimpressionist movements of the end of the century all came, to some degree, from the attempt to break away from the restrictions of the official academic manner.

Ingres was the draftsman who gave fullest expression to the precepts of the neo-classical manner. One of the master draftsmen of all time, his temperament was such that the discipline of the academy was particularly suited to his gifts, and, rather than being restricted by academic practice, his own way of working contributed to its formulation. He commenced his career as a recipient of the coveted Prix de Rome and spent a number of years in Italy copying the old masters, particularly Raphael. It was during these years as a student in Paris that, to supplement his income, he commenced making the pencil portraits which for many represent the pinnacle of his remarkable powers. His "Portrait of Docteur Robin" (Figure 16–8) is one of the many masterful pencil drawings from his years in Rome. The neo-classical virtues of logic and clarity are beautifully exemplified here. The vertical of the figure, placed slightly to the right of center, is balanced by the vertical movement of the dome of St. Peter's. The lines of the distant roofs and entablatures provide the desired horizontal stabilizing line movement. The strongest tonal contrasts are in the head, the logical spot on which to focus attention. The gray tones in the head and waistcoat are repeated in the two lower corners, again reinforcing the stability of the composition by establishing a triangular relationship of parts. The medium of pencil is used with the same logic. The precise contour line defines the edges of the forms without ever restricting them or confining the eye. For instance, the right arm moving back from the body into space, relates to St. Peter's in the distance, causing the entire figure to exist as a solid three-dimensional volume.

FIGURE 7–2

Pierre-Paul Prud'hon (1758–1823; French).
"La Source." Black and white chalk, 21¾₁₆" x 15⅝₁₆".
Courtesy of the Sterling and Francine Clark Art Institute,
Williamstown, Massachusetts. (See Plate 12.)

The lines are kept clean and pale, with delicate light hatchings reinforcing the outlines. Where darker tones have been created by the pencil, as in the modeling of the head and the accenting of the eyes, the areas of dark are sharply limited. The master draftsman knew better than to try to force the pencil to do something other than what it did most naturally. The entire drawing summarizes the virtues of the classic concept: restraint, clarity and logic, tempered by the refined judgment that grew from long study of the masterpieces of the past, and executed with exquisite technical grace.

Two figure studies by Ingres illustrate the classical ideals as they apply to the rendering of the human figure. We have already seen the "Studies for the Dead Body of Acron" (Figure 1–10). Here one again witnesses the brilliant use of line. The clear pencil lines, reinforced with only very slight modeling, convey a full sense of the three-dimensional form. The interplay between the sharp eye, the clear mind, and the obedient hand, all tempered by the most exquisite taste, is masterful. Despite his amazing native facility, Ingres never indulges in a vulgar display of his virtuosity.

His drawing of Two Nudes, a study for "The Golden Age" (Figure 7–1) provides an interesting contrast to the incisive "Studies for the Dead Body of Acron." Here one can see the conventionalized treatment of the human figure favored by the classic-revival artists when they pictured symbolic or mythological themes. The proportions are based on the ample figures of the High Renaissance tempered by a study of Hellenistic sculptures, with small heads, hands, and feet, and long, gracefully proportioned bodies creating ideal godlike men and women. The impassive dreamy faces have the features of Greek statues, and the modeling throughout the drawing is pale and remains subordinate to the contour line so that white marble surfaces are suggested rather than flesh. The cold, pale hand of the academy, rather than the incisive eye of Ingres, is forecast in this drawing.

Neoclassical theory placed drawing, rather than color, as basic to the art of painting, and a number of the finest expressions of classic revival taste appear in the drawings of the men working in this school. Pierre-Paul Prud'hon was also a proponent of the neoclassic manner, and as with Ingres, drawing of a most disciplined nature was particularly suited to his talents. "La Source" (Figure 7–2), in black and white chalk, provides an excellent illustration of the disciplined techniques of the classic-revival artist used later by the academicians who systematized neo-classical practices. The chalk was applied to the paper very carefully, in general through diagonal lines subsequently smoothed into an even tone by cautious rubbing. In this way even movements of value from pure white through delicate gradations of gray to velvety darks was achieved. All indications of the manner of applying the chalk were eliminated in the main forms of the body until the finishing touches were applied, when a beautiful texture of chalk lines was added to produce an elegant granular surface. In a few areas, such as the hair and draperies, a freer use of chalk provided variety to the textures and a certain freshness of execution.

These smooth gradations of gray were employed in conjunction with the systematic use of planes of light and shade separated by the "core" of the

FIGURE 7–3

Théodore Géricault (1791–1824; French).
Study for "The Bull Market." Black chalk, gray wash, and
white gouache on brown paper, 8¼" x 11¹¹⁄₁₆".
Courtesy of the Fogg Museum of Art, Harvard University, Cambridge,
Massachusetts (Grenville Lindall Winthrop Collection).

shadow and supplemented by highlights, cast shadows, and reflected lights. These elements of modeling can also be clearly observed in a fine head by Prud'hon (Figure 16–5) in which the naturally handsome features are colored by the classic concept of ideal beauty, the broad forehead, long straight nose, full mouth, and rounded chin.

Géricault and Delacroix were the two most forceful exponents of romanticism in France. As stated before, the Romantic movement in painting like the subsequent turn toward naturalism and realism came, to a considerable degree, as a reaction against the cold eclecticism of classic-revival theory and the restrictive nature of academic practice. Many social, political, and intellectual factors such as religious revivalism and humanitarian social concerns contributed to the Romantic movement, subsequently colored all nineteenth-century artistic expression. A concern with the realm of highly wrought emotions and exciting visions became the particular province of the Romantics. A deep capacity for emotion, inner tumult, visions, compassion, and heroism motivated their art, and the ideal of tempered lucidity found in Raphael and other Italian painters of the High Renaissance gave way to a preference for the turbulent emotionalism of Michelangelo and the free painterly manner of the Baroque masters, particularly Rubens.

Two studies by Géricault reveal two facets of his genius. One is a page of "Sketches of a Cat" (Figure 16–10), the other a "Study for the Bull Market" (Figure 7–3). His drawings of a cat were quick notations in pencil made from direct observation of the animal. The Romantic taste for highly wrought and exciting subjects is revealed by the artist's selection of twisting, snarling, and biting movements. Though the model may have been a gentle household pet, the sketches suggest a fierce ocelot. The drawing is done in pencil and remains factual, but the sketchy line catches every undulation of surface, records the patterns of fur and at times throws a light but evocative shadow over the twisting body of the cat.

The full impact of the Romantic manner is felt in the more developed compositional "Study for the Bull Market." Executed in chalk and wash, highlighted with opaque white, the study employs the full gamut of Romantic devices. The forms are established through broadly massed areas of tone rather than through line, with limited areas of white shining out from the surrounding darker tones to provide dramatic focal accents. The face of the foreground rider, in contrast, silhouettes itself as a shadowy center of interest at the apex of the great triangular mass that forms the chief structural element in the composition. The vigorous movements, so essential to the Romantic composition, are established by the sweeping lines which start at the lower left and move to the right in a series of concentric arched movements. The rendering is loose and painterly, freely drawn lines of charcoal reinforce the washes, broadly brushed masses of white establish the light accents. The handling of the white is particularly rich in the lowered head of the bull.

FIGURE 7–4

Ferdinand Victor Eugène Delacroix (1798–1863; French).
"An Arab on Horseback Attacked by a Lion." Pencil, 12″ x 18⅛″.
*Courtesy of the Fogg Art Museum, Harvard University, Cambridge,
Massachusetts (Meta and Paul J. Sachs Collection).*

Delacroix, who followed Géricault, is one of the masters of action drawing. His notations of forms in violent movement appear to have been executed in the heat of excitement, a scribble of lines initiating the movement, and from this whirling vortex the charging forms emerge. "An Arab on Horseback Attacked by a Lion" (Figure 7–4) is at the opposite end of the pictorial spectrum from Ingres. The ideal of Ingres was controlled delineation of the objects under observation; Delacroix desired to recreate the excitement of action and interaction, with observation almost subordinate to empathy. As one would expect, small niceties of technique are outside the realm of Delacroix's concern, but the impassioned lines are charged with energy. In "The Sultan on Horseback" (Figure 17–2), a few essential relationships are established with unequivocal force by a kind of pictorial shorthand. Using a minimum of telling lines, Delacroix recreates a dynamic gesture and proud attitude. The vitality and expressive force of this drawing is as exciting as the technical wizardry of Ingres is admirable.

Romanticism in England and Germany

In England and Germany the Romantic movement assumed a direction which was far removed from the intensely emotional, painterly manner of Géricault and Delacroix. In both countries the Romantic painters sought to avoid both the frivolity and worldliness of the Rococo school and the cold archaeological exactitude of the classic revival. One group of Englishmen, the Pre-Raphaelites, turned to the art of the early Renaissance in Italy for their inspiration and treated themes of a moralistic or poetic nature. Dante Gabriel Rossetti, one of the leading Pre-Raphaelites, was both poet and painter. His "Portrait of Elizabeth Sidall" (Figure 17–1) exemplifies both the serious nobility of tone and the disciplined technical methods which the Pre-Raphaelites derived from the early Italians. Pen and ink were applied line by line much as tempera was used in the fourteenth century and the same idealization of the past is reflected in the Botticellilike interpretation of Elizabeth Sidall's features.

At the turn of the century a number of German artists, trained according to classic concepts but sensitive to the impending Romantic mood, created works of art which combine classic restraint and elegance with romantic symbolism and sentiment. Such an artist was Phillip Otto Runge who created a number of drawings of exquisite beauty. In "Die Lichtlilie mit Schwebenden Genien" (Figure 7–5) the idealizations of anatomy, the rhythmic purity of line and the controlled pen and ink technique reflect the discipline of neoclassicism, yet the drawing is dominated by a tone of poetic sentiment that is essentially romantic.

Caspar David Friedrich was the leading German Romantic painter, and he too worked in a precise clear technique; the observer is almost unaware of the picture surface, so smooth and flawless is the application of paint. Friedrich allied himself with the Romantic movement through the intense lyric mood

FIGURE 7–5
Phillip Otto Runge (1777–1810; German).
"Die Lichtlilie mit Schwebenden Genien."
Pen and ink, 26½″ x 17¹¹⁄₁₆″.
Hamburger Kunsthalle

which dominates even his most realistic works as well as by the sentimental idealism by which he frequently united realism and poetic invention. His pencil and wash drawing "Rock Quarry" (Figure 16–6) provides a fine example of this combination of exactitude and poetic feeling. The empty quarry conveys an atmosphere of loneliness and immobility, almost symbolizing some deep indifference to the human spirit implicit in the hard core of the earth. The carefully planned lighting reveals the forms with chill clarity. The almost parallel lines, controlled but never mechanical, locate the facets of stone in space with sharp and exact planes. Essentially the work of a draftsman and reflecting the artist's early training in architecture, the drawings of Friedrich help span the gap between the romanticism of the early nineteenth century and the sensitive realism of mid-century.

A number of German draftsmen of exceptional skill emerged in the first half of the nineteenth century, some of whom were pupils of Friedrich's. Their drawings combine brilliant technical discipline, intimate observation and romantic sentiment. "Weinberg, Olivano" (Figure 7–6) by Heinrich Reinhold is such a work. In it an intense poetic mood is achieved through the most exacting technique. Every disciplined pen stroke reflects the artist's delight in the beauty of the rustic scene, yet his technical dexterity never became an end in itself as it did in the hands of lesser men later in the century.

Mid-Nineteenth-Century Realism: France

A current of realism dominated the art of the mid-nineteenth century, an outgrowth of the expanding horizons of science as well as the political and industrial changes which both threatened the established social order and held great promise for the future. Certain of the mid-century realists concerned themselves with the urgencies of social and political conflict; others turned their eyes less to people and their problems, and more to the cityscape, the landscape, and the pastoral scene. A traditional system for classifying the relationships between the various groups of nineteenth-century realists was to classify them as naturalists and realists. The naturalists were those artists whose work was focused on nature and the landscape, whereas the realists were those men who related themselves in some way to the struggle between the emerging democratic and socialist forces and the older conservative and reactionary elements of society. Few men concerned themselves with one pole of realism to the exclusion of the other, but such a definition had the value of establishing the two poles of nineteenth-century realism. In any case, both groups avoided the grand manner that characterized the art of the academy and the Romantic painters alike.

Daumier was one artist who concerned himself exclusively with man as a social and political animal. He made his livelihood as a satirist who caricatured the political personalities and the social issues of his day. His lithographs, which appeared in the pages of *Caricature, Charivari,* and other liberal journals of his time, represent the beginning of the great body of journalistic pictorial art

concerned with social, political, and economic problems and personalities which
has played an important part in shaping the democratic process ever since. The
role of such an art is to command attention and persuade the beholder. To
accomplish this it must be terse, bold, and witty. Daumier developed a style of
drawing eminently suited to the art of persuasion. His lithographs were bold in
their tonal contrasts, simple in composition, and endowed with an electric linear
energy. He had an innate feeling for the expressive gesture and the charac-

terizing detail of feature or posture that enabled him to make a character or situation come alive with a few quick strokes of the brush. These abilities are most apparent in a delightful study of "Don Quixote and Sancho Panza" (Figure 7–7). The sketch was laid out initially in charcoal, and the animated charcoal lines can be felt behind the brushed ink accents. The ink accents reveal a masterly ability to summarize through a minimum of means. If brevity is the soul of wit, the contrast between Panza's paunch and Don Quixote's straight back cannot be surpassed for witty commentary. Equally charming is the difference between the mule's slack movements and the tense energy of the horse, particularly as these qualities are contrasted in the haunches of the animals.

One of the most distinctive qualities of Daumier's drawing is the dynamic energy of the line by which he builds his drawings. "The Clown" (Figure 15–11) was developed from an initial tangle of charcoal lines, reinforced by wash. Out of a matrix of interweaving lines, like snarled bits of yarn, the solid gesturing figure emerges, charged with energy and communicating form, movement, and emotions with equal force. In "Fright" (Figure 7–8) the pencil and charcoal lines play over the entire surface, to a considerable extent taking over the role of chiaroscuro in describing the alternations of bulge and hollow on the inner surfaces. This is most apparent if one observes the drawing of cheekbone, jaw, neck, and esophagus. Mid-nineteenth-century France, attuned to the niceties of academic practice, dismissed the vital art of Daumier as political pamphleteering. Today the pulse of life which flows through the art of Daumier makes us value his political commentaries as great works of art, whereas the output of his academic contemporaries appear, at best, as interesting sociological artifacts.

Jean Louis Forain, like Daumier, found an outlet for his criticisms of society in the liberal Parisian journals. His sharp comments reveal a straightforward style of reporting which expresses its forces through incisive line and an ability to sort out the most essential elements of form and summarize them in a few telling lines and blots of wash (Figure 1–7).

The great etcher, Charles Meryon, loved the city of Paris with a passion, but less perhaps as a setting for human activity than as a cityscape. His etchings record the monumental aspects of the city, the weight of its stones, the height and dignity of its grave façades, the structured power of even its most picturesque alleyways. His drawing for the etching "Le Pompe de Notre Dame" (Figure 7–9), like so much of Meryon's art, selects and stresses the elements that contribute a sense of stability and grandeur to a subject that could easily have been made cheap by emphasizing its quaint irregularities. The framing play of vertical and arched lines relate beautifully to the pyramidally massed pilings surmounted by the low buildings, and finally, the culminating tower. Each part of the architectural complex is drawn with the same firm sense of structure that distinguishes the entire composition. With Meryon one comes to realize that the most beautiful city in the world has not only a charming surface but an underlying, matching power and strength. "Le Stryge" (Figure 14–11) broods over the city like an ominous and fateful spirit. Here too we see Meryon's capacity to endow the picturesque, even the grotesque, with grandeur and power.

FIGURE 7–7

Honoré Daumier (1808–1879; French).
"Don Quixote and Sancho Panza."
Charcoal washed with India ink, 7⅜″ x 12⅛″.
The Metropolitan Museum of Art, New York
(Rogers Fund, 1927).

FIGURE 7–8

Honoré Daumier (1808–1879; French).
"Fright."
Pencil and charcoal, 7⁵⁄₁₆" x 9¼".
*Courtesy of The Art Institute of Chicago
(Gift of Robert Alberton).*

The Barbizon School

In the mid-nineteenth century a number of painters left Paris and settled in a small village near Fontainebleau to paint the landscape and rural life. Called the Barbizon School after the name of the village, this group initiated the practice of working out of doors directly from nature, rather than painting in a studio. In their drawings and paintings one feels an almost religious reverence for the facts of nature, coupled with deeply poetic sentiment. The great French art critic, Elie Faure, once described Corot in terms that could well be applied to the entire Barbizon School, though they are particularly fitting for Corot. "He copied what he saw but the quality of his vision was divine. . . . If the lens of the photographer—by your leave, O Corot!—were endowed with a heart, it is thus it would doubtless see the world." One need only glance at Corot's "Study in the Forest of Compiègne, with Seated Woman" (Figure 7–10) to sense the truth and insight of this remark. The drawing, executed in crayon and pen on white paper, reveals the most sensitive scrutiny of the facts of nature: the slightly undulating movements of the slender trunks of trees formed by the search for sun and sky as each tree moved upward over many years, the dark pattern of extended branches seen against the overhead light in contrast to the shine of an occasional branch against the distance, the deep quiet of the shadowy underbrush, the dim mottled light and feathery spurts of foliage, all coupled with a certain gravity of vision that grew from genuine modesty. Corot appears happy to transfer the facts of nature to the paper, attempting neither to add to nor take from nature, neither modifying the material character of his subjects, their local tone, nor the relationship between parts. One only notices the two figures after extended study, so much a part are they of the woodland interior. The technique in which the drawing is executed is as sensitive, discreet and controlled as the quality of the artist's vision. Nowhere does the line of the fine hatching take over at the cost of the subject. Corot drew and painted people with the same poetic realism that distinguishes his landscapes. His pencil study of a "Little Girl with Doll" (Figure 7–11) cannot be surpassed in the quiet sensitivity with which he has captured the shy self-consciousness of a timid child.

Corot was but one of the many painters who concerned themselves with the landscape in the vicinity of Fontainebleau. Théodore Rousseau also loved trees and painted the shadowy splendor of dark woods, but he was equally exhilarated by a stretch of open country, airy distances, and spacious skies. "The Hunt" (Figure 7–12), a charcoal drawing by Rousseau, is a miracle of atmospheric veracity. The soft smudge of charcoal suggests a light so diffused that the very air seems to have substance or body in itself. One feels the damp illumination everywhere, in the sky, shining on the distant road behind the two figures, touching the facets of distant houses and illuminating the shadows. An occasional crisp accenting line keeps the drawing from becoming mushy in texture; the firm perspective of the converging road and the long horizontals of the distance provide the necessary stabilizing structure.

Jean François Millet also joined the painters working in and around the village of Barbizon, but not so much to paint the landscape which he knew and loved as to record the life of the peasants "with breadth and simplicity," to

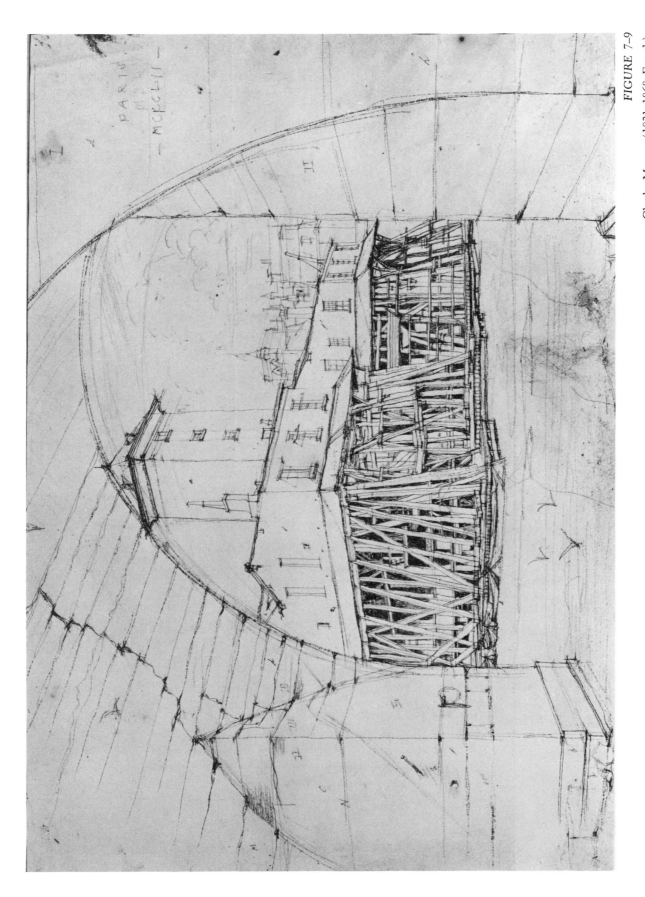

FIGURE 7-9

Charles Meryon (1821–1868; French).
Study for the etching: "Le Pompe de Notre Dame." Pencil, with sanguine notations, 11⅝" x 13⅞". *Courtesy, Museum of Fine Arts, Boston.*

FIGURE 7–10
Camille Corot
(1796–1875;
French). "Study
in the Forest of
Compiègne, with
Seated Woman."
Crayon and pen
on white paper,
15¾″ x 10⅝″.
*Musèe d'Art et
d'Histoire, Lille.*

FIGURE 7–11

Camille Corot. (1796–1875; French). "Little Girl with Doll." Pencil on white paper, 9⅝″ x 7⅞″. *Musée du Louvre, Paris.*

quote Millet's own words. Usually executed in soft charcoal, his drawings, done largely as figure studies for his paintings, are without any flourish of execution, being simplicity itself in the quiet rendering of fact, whether it be the fact of form or of gesture. As in "Peasant with a Barrow" (Figure 16–1), there is little modeling though there is an insistent feeling for broad surfaces and expressive planes communicated by strong, honest contour lines. Like Corot, a deep reverence for the dignity of the fact keeps Millet, when drawing, from

FIGURE 7–12

Théodore Rousseau (1812–1867; French).
"The Hunt." Charcoal, 12³⁄₁₆" x 19¼".
Courtesy, Museum of Fine Arts, Boston.

dramatizing any facet of his own artistic personality. As a consequence, an art of the greatest reticence and modesty is created, an art that is closely related to both the evolving scientific respect for objective fact and the growing sense of democracy with its balanced components of feeling for human dignity and willing subordination of the individual personality to the good of the group.

Courbet was another mid-nineteenth-century French painter to react against the academy and bourgeois pretense. His work runs the entire gamut of the realist vocabulary, for he painted landscapes, seascapes, animals, portraits, and genre scenes. Courbet was not a self-effacing, modest man like Corot or Millet, but rather a pugnacious aristocrat who painted the commonplaces almost as much because his doing so annoyed his conservative friends as through ideological conviction. Realist though he was in his choice of subject matter and his unwillingness to editorialize, Courbet more than any other mid-century French artist retained the Romanticists' richness of texture and feeling for the evocative power and mystery of the shadow. Time after time, as in his "Self-Portrait" with pipe (Figure 7–13), he dramatizes the shadow and its unique capacity to endow form with feeling. In so doing, he achieves a textural richness through his use of charcoal that is quite unlike Millet's restrained use of the medium. In his self-portrait one sees Courbet applying the charcoal in a half dozen ways—rubbed smooth, left rough, erased to leave small white lines, hatched and even accented with small jabs of dark. His drawings, like his paintings, represent the triumph of the artist's sensibilities against the limitations of doctrinaire theory, for he claimed to be a realist, was in theory contemptuous of any esthetic enrichment of vision, yet at the same time created magnificently textured surfaces that enhance whatever he drew.

Nineteenth-Century Realism: England and the United States

England too had a vigorous school of landscape painting in the nineteenth century, and like the painters of the Barbizon School, the English too preferred to paint and draw out of doors rather than in the studio. Constable was one of the English masters who used a variety of media to make quick studies of the landscape, stressing atmospheric effects. A small study of "Poplars by a Stream" (Figure 7–14) reveals a fine eye for the quiet beauty of the English countryside and its misty ambience. This simple sketch gains much of its distinction from the broad simplifications that Constable used, simplifications that record the general patterns of nature rather than its multitudes of detail. Strength through simplification is also the essence of a brilliant wash study of "Trees and a Stretch of Water on the Stour" (Figure 17–12). Almost magical in effect, this drawing was done with the boldest possible contrasts of light and dark so as to convey the sharp glare of light reflected on shining water. This study reveals the intense excitement with which the early nineteenth century landscape painters studied nature and in so doing discovered much concerning air and light that in the succeeding generation led to the experiments and methods of the Impressionists.

Mid-nineteenth century enthusiasm for the familiar landscape was wide-

FIGURE 7–13

Gustave Courbet (1819–1877; French).
"Self-Portrait." Charcoal, 10⅞" x 8".
Courtesy, Wadsworth Atheneum, Hartford, Connecticut.

FIGURE 7-14

John Constable (1776–1837; English).
"Poplars by a Stream." Pencil, 4¾" x 7⅛".
Henry E. Huntington Library and Art Gallery,
San Marino, California.

spread. The example of both the French and English stimulated American painters to abandon the grandiose landscapes preferred during the earlier years of the century for an intimate treatment of more pastoral scenes. Alexander Wyant's "Landscape" (Figure 7–15) with its richly delineated textures and its concern with atmospheric effects exemplifies the solidity of technique and the honesty of vision which characterized the American landscape school in the last half of the century.

Landscape was not the exclusive concern of English and American painters nor were all nineteenth century painters concerned with serious social and esthetic problems; a lighter vein pervaded much of the more popular forms of expression. An expanding middle class witnessed the apogee of such middle class

FIGURE 7-15

Alexander H. Wyant (1836–1892; American).
"Landscape." Charcoal, 11¾" x 17".
Los Angeles County Museum
(Gift of Dr. and Mrs. F. W. Callmann).

FIGURE 7-16

Eastman Johnson (1824–1906; American).
"Berry Pickers." Pencil and watercolor, 7½″ x 19½″.
Addison Gallery of American Art, Phillips
Academy, Andover, Massachusetts.

values as a respect for careful surface finish, for virtuosity of technique, and for an amusing or instructive anecdote. Sir David Wilkie delighted his Victorian contemporaries with his meticulous renderings of genre scenes drawn from daily life. He made innumerable delightful sketches as a basis for his popular pantings, frequently using pen and ink with an incisive energy to record all the fascinating minor details of gesture, expression, costume, and background which gave his paintings their admirable tone of authenticity. His "Arrival of the Rich Relation" (Figure 17–6) provides an excellent example of his entertaining talents. The flood of light from the open doorway piercing the dark night, the excitement and confusion of the arrival, the complex interaction between the leading characters, all are presented with enviable ease. The dour visage of the spectacled figure in the doorway provides a particularly amusing wry note.

In America picturesque incidents from frontier life and typical aspects of familiar activities provided popular subjects for the painter's brush. "The Berry Pickers" (Figure 7–16) by Eastman Johnson is one of his typical vignettes picturing the warm communal activities that characterized small town life in the last century. With an unerring eye Johnson has made notations of familiar silhouettes, costume details, and the effects of light—for the rendering of light was a major concern of nineteenth century painters.

The step between poetic sentiment and mawkish anecdote is slight. By the end of the century the honest description of nature's beauties had degenerated in the hands of many into an ostentatious rendering of surface textures, while the healthy delight in picturing folkways of the mid-century gave way to a taste for sentimental anecdote. But at the same time a new kind of visual realism appeared—a concern with light, color, and with formal esthetic values. This new realism, popularly termed *impressionism*, is our next concern.

Summary

Paris was the artistic center of nineteenth-century Europe; from it the significant movements that characterized the century spread to other countries. The classical revival, with Ingres as its chief draftsman, was the dominant movement at the opening of the century. Ingres most frequently drew in pencil and his drawing is characterized by disciplined observation, refined sensibilities, and technical virtuosity—qualities most effectively displayed in his portrait and figure studies. Delacroix was one of the important leaders of the French Romantic movement. His drawings, often in pen and ink, are charged with energy. The lines move freely to describe movements and feelings rather than visual facts. Unlike the French, the drawings of the English and German Romanticists were disciplined and controlled, giving expression to idealized and sentimental interpretations of landscape, portrait, and allegorical themes.

In the mid-nineteenth century French artists turned away from grandiose historical themes and allegories to portray the life around them. Daumier drew the people of the city, alternately with humor, satire, or sympathy, using dynamic, free linear movements and expressive exaggerations of form. A number of artists, foremost among them Corot and Millet, worked in Barbizon, a small

PLATE 7

Antonio Canaletto ([Canale] 1697–1768; Italian).
"An Island in the Lagoon."
Pen, brown ink and carbon ink wash over ruled pencil lines, 7¹³⁄₁₆" x 10¹⁵⁄₁₆".
By courtesy of the Ashmolean Museum, Oxford.

PLATE 8

Jan van Eyck (1390–
1441; Flemish). "Saint
Barbara." Brush on chalk
ground on wood, 7⅜" x
13⅜". *Musée Royal des
Beaux-Arts, Antwerp.*

village not far from Paris, and by their work extolled the rural landscape and the life of the peasants. Charcoal and chalk were preferred by Barbizon artists. The vigorous schools of landscape art that flourished in England and the United States reflected the characteristics of this Barbizon group. Anecdotal and genre painting and drawing reflected middle-class tastes. In Victorian England Sir David Wilkie produced amusing and skillful pen-and-ink genre sketches with enviable facility.

8

IMPRESSIONISM

AND

POSTIMPRESSIONISM:

1860-1900

Almost any area of human concern observed analytically reveals infinite complexities. Just as the scientists, when they began to analyze matter, found it ultimately to be only charges of energy, so the artists, upon going outside, found that the world was seen as an infinite interchange of energized dancing colors. Thus the open-air painting initiated by Corot and other members of the Barbizon School led to a more sensitive analysis of the color components that make up light, shadow, and the endless variations of atmospheric effects that constitute the landscape painter's world. For certain painters who later were part of the group whom the critics somewhat derisively termed the *impressionists,* color became the primary vehicle by which the world of sunlight and shadow, morning, noon, and evening, spring, summer, autumn, and winter was rendered. Color was seen not as a static element but as a matter of radiating surfaces that absorbed and reflected light.

FIGURE 8–1
Claude Monet (1840–1926; French).
"Two Men Fishing." Black crayon on white scratchboard with light accents obtained by
scratching through to white ground, 10″ x 13½″. *Courtesy of the Fogg Art Museum, Harvard
University, Cambridge, Massachusetts (Meta and Paul J. Sachs Collection).*

The Drawing of the Impressionists

Claude Monet was one painter who did much to develop a method for recreating the surface vitality on canvas that characterized the out-of-door light in nature. Monet, and the painters who shared his methods, applied their color in rough, separate strokes, forcing the eye to fuse the dabs of color and thereby creating an active and dynamic painted surface. Since color was normally his chief preoccupation, Monet did not leave many drawings, but when he did draw without color he achieved this same surface dynamism by applying his pencil, chalk or pen strokes to create animated textures. "Two Men Fishing" (Figure 8–1) was done on scratchboard with black crayon. White lines have been re-established by scratching through the darks with a sharp instrument. The entire surface of the paper radiates light, yet each surface described in the drawing has a separate textural identity. The deep grass on the river bank contrasts with the flowing surface of the water. The heavy boards of the boats differ from the finer-textured jackets. The various surfaces are unified by the all-encompassing light and by the fresh unlabored rendering which permeates the drawing.

Not all of the individuals who have come to be termed the *impressionists* concerned themselves with the outdoors. As a group, all they shared was mutual sympathy, a distaste for the fashionable art of the salons and a few exhibitions, for they were more concerned with preserving the fidelity of each artist's particular view of life than with any single doctrine or method of work. The life of Paris proved as fascinating to two of the group, Manet and Degas, as did the subtleties of atmosphere to Monet. Both men were aristocrats and sophisticates who enjoyed the flavor of metropolitan life, moving from the world of fashion, the theatre, and the cafe to the demimonde with its overtones of depravity. No matter what the subject, however, their drawings remained committed to truth, both visual and social. Sentimental idealization and romantic symbolism were for them both moral and esthetic vices.

Many traditional elements in the hierarchy of artistic values were discarded. Manet was the first to disclaim the shadow as a sentimental and romantic device that falsifies. He drew and painted frankly, without the delicate passages of tone that made ordinary objects, particularly the human body, precious and so removed from the everyday world into the realm of illusion. For Manet the human being was no more important than the other elements that make up the fascinating spectacle constituting the world of fashion, which he viewed as a vast still life. In his "Portrait of a Woman, Half-Length" (Figure 8–2) or his sketch of "George Moore" (Figure 17–7), we can see the audacious honesty of his style and the sense of style that grows from his audacious honesty. The pencil line or brush stroke is candidly just that and there is an equally frank acknowledgment of the gesture by which the drawing was created. The sitter is drawn as a seen thing, rather than as an embodiment of sentimental or spiritual values. Even that almost sacred feature, the eye, was no more important to him than a bit of costume. In "At the Café" (Figure 8–3), the details of figure, costume, and cafe are scrambled with the casual irreverence of a snapshot. The pen strokes have the fresh vitality of unpremeditated speech, suggesting that neither his clear vision nor the act of drawing was hampered by precedent. The impressionists retained their fresh impressions only by rejecting many of the oppressive refinements that at one and the same time constitute both the great lessons of the past and the dead hand of tradition.

Not all of the past was rejected. Much of the strength and distinction of the art of Degas grew from his ability to reconcile what at first glance appears to be the most divergent and contradictory elements. Degas began his career as an

FIGURE 8–3

Édouard Manet (1832–1883; French).
"At the Café." Pen and blue-black ink, 11⅝" x 15½".
Courtesy of the Fogg Art Museum, Harvard University, Cambridge,
Massachusetts (Meta and Paul J. Sachs Collection).

admirer of Ingres; his first master was a disciple of Ingres, who transmitted to him the drawing discipline of the master. He visited the Louvre as a child under the tutelage of his father, a man of cultivated tastes, and in later years continued to study the treasures accumulated there. When he came in contact with Manet and other members of the literary and artistic avant-garde, he gradually turned his sharp eye, trained hand, and disciplined taste to the depiction of Paris life. Degas, like the master Ingres whom he so much admired, was above all a draftsman, and it is in the depiction of form in movement, of gesture, whether in the street, the cafe, the theatre or the race track, that he achieved the sharpest rendering of visual truth. His "Four Studies of a Jockey" (Figure 8–4) is one of the many sketches he made in preparation for his paintings of the race track. The exact turn of a head, the difference between the shape of the trousered buttocks when the figure sits comfortably relaxed, as in the upper right, and when the body bounces off the horse and the weight of the figure is transferred to the legs, as in the lower left, are recorded with unerring certainty. The economy of means is as admirable as the certainty. The brush line responds to every momentary impression, thickening to describe a shadow or loose fold of fabric, narrowing to a sharp edge when the flesh pushes against the cloth. A quick smear of white tempera suggests the sheen of the jockey's satin blouse. Yet nowhere does this admirable facility degenerate into a mere display of virtuosity. "Gentleman Rider" (Figure 16–9) is equally admirable.

Degas' portrait drawings are among the most subtle of his performances (Figure 8–5). In "Portrait of Diego Martelli" the individualized character of the sitter is communicated as forcefully as the man's physical bulk, solidity and weight. By contrast his "Study for a Portrait of Madame Julie Burtin" (Figure 15–5) imparts restraint, reticence and shimmering surface, with a minimum of body weight.

But visual truth is not all that gives distinction to Degas' work, for accompanying the knowing eye and telling hand is a restrained and balanced taste that frowned on excess of any kind. Even the compositional arrangements were planned to achieve a kind of structured formal balance. In his "Groupe de Danseuses Vues en Buste" (Figure 16–2), the long diagonal made by the raised arm at the right, continued in the shoulder-to-elbow movement of the figure at the left, is planned carefully to counterbalance the movement established by the right-hand edge of skirt, left edge of bodice, and the foreshortened arm adjusting a shoulder strap. His freest sketch is controlled; the lines never live for their own sake but exist only to describe. Thus the scribbled shadow-contour that defines the raised forearm at the upper left never foregoes its descriptive function to enjoy the exuberance of a flourish. His freedoms are always balanced by control.

Toulouse-Lautrec continued the trend established by Degas, both in terms of manner and subject matter. Like Degas he was a draftsman of great power, capable of recording an entire complex of forms, movements and gestures in a few telling lines (Figure 1–2). But the measured balance that always persisted in Degas, providing a classical note of restraint irrespective of subject, gave way to an acrid intensity in Toulouse-Lautrec. "La Buveuse ou Guele de Bois" (Figure 8–6) is one of his many studies of the twilight world of prostitution and corrup-

FIGURE 8–4

Edgar Degas (1834–1917; French). "Four Studies of a Jockey." Oil heightened with Chinese white, 17⅝" x 12". *Courtesy of The Art Institute of Chicago* (Mr. and Mrs. Lewis L. Coburn Memorial Collection). (See Plate 13.)

tion. His morbid oversharpened sensibilities made him particularly apt at describing its bitter flavor—his lines cut and his textures bite. The analytical eye seems hostile rather than cool, the drawing seems almost to eat into the paper.

The art of Toulouse-Lautrec moves beyond the objective vision of impressionism toward the subjective feelings of expressionism. The limitations of an art based upon the objective eye were felt by many of the men who for a time affiliated themselves with the impressionists. Recording the perceptions of the eye alone could end up as limiting to the artist as were the restrictions of the academy. A great world of sentiment, of esthetic refinement, of social and political commitment, was excluded by this rigid subjection to visual analysis.

FIGURE 8–5

Edgar Degas (1834–1917; French).
"Portrait of Diego Martelli." Black chalk heightened with
white chalk on gray-brown paper, 17¾" x 11¼".
Courtesy of the Fogg Art Museum, Harvard University,
Cambridge, Massachusetts (Meta and Paul J. Sachs Collection).

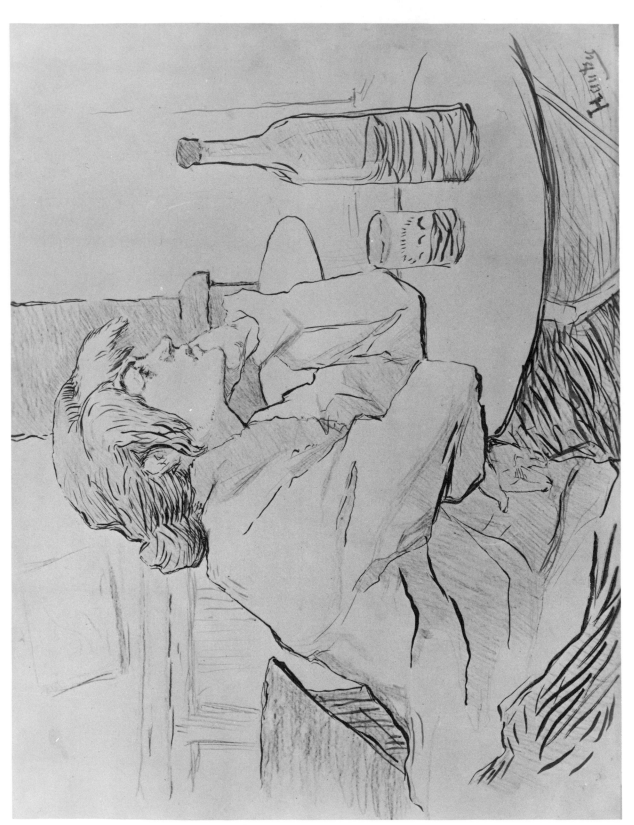

FIGURE 8–6

Henri de Toulouse-Lautrec (1864–1901; French).
"La Buveuse ou Guele de Bois."
Black ink and blue crayon, 18⅞″ x 24¾″.
Musée Toulouse-Lautrec, Albi, France. (Photo: Georges Groc.)

Postimpressionist
Drawing

In the last two decades of the nineteenth century certain of the painters who for a time worked and exhibited with the impressionists, either under the aegis of the old masters or directed by their own inner impulses, built upon impressionism a series of more personal and complex forms of expression. These men, for convenience of discussion, have been called the *postimpressionists,* and from their individual and highly personalized styles and the implications thereof have been built the radical departures from the western European tradition of painting that characterize the twentieth century. Renoir, Cézanne, Van Gogh, Gauguin, and Seurat are the masters usually described as postimpressionists.

Each of these five men developed a highly personal style of painting and a corresponding method of drawing. Renoir in many ways stayed closest to tradition. Though he retained the clear light colors and the freely textured paint beloved by Monet, he sought to enrich these devices by increasing the solidity of the forms and by designing his canvases with more continuous and rhythmic relationships of line. These qualities are all very evident in his study for "The Bathers" (Figure 8–7). Though the actions appear spontaneous, there is nothing casual or accidental in the grouping. The three figures build together into that most traditional and stable of compositional units, the pyramid. The extended figure in the lower right projects the diagonal line that forms the right side of the pyramid while the carefully designed negative space between the right-hand figure and the other two moves up and to the left with as much force as the figure itself.

Though this drawing was done as a study for a painting in which Renoir defined contours with an uncharacteristic precision, his was an art of light, air, and unfettered movement. In this preliminary study, rather than attempting to imprison the form in hard outlines, he employed a free bundle of pencil lines which seem to envelop the form and suggest its continuity in three dimensions, beyond the limited vision of the beholder. These soft flowing lines also suggest the luminous ambience in which the forms exist. The very act of making the drawing seems as pleasurable as the movements of the playing girls. No compulsive need to define with exactitude inhibited the lyric impulse of the artist. Much of the beauty of the drawing results from Renoir's effortless suggestion of firm, weighty pale bodies moving freely in space. This quality of effortless description is particularly evident in the top figure, where the volume of the breasts and the forms of the neck, shoulders, and abdomen have been suggested by the direction and overlapping of the soft lines.

In studying the drawing of "The Bathers," one is also impressed by the easy grace with which the potentialities and limitations of pencil as a medium have been accepted. The long sweeping pencil lines which provide the structural elements in the drawing reflect the arc of the hand moving easily across the page. Rather than force the pencil into deep shadow tones, Renoir kept the drawing light, thereby achieving both a sense of the out of doors and of pale skin. By occasionally smudging the pencil lines with his fingers, he suggested the roundness and smooth texture of the firm flesh and with telling wisdom he has used the smudged effects sparingly, concentrating them on breasts and other areas where roundness and softness are most striking.

Like Renoir, Cézanne first went through a period of apprenticeship as an Impressionist concerned with rendering the light and air of the out of doors, and then proceeded to create from impressionism an art that was as "solid and durable" as the masters whose work he studied in museums. Renoir also derived something of his compositional solidity from the study of the old masters, but here the similarity between the two men ends. Cézanne's art is not an effortless expression of lyric impulses, but rather a most searching and exacting analysis of the nature of form, space, and the process of vision. Cézanne was always dependent upon the physical act of seeing. He has almost none of the ability to imagine, to conjure from the depths of his mind a pictorial image; he is always dependent upon "nature" for his inspiration, whether that nature be landscape, still-life, genre, or portrait. No matter what the subject, Cézanne drew it or painted it as pure form—that is, without sentimental, literary or symbolic connotations, for there was no other subject for him than form and space. For him form became "the plane." So great was Cézanne's concern with the planes which constitute the surface of a form that he did not even find it necessary to define the exact contours of an object. What was necessary, however, was that he place each set of faceted planes in its proper relationship to the other objects in the space of a painting or drawing. Thus, in "Quais de la Seine" (Figure 8–8) the eye moves in space across the fragmented notations of barges, boats, bridge, by means of the directional planes that place each object in exact spatial relationship to every other object. There is no primary concern with the grace, sensuous charm or the picturesque atmosphere of the Seine in Paris. Instead, his primary concern was the creating a solid structural relationship between the objects within the drawing. This concern is so intense that it rendered Cézanne indifferent to a multitude of the other aspects of his subject matter that usually intrigue artists.

Another particular aspect of Cézanne's style grew from his concern that the faceted gradations at the edge of an object define its full form and volumes. This particular aspect of his mode of drawing can be seen most clearly in his "Study after Houdon's Écorché" (Figure 13–12). Here the sensitive way in which the planes that make up form appear as fragmented contour lines is particularly evident. Cubism (Figure 10–7), the most immediate offshoot of Cézanne's personal style, took his faceted surfaces as a point of departure and created an art of intersecting planes composed, much as Cézanne had composed, with a classic formalism and monumental sense of order. From the specialized nature of his concern and this indifference to other aspects of what he described, developed his highly personal style, a style which had a greater influence on the subsequent development of painting than that of any other nineteenth-century painter. Perhaps even more important in its impact upon successive generations than any single aspect of Cézanne's style is the fact that his example encouraged successive generations of artists to fragment the experience of seeing and to concentrate on that part of the total experience which was meaningful to them. Thus, rather than pursue the concept of a balanced vision in which one attempts to coordinate and unify all the varying sensations that beset the eye, twentieth-century painters and draftsmen sought to particularize visual experience in their art, to select and stress some one aspect of vision or the art of picture-making rather than strive for a balanced whole.

Vincent Van Gogh was another of the men who drew from the impressionistic method of rendering light and air the elements for his own particular form of expression. Van Gogh was an intense and ardent man who commenced his

FIGURE 8–9

Vincent Van Gogh (1853–1890; Dutch-French).
"In San Rémy." Black chalk or charcoal and white chalk on tan paper,
11¾" x 15⅜". *Courtesy of Mrs. Ruth Lilienthal.*

FIGURE 8–10

Paul Gauguin (1848–1903; French).
"Standing Tahitian Nude."
Pastel, 38¼″ x 19″.
*Des Moines Art Center, Iowa
(John and Elizabeth Bates
Cowles Collection).*

professional life as a minister of God in order that he might translate his love for his fellowman into concrete acts of help for his poor parishioners. His life is a tragic record of frustrated human relationships, but the burning intensity of his feelings found an outlet in his art. He drew and painted with the overwhelming ardor that was denied him in love and friendship, and the direct passion with which he executed his work shaped his style. A powerful empathy with the physical world made him feel each surface as an alive thing that seemed to move, and his brusque direct pen or brush strokes recorded this animation of surface. Thus, in "In San Rémy" (Figure 8–9) every surface seems to move, the great rounded masses of shrubs and trees appearing like organic animal forms in which one sees the movements of muscles underneath the pelt. The bundled figure hurrying home seems no more alive than the road which twists as it moves into the drawing. Each shrubby mass had its individual rhythm. On the right the heavy vines hang over the wall; above it the rounded trees well up like a wave to carry the eye to the sweeping vertical curves of the dark cypresses. On the left the textures are more tangled and complex, expressing the turbulent richness and variety of plant growth. The heavy black chalk lines were drawn in and the few white accents added without hesitation or caution to create an organic whole that seems as natural as a rush of affection.

In "The Bridge at L'Anglois" (Figure 15–2), the spiky grass radiates up and out of the ground, the rectangular texture of stones is briefly indicated, and the cypresses twist toward the sky. In opposition are the quiet flowing horizontals of the smoothly flowing water. One cannot conceive of a more simple, direct and expressive use of pen and ink; it is clear why Van Gogh has been described as the father of modern expressionism, since intensity of expression and the expression of intense feelings are his primary and almost his only aims.

Both Gauguin and Seurat are less concerned with the outward seeing eye and more with their inner vision. Gauguin's art reflects his longing for a world of primitive simplicity, where his physical passions, his egocentric drives and his esthetic tastes could find release and freedom. In his drawing he eliminated complexities of modeling and subtleties of form, preferring broad simplifications to suggest the elemental qualities that differentiated the girls of Tahiti from the women of Paris. Thus, in his pastel drawing of a "Standing Tahitian Nude" (Figure 8–10), the awkwardness of heavy legs and broad feet, the firm simplicity of contour lines, and the simple flat planes of modeling, all help to convey the gauche charm of the unsophisticated native girl. These same stylistic elements relate the drawing to the flat-patterned decorative arts of the South Sea Islands. The work was conceived more as a symbol of primitive life than as a representation of visual fact.

Seurat, too, was guided by an inner vision, but it is an inner vision of order and relationship. Unlike Gauguin, Seurat accepted the sophistication and complexities of modern life and attempted to control them through a systematic relationship of parts to a unified whole. In this way he reduces whatever form he depicts to an almost geometric component in a larger formally organized system of verticals, horizontals, and diagonals. In the same way Seurat reduced the complex textures by which Monet suggested the amplitude and vitality of visual

FIGURE 8-11

Georges Seurat (1859–1891; French).
"The Café Concert." Drawing, black conté, 12" x 9".
Permission of Museum of Art,
The Rhode Island School of Design, Providence.

experience into an orderly application of dots of pure color which unite all the complexities of form, light, and color into a unified totality. In his drawing "The Café Concert" (Figure 8–11) the conté crayon was applied on a rough but regularly textured surface to produce an even-toned glitter which reduces all the complications of surface to a uniform and therefore unifying texture. The contours are equally simplified, so that figures, related forms, and the architectural background are reduced to almost geometric equivalents. The singer becomes almost a triangle, the head of the orchestra leader a sphere, the baton a ruled line and thus geometricized; these lines fit into the larger architectural framework by which Seurat structured the entire composition. The same regular texture and geometrically simplified forms distinguish "Seated Boy with Straw Hat" (Figure 16–20). His is an art predicated upon a rational and scientific attitude toward life, not consciously based upon particular scientific theories but intuitively based upon an esthetic set of values which are in harmony with science and its methods. The method of drawing confirms this. It is carefully planned, methodically executed, glorifying system at the cost of impulse, at the opposite end of the spectrum from Van Gogh's intense self-consuming outbursts. It established a precedent from which the geometric abstractions of the twentieth century were the logical development.

Before closing the discussion of drawing in the nineteenth century the work of one English illustrator, Aubrey Beardsley, should be mentioned also. Beardsley is best known for his remarkable illustrations for Oscar Wilde's "Salome." "J'ai Baisé ta Bouche, Jokanaan" (Figure 8–12) is a study that probably secured for Beardsley the commission to illustrate "Salome." These illustrations reflect some of the stylistic features of that phase of turn-of-the-century illustrations which was influenced by the impressionists and postimpressionists. One senses the enthusiasm for both the Japanese prints and the striking posters designed by Toulouse-Lautrec and others behind the particular blend of sensuality and sophistication that distinguishes the Beardsley drawings. These are among the most brilliant and original illustrations of literary work to appear in modern times. They do not illustrate the text in the conventional sense, but rather provide a visual counterpoint to reinforce and enrich the mood of their literary source of inspiration. The Beardsley drawings were done in precise firm outlines without modeling or conventional chiaroscuro. Tonal variations were obtained by texture patterns such as can be seen in the scalelike overlapping circles behind the head of Salome. Such typically art-nouveau elements as the elongated vertical lines, the involved linear arabesques and the taste for flat-patterned decorative elements were derived from Oriental sources, particularly Japanese prints. Behind the sophisticated drawings by Beardsley one senses the turning away from traditional Western forms of artistic expression toward more exotic sources of inspiration which finally lead to the highly stylized and abstract modes of today.

An outline of all the tumultuous developments and conflicting movements that have characterized the art world since the postimpressionists initiated their bold and independent innovations could occupy this entire volume, but this book is not primarily a history of drawing. A chronological overview of the past

FIGURE 8–12
Aubrey Beardsley
(1872–1898; Eng-
lish). "J'ai Baisé ta
Bouche, Jokanaan."
*Ink and pen, 10⅞″ x
5¾″. Princeton Uni-
versity Library.*

merely seemed a logical way to introduce the reader to the magnificent body of work that constitutes our drawing heritage from earlier periods. The impact of impressionism and postimpressionism spread from country to country and at the turn of the century bold reactions to the new movements were widespread, as will be evidenced in the subsequent chapters on twentieth-century drawing.

Summary

The realism of the French mid-nineteenth-century painters provided the background from which impressionism and postimpressionism emerged. The impressionists were a group of Parisian artists who exhibited together and shared a common distaste for late nineteenth-century academic salon art. Monet was the principal landscape painter in the group and his infrequent chalk drawings have a linear texture that provided a graphic equivalent of the alive painted surfaces by which he created a sense of outdoor light. Manet and Degas were the principal Impressionist painters of upper middle-class Paris, particularly the genre of cafe, race track, and theatre. Degas, a student of Ingres, was a master draftsman and his unerring eye established characterizations and caught gestures with sharp exactitude. Manet often drew with pen, brush, and ink, whereas Degas drew with pencil, chalk, or charcoal with equal facility.

In the last twenty years of the century the Postimpressionists—Cézanne, Van Gogh, and Seurat in particular—moved beyond impressionism toward very personal methods of drawing and painting which laid the basis for the highly individualized and varied styles that dominated twentieth-century art. Cézanne pushed drawing and painting toward a fractional and faceted interpretation of form and space, Van Gogh toward expressionist intensification, and Seurat toward formal simplification and abstraction. In England Aubrey Beardsley gave expression to the turn-of-the-century *art-nouveau* mode in a decorative pen-and-ink illustrative style of great brilliance and originality.

9

DRAWING

OF

NON-EUROPEAN CULTURES

Until the late nineteenth century, certain prejudices as to the nature of artistic expression limited Western appreciation of the arts of the Orient, the Near East, of primitive societies and of other so-called exotic cultures. Art critics before the end of the nineteenth century assumed that the only significant artistic expression was devoted to the naturalistic or idealized treatment of the human figure or the landscape portrayed by creating the illusion of form, space, naturalistic light, and surface texture. Admirable though Renaissance and post-Renaissance art might be, the modern movement freed us from its biases and enabled us to perceive and cherish the arts of many peoples and cultures which had heretofore been viewed as merely curious bits of exotica or as subjects of anthropological significance. The arts of China, Japan, India, and the Middle East, of primitive societies in the South Pacific, Africa, and Pre-Columbian America, as well as archaic and folk cultures elsewhere, provide a rich reservoir of materials developed with relatively little reference to the traditions and conventions of the Mediterranean world and western Europe. For this very reason, these arts have supplied contemporary artists with fresh viewpoints and new stimuli and so are highly valued today.

The earliest settlements in the Far East appear to have occurred in India in the Indus Valley as far back as 2500 B.C., and the few artistic remains uncovered there suggest that the first developments were related to earlier civilizations in the Tigris-Euphrates Valley. The oldest urban settlements in China appeared in the valley of the Yellow River around 1500 B.C., and these, too, show

198

FIGURE 9–1

Li Ch'eng ([Ying-ch'iu] c. 940–967; Chinese). "Buddhist Temple amid Clearing Mountain Peaks." Ink and slight color on silk, 44″ x 22″. *Nelson Gallery - Atkins Museum (Nelson Fund), Kansas City, Missouri.*

FIGURE 9-2

Li K'an ([Li Hsi-chai] c. 1260-1310; Chinese).
Detail, "Ink Bamboo." Ink on paper, 14¾" x
93½". Nelson Gallery-Atkins Museum (Nelson
Fund), Kansas City, Missouri.

FIGURE 9-3
Wên Chêng-ming (1470–1559; Chinese).
"Cypress and Rock." Ink on paper, 10¼" x 19¼".
Nelson Gallery-Atkins Museum (Nelson Fund),
Kansas City, Missouri.

Emperor Hui Tsung (1082–1135; Chinese).
"Ladies Preparing Newly Woven Silk" (Detail of Ironing).
Color on silk, 14⁹⁄₁₆″ x 57¼″.
Courtesy, Museum of Fine Arts, Boston. (See Plate 14.)

characteristics which indicate contact with the prehistoric civilizations of India and thus Mesopotamia. For the most part, the conventions which dominate the arts of the Far East evolved independent of the traditions of the Mediterranean world and western Europe, although from time to time contacts were made and a cross fertilization of cultures ensued. This occurred in the fourth century B.C. when the conquests of Alexander the Great extended Greek influences into Persia, and this impact was felt as far east as India. In the seventeenth century an Italian painter settled in China, introducing certain conventions of the Italian Renaissance into the ancient and dignified art of China. In the nineteenth century contact with the art in Europe proved most stimulating to the practice of drawing, painting, and wood block printing in Japan. It has only been since the middle of the twentieth century, however, and then only in the advanced centers of development, that artistic expression in the Orient has joined the mainstream of world art.

In general, drawing and painting were less separate and specialized activities in China and Japan than in the West. For the most part, drawing and painting were one, for it is the mark made with the brush that constitutes both drawing and painting in the Far East, and the excellence and stylistic variations of the brushwork distinguish the various schools and artists from one another. It was, in fact, this distinguishing characteristic, the fact that painting in China and Japan was executed in ink or watercolor on paper or silk scrolls which earlier tended to discredit it in the West where the only valid forms of painting were considered to be fully developed oil paintings executed on canvas or mural painting in fresco. In like manner the spontaneous and sketchy character of Oriental drawing made it appear less intellectual than the elaborate, fully developed drawings that were the pride of the nineteenth-century academic ateliers.

The oldest developments of drawing appeared in China. The calligraphic style of brushwork that characterized the great periods of Chinese art appear fully developed before 1000 B.C., and there is evidence that the antecedents for this manner of working go back to the time of Christ. The artists of the great schools of the tenth century concerned themselves largely with landscape, continuously contrasting the grandeur and poetry of nature with the insignificance of man, as can be seen in "Buddhist Temple amid Clearing Mountain Peaks" (Figure 9–1), attributed to Li Ch'eng (Ying-Ch'iu). This handsome scroll painting represents the height of this development, with mist-enshrouded mountains rising in the distance behind a foreground of twisting waterways, picturesque pines, great stratified rocks, and tiny buildings, bridges, and perhaps people. A number of fine works of this type still exist, and the greatest exude an air of solemn majesty. Their distinction comes both from the awe and reverence of the artist in transferring the scale and magnitude of nature to silk or paper and from the elegance and refinement of the brush marks he uses to characterize the forms and textures of nature. In later schools of landscape painting, frequently both subject matter and style of brushwork became highly conventional, a certain set of brush strokes applied in a prescribed way being used to depict each separate subject. Thus pine-tree branches, bamboo leaves, rocks, rippling wavelets, each has its own particular calligraphy, and the mark of the master is shown by his deftness, taste, and originality in using this conventionalized imagery. A section of a hand scroll by Li K'an, who was active roughly from A.D. 1340 to 1360, shows the exquisite taste used by the masters of Chinese painting in handling these familiar subjects (Figure 9–2). Despite the standardized character of the motifs, the most admired artists not only arranged these motifs with distinction but also impregnated each mark with their own artistic personality in much the same way that a fine musician, when performing, leaves the imprint of his personality on the established composition he is playing.

Wen Cheng-ming, who painted in the late fifteenth and the first half of the sixteenth century and is best known for his landscapes, also specialized in bamboo, orchids, old trees, and rocks. "Cypress and Rocks" (Figure 9–3) reveals

Chinese Drawing

his characterful handling of the weathered rocks, the twisting branches of the cypress and the dense texture of the cypress foliage. The chief distinction of the drawing in the eyes of connoisseurs lies in the facile variations of brushwork and the richness of surface textures. The tones of ink range from pale washes to rich darks, the textures from wet spreading splotches to dry brush, and the strokes from the strong straight lines used in the dead cypress branches silhouetted against the sky to the broken stippled pattern of the cypress foliage. We see here a highly refined art combining taste, virtuosity, and sensitivity.

Though in the great periods of Chinese art landscape provided the vehicle for expression of the most exalted and profound sentiments, the human figure was also handled with great insight, skill, and reverence. Scenes of court life, the depiction of episodes from the life of Buddha, even portraits of important personages made up the repertoire of the ancient Chinese figure painters. Two scrolls provide an idea of the impressive level of achievement in rendering figure compositions that occurred in China well before the Gothic period in Europe. A hand scroll on silk with color, attributed to Hui T'sung in the twelfth century, is supposedly a copy of an earlier work by one of the masters of the T'ang Dynasty which lasted from A.D. 618 to 907 (Figure 9–4). Representing "Ladies Preparing Newly Woven Silk," the facility with which the figures are depicted, the refinement of the conventions for describing facial features, folds of cloth, and the sophistication of the composition suggest a long and sustained earlier

development. Pictorial representations of the life of Buddha stimulated some of the most vital developments in Chinese painting as can be seen in a handscroll representing "Barbarian Royalty Worshipping Buddha" (Figure 9–5). This particular scroll was executed in the tenth or eleventh century in the relatively provincial court of the Northern Sung Dynasty. From such works we can surmise the splendor of pageantry portrayed by the earlier masters of the T'ang Dynasty who established the prototype for these subjects. The vivacity and variety with which the various personages are portrayed, the complexity of costumes, attitudes and the skillful groupings of the figures in space all indicate a high order of artistic expression. Particularly effective is the placement of both the barbarian emperor and Buddha which establishes their eminence in relation to the retainers.

A handsome portrait done in ink and color on silk (Figure 9–6) by a painter of the Ming epoch (1368–1644) reveals an admirable elegance of line and subtlety of value relationships which in no way weaken its incisive delineation of character. Such works prove the falsity of the frequently voiced opinion that, because of the burden of convention and the effete refinement of court tastes, Chinese art lost contact with reality.

The same combination of elegance and skill characterizes the painting of a "Bird" (Figure 9–7), by Chu Ta, a seventeenth-century painter who left an album containing ten paintings in ink on paper of birds, flowers, insects, and

FIGURE 9–6
Ming-Ch'ing Periods (seventeenth to eighteenth centuries; Chinese).
"Portrait." Ink and color on silk, 59¾" x 37".
Courtesy of the Fogg Art Museum, Harvard University,
Cambridge, Massachusetts (Gift of Dr. Denman Ross).

FIGURE 9–7

Chu Ta (1626–1705; Chinese).
"Bird, from an Album of Flowers, Birds, Insects and Fish." Ink on paper,
10¹⁄₁₆″ x 9¹⁄₁₆″. *Courtesy of the Smithsonian Institution,*
Freer Gallery of Art, Washington, D. C.

fish. Although the performance is in many ways highly formalized, one cannot help but admire the way in which the branch moves into the composition from the lower right, and a counterbalancing movement from lower left to upper right is achieved by the branch, leg, and head. The contrast is admirable between the drybrush texture of the branch, and the velvety wash of dark on the body of the bird, which fades out just enough to suggest the plane of the neck and to show the pattern of wing feathers. Even the seals of the owners and the artist's calligraphy in the lower right-hand corner relate skillfully to the rest of the composition.

FIGURE 9–8

Nonomura Sotatsu (d. 1643; Japanese). "The Zen Priest Choka." Hanging scroll, ink on paper, 37¾" x 15¼". *The Cleveland Museum of Art (Norman O. Stone and Ella A. Stone Memorial Fund).*

PLATE 9
Albrecht Dürer (1471–1528; German).
"The Great Piece of Turf."
Watercolor, 16¼" x 12⅜".
Albertina, Vienna.

PLATE 10   Jean Antoine Watteau (1684–1721; French).
"Four Studies of Italian Actors." Red, white, and black crayon, 10¼" x 15⅝".
Courtesy of the Art Institute of Chicago (Gift of Tiffany and Margaret Blake).

The basic elements of Japanese art were inherited from China. These were ideographic characters which constitute their writing and the brush and ink in which both writing and painting were executed. The elements of pictorial art first appeared in Japan in the fifth century when mainland culture was introduced. As with China, the art of Japan was an art of highly refined conventions, in which natural forms were delineated by means of black lines reinforced with light colors. In Japan, as in China, stylistic distinction and imagination in the handling of the brush constituted an important characteristic of the pictorial arts, and unlike Chinese drawing and painting, an element of humor and satire frequently adds spice to their refined and conventional practices.

The artists of Japan based their finest works on religious themes, religious ceremonies, and court life, although they also painted landscape and nature forms. Many of the characteristic qualities of Japanese art can be seen in the Kumano Mandala hanging scroll from the great Kamakura period between 1185 and 1333, a period when many distinctly Japanese attributes began to modify the Chinese heritage (Figure 14–6). In such works, the landscape provides the setting for a religious and aristocratic narrative. The role of this particular scroll painting was to provide the viewer with a symbolic visit to three Shinto shrines. Though in reality these three mountain shrines were separated by many miles, they were brought close together for pictorial purposes in this sacred diagram of holy places. Hills, flowering trees, and other beautiful aspects of nature contribute to the devotional atmosphere. This particular scroll illustrates the conventions by which perspective and deep space were rendered. Successive levels indicate spatial recession, and the diminishing sizes, as one moves back and up make the space concept visually convincing, even to a viewer steeped in Renaissance perspective. The architectural forms were rendered in isometric perspective so that parallel lines, rather than converging as they move into pictorial space, remain parallel.

In the painting that followed the Kamakura period, typical Japanese characteristics become intensified, and a high degree of esthetic sophistication distinguished the work of certain artists who were sufficiently famous that their names have been perpetuated. Such was Nonomura Sotatsu, a seventeenth-century painter whose ink scrolls reveal great originality and brilliance. In "Zen Priest Choka" (Figure 9–8), one can see his bold innovations which left an indelible mark on subsequent Japanese styles of drawing and painting. Extreme asymmetry of composition was often preferred. In this example, the pictorial elements are arranged far to one side of the scroll, balanced by an extended empty area, thereby creating a negative space of great visual interest which probably also had symbolic significance. Amazing variety and ingenuity characterized his handling of the brush and ink, with each separate surface displaying a special and unique technique. Brushed line, dragged and splashed ink, the uneven dilution of wash to produce blurred and pooled effects, and other textural devices provide elements of variety and surprise. The people he depicts are often caricatured so that a dimension of humor adds to the sophisticated charm of his work.

Some of the finest examples of Japanese brushwork can be seen in the richly decorated folding screens on which Japanese artists displayed their formidable virtuosity. One panel of a six-fold screen from the late sixteenth century reveals the elegance with which the conventions for representing foliage and other landscape elements were manipulated (Figure 17–9). While this lacks the sober grandeur of the great tenth-century Chinese landscape paintings from which this tradition was derived, the frankly skilled dispositions of patterns and textures in this panel create a work of great decorative charm and visual distinction.

The succession of masters who accented the general high level of artistic production during Japan's long history culminated in a number of individual artists of great distinction in the late eighteenth and the first half of the nineteenth centuries; most notably Hokusai and Hiroshige.

Of all Japanese artists, Hokusai is best known to the Western world. Not only was he a prolific artist who produced a tremendous number of paintings, drawings, and designs for woodblock prints, but the humor, vivacity, and warmth of his work make him liked even by those who are not sensitive to his esthetic and technical assets. In the course of his life he worked in many styles and treated a broad range of subject matter, much of which concerned itself with the genre of Japanese lower-class life. Such is the theme of "The Mochi Makers" (Figure 9–9), a topic frequently depicted by Japanese artists. The subject of the mochi makers was popular, since it involved the ritual making of rice cakes in preparation for the Autumn Festival of the Full Moon. The difficulty of preparing the dough was widely recognized; in fact, there was a popular Japanese saying to the effect that amateurs had best avoid undertaking this tricky task. Some artists handled the subject seriously, emphasizing the skill involved in carrying out the difficult process, while others treated it humorously, stressing the hazards of an awkward handling of the sticky and intractable mass of dough. Hokusai touched on both attitudes. He stressed the skill involved in hammering the rice with a great mallet and at the same time revealed the impatience of the malleteer with the co-worker who is unable to cope with the sticky dough—to the intense amusement of the audience witnessing the clumsy performance.

In a kakemono of "The Old Woodcutter" by Hokusai (Figure 13–4), the line quality is reinforced by rich value contrasts and a variety of textures. But rich and satisfying though these elements are, one cannot survey a group of Hokusai's drawings without being aware that, above all, he is a master of line. In certain drawings the line is fluid and rhythmic, with slight variations in width accenting movements and providing visual variety. Elsewhere the line moves with fierce energy, enlarging from a hair's breath to the width of the brush. Again, it is rough, tense, and crabbed, seeming to be contorted by some inner convulsion and radiating a constricted and thwarted force. There seems to be no potential of line as an expressive device that this great draftsman does not exploit. For instance, each part of the "Mochi Makers" has a particular linear quality which intensifies its expressive character. The tangle of lines in the lap of the laughing onlooker provides an obligato to his humor, in contrast to the twisting movements which so effectively describe the actions of the man

manipulating the dough. There appears to be no aspect of human emotion that Hokusai did not encompass from poetic and sentimental revery through humor to violent satire. Such is the expressive power of his work that we become intimately involved in it and cease to be aware of the unfamiliar flavor of the culture that produced it—for the Japan of Hokusai's day was culturally much farther from Western mores than the Japan of today. Such was the modesty of this great artist that though he lived to be eighty-nine, he declared that only after a hundred or even a hundred and ten years would he achieve the true ability of an artist.

Ando Hiroshige was a contemporary of Hokusai whose eminence is based chiefly on his well-known block prints. His greatness is probably most evident in the many drawings made as studies for his prints, since the drawings are directly from the artist's own hands, while the prints include the handwork of the engravers and printers who prepared the blocks and printed them. Hiroshige's block prints were usually issued in series, and many describe the great scenic beauties of Japan, particularly as seen from the main routes of travel. Others depict courtesans and elegant ladies at their toilette, or ladies and gentlemen entertaining themselves. Hiroshige preferred court life and the entertaining activities of the upper classes to the lower-class genre that fascinated Hokusai. A drawing of a "Gentleman and a Courtesan," attributed to Hiroshige, shows the fluent line and graceful disposition of forms that characterize his drawings (Figure 9–10). The sense of composition revealed here seems spontaneous and impeccable. The curved stance of the standing male figure is complemented and completed in the reverse curve of the back of the woman, and the two heads moving in the same direction with the woman's raised hand relate the two figures. The facial features are at the same time highly conventionalized and very expressive.

Persia and India

India and Persia have a rich tradition of pictorial art, to which we cannot possibly do justice in a few pages. In the drawings and paintings of the great periods of artistic development, both countries have much in common. The art of China was an important influence on each, for in the fourteenth century, Chinese models set an example of elegant linear calligraphy accompanied by the use of delicate washes of clear color. At a later date the impact of the Italian Renaissance expressed itself in the use of more brilliant and solid color and the increased spatial emphasis.

The most fully developed examples of pictorial art to come out of the Near East are painted miniatures—exquisitely rendered colored depictions of court life or illustrations of well-known literary works. Many Persian and Indian drawings were studies for these miniature paintings, although some of the finest drawings are finished studies done in the spirit of the miniatures but not completely colored.

"A Youth Kneeling and Holding Out a Wine Cup" (Figure 9–11) by Riza-i'Abbasi, a famous draftsmen of early seventeenth-century Persia, reveals many characteristics of the school of miniature painters. The carefully modu-

FIGURE 9–10

Attributed to Hiroshige (1797–1858; Japanese).
"Gentleman and a Courtesan." Brush drawing, irregular shape, 5" x 5¾".
Stanford University Museum, California (Museum Purchase Fund).

lated lines flow smoothly, and by their swelling and diminishing widths suggest the volumes of the figure. The background patterns of leaves and plants are placed with a sensitive feeling for their decorative potentialities. A small amount of color and gold has been introduced to add to the decorative charm. It is an art of highly refined conventions rather than one of exploration and discovery.

The most vigorous school of pictorial art to develop in India appeared during the reign of the Mughal emperors in the seventeenth century. Familiar

FIGURE 9–11

Riza-i'Abbasi (early seventeenth-century; Persian).
"A Youth Kneeling and Holding out a Wine Cup."
Line drawing; ink, color, and gold, 5½″ x 3⅝″.
Courtesy of the Smithsonian Institution,
Freer Gallery of Art, Washington, D.C.

with the refined art of Persia, these vigorous rulers encouraged the practice of the arts, even overlooking the Moslem injunction against making pictures. Some of the artists practicing in the Mughal court were imported from Persia, although the emperors preferred Indians, since they seemed more free from the effete conventions that dominated much Persian art. Paintings were brought from Europe to better acquaint the Indian artists with the European methods of achieving convincing visual effects. The paintings of the Mughal court, like those of Persia, are small, precise and dependent on line and color rather than on effects of chiaroscuro, but in the vigorous climate of the Mughal court the Persian conventions took on a new life. The introduction of portraiture was one of the innovations of this period, and no more remarkable example exists than the "Death of Inayat Khan" (Figure 9–12). The angular pose, emaciated face, and skeletal body contrast strikingly with the full, rounded forms of the pillows. This incisive drawing of a dying man has a strength, clarity, and singleness of purpose that makes it one of the great portraits of all time.

A delightful seventeenth-century drawing by an anonymous artist, "The World of Animals" (Figure 9–13), is another of the famous drawings to come from Mughal India. A brush drawing executed in pale warm colors, it is unusual both because of its complexity and its sense of space and movement. For the most part, the animals are depicted in pairs, although certain fantastic imagined monsters appear singly. The individual forms are delicately modeled and because of their rhythmic relation to one another, the rather precise edges and sensitive contrasts of value, the composition remains unconfused and pleasing. One encounters this rich sense of patterning and movement more frequently in Indian architectural sculptures and the decorative arts than in drawing and painting.

Pre-Columbian, African, and South-Sea Island Cultures

The picture, as such, hardly exists for primitive man. For him, the objectifying of experience through pictorial symbols tends to accompany the making of ritual objects rather than being an end in itself. In the South Seas, Africa, pre-Columbian America, and elsewhere, primitive peoples decorated their bodies, household implements, ceremonial objects, temples, and dwellings with many types of drawn and graven images, and these images provide a valuable addition to the sources from which modern artists draw instruction and inspiration.

The field of primitive art is extensive and varied, and each day archaeological research and anthropological study reveal new information and materials. A few token examples have been included here, if only to make the reader aware of the fascination and promise of the subject.

Four examples of what might liberally be termed drawing from pre-Columbian America suggest the symbolic and decorative character of such works. Starting in the Arctic north, the engraved walrus-ivory stem of a tobacco pipe pictures Eskimo hunters in pursuit of their prey (Figure 9–14). The terse symbols of men, boats, spears, fish and animals were engraved in the ivory with a sharp instrument, and the engraved lines were then filled with red ochre or black

soot. These engraved symbols represent a kind of pictorial writing—observant, factual, and vividly descriptive. We see the men carrying on varied aspects of the hunter's life, traveling over the sea in their kyacks, brandishing their spears, bows and arrows, spearing seals, whales, and fish and skinning and otherwise preparing the animals for consumption. Engravings of this type have been found dating back to the time of Christ.

From the Pueblos of the southwest United States, probably from before A.D. 1900, comes a handsome bowl decorated with deer, floral arabesques, and

FIGURE 9–13

School of Jahangir, Mughal (early seventeenth century; Indian). "The World of Animals." Brush drawing in pale tints, mounted as an album leaf, with illuminated border, Paper: 13⅝₁₆″ x 8⁹₁₆″; Painting: 9³₁₆″ x 4¹¹₁₆″. *Courtesy of the Smithsonian Institution, Freer Gallery of Art, Washington, D.C. (See Plate 15.)*

symbolic designs (Figures 2–2). By the time the bowl was created these lively patterns had probably lost their original magic function and were cherished for their decorative charm rather than because they were believed to bring fortune to the hunter. This follows a universal law: that esthetic values gradually replace utilitarian purposes as a society becomes more sophisticated. While the patterns on the Eskimo pipe discussed above have a terse angular linear quality that grows from the constrained act of cutting into the hard horn, the patterns on this pot were applied in thinned clay slip, and the heavy, fluid medium has influenced the character of the decorations, producing lines of rather even width which move with slow, full rhythms.

Stepping down farther south to Guatemala and farther back in time to well

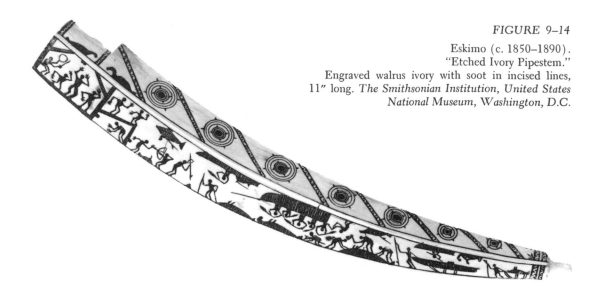

FIGURE 9–14

Eskimo (c. 1850–1890).
"Etched Ivory Pipestem."
Engraved walrus ivory with soot in incised lines,
11″ long. *The Smithsonian Institution, United States
National Museum, Washington, D.C.*

before A.D. 900, we find an example of great pictorial sophistication in the famous "Chama vase," one of the finest examples of classic Maya vase decoration (Figure 9–15). A corpulent figure is depicted kneeling between two black-painted priests. The differing visages of the three figures are sharply emphasized, as is the splendor of the ritual costume of the priest at the far right. The glyphs placed close to the borders between the figures probably identify the individuals or explain the nature of the ceremony described by the drawing. The drawing is in black and red on tan clay, with firm black outlines defining its forms. The various elements of the design are placed on the cylindrical vase with a strong feeling for both narrative clarity and decorative effect.

The Mochica culture flourished along the northern coast of Peru, extending back almost to the time of Christ. Among the most refined products of the Mochica were the elaborate ceramic vessels made for burial in the graves of important personages. These stirrup-handled vessels were often modeled in the form of a highly realistic portrait of the deceased or were decorated with elaborate pictorial scenes designed to describe some aspect of Mochica life or belief. A vase which depicts a mythological battle of the bean warriors displays the brilliant decorative sense and technical skill of the Mochica potter (Figure 9–16). Maintaining an even, controlled width of line and uniform sizes on a curved ceramic surface is extremely difficult, yet the pattern has been applied with precise control and lively imagination. Though no two figures or intervening spaces are identical, a brilliant effect of a consistent all-over pattern has been produced. Equally satisfying when viewed as a whole or studied in its separate parts, this handsome vessel represents an artistic achievement equal in its refinement and sophistication to the achievements of the classic Greek potters.

Africa and the South Pacific have also provided an abundant source of primitive *objet d'art*. Though most primitive African art is three-dimensional, a number of rock paintings have been found which display the same bold sense of form and decoration as has characterized African sculpture. Rock paintings have been found on prehistoric sites, and the practice has been continued into modern times. A rock painting from Khargur Tahl in the Libyan Desert describes a fight, apparently for the possession of a bull (Figure 2–4). The drawing displays a vivid faculty for summarizing action through slight variations in the postures of effectively composed symbolic figures. In such works, one sees the human figure reduced to cryptic symbols which represent a step toward pictographic writing rather than toward realistic representation. From such art forms evolve pictographs, then hieroglyphics, and finally writing.

The arts of Oceania are extraordinary in their variety and extravagance of invention. In Melanesia, in particular, a fantastic degree of elaboration characterizes many of their ceremonial artifacts. Ancestor worship, totemism,

FIGURE 9–15

Mayan (eighth to ninth century A.D.; Guatemala). Chama vase. Painted ceramic, 9½" high. *University Museum, University of Pennsylvania, Philadelphia.*

FIGURE 9–16

Mochica (third to ninth centuries; Peru).
Stirrup-spout vessel, "The Mythical Battle of
Bean Warriors." Ceramic, 10¾₆″ x 5¾₆″.
*Courtesy of The Art Institute of Chicago
(Buckingham Fund)*.

and a belief in magic and spirits are the principal forces motivating the involved, carved and painted masks, doorposts, utensils, and weapons which, along with the decorations of their bodies, ceremonial houses and canoes, constitute the chief artistic creations of the South Sea Island peoples. The motifs employed in these decorations represent or symbolize human and animistic ghosts, spirits, and supernatural beings, but the forms are conventionalized, elaborated, and entertwined in such a way that it is usually difficult to disentangle and identify the various elements. This is evident in even a relatively simple wooden shield from the Trobriand Islands (Figure 9–17), which is unusual in that the flat surface of the shield is not also enriched with sculptural, bas-relief or inlaid enhancements. Decorated with black and reddish-brown patterns, the lower part of the shield has a shark or fish motif, topped by what appear to be two birds, and enclosed by an elongated, eel-like form. The upper half is decorated with what seems to represent a flattened animal form with six outstretched legs, clawed feet, and symbolic representations of intestines and other internal organs. The rhythmic pattern of dots that surrounds the principal motifs provides the animation of surface that is usually achieved through polychrome carvings. As is frequently the case in Oceanic art, many of the motifs are treated in a manner that suggests a kinship with the pre-Columbian and northwest Coast cultures of America.

FIGURE 9–17

Trobriand Islands (Late nineteenth century; Oceania). Wooden shield. Incised design painted black, white, and brown, 30¾″ x 13⅜″. *University Museum, University of Pennsylvania, Philadelphia.*

The aboriginal tribes of Australia were stil living in an Old Stone-Age level of culture when the first settlers arrived from England at the end of the eighteenth century. Nomadic hunters and fishermen without settled habitations, the aborigines continued their way of life in the remote and central areas of Australia well into the twentieth century. Like the Old Stone-Age hunters who decorated the caves of France and Spain, the artistic output of the Australian natives was used as part of the magic ritual dedicated to appeasing the forces of nature and insuring success in the chase. Rock paintings on the vertical walls of cliffs under overhanging ledges and paintings on bark constitute the chief art of these peoples. A bark painting of two crocodiles and a wallaby in red, white, and yellow earth colors on dark bark represents the art of these peoples at its most naturalistic (Figure 9–18). The animals are pictured in their most characteristic aspect, thus the alligators are shown from above where the flattened shape and awkward four-legged mode of locomotion is most evident, while the wallaby was done in profile, suggestive of a leaping position. The pattern of lines and dots which cover the body of the animals may represent either surface patterns or the internal organs, for primitive man does not hesitate to picture parts of the animal which he considers important, even though he cannot see them.

Summary

By the end of the nineteenth century, an appreciation of the arts of the Far and Near East became widespread. In the twentieth century, European and American cultural horizons broadened to include the artistic expression of primitive African and South Sea Island cultures, as well as the arts of the pre-Columbian inhabitants of the Americas.

In Asia the first settled civilizations appeared in the Indus Valley of India as far back as 2500 B.C., and before 1500 B.C., a Neolithic level of culture had appeared in the Yellow River Valley of China. But, despite occasional contacts with the Mediterranean world and Western Europe, the arts of Asia developed in relative independence and exhibited certain unique aspects.

China witnessed the first development of the pictorial arts in Asia. Drawing and painting hardly existed as separate entities, and both were closely related to the art of calligraphy. Both relied primarily on brush and black ink used on silk scrolls, with color employed sparingly. Before A.D. 1000 vigorous schools of landscape painting had developed in the dynastic courts of China, in which the poetic grandeur of nature and the insignificance of man was a frequent theme. Figure painting depicting Buddhist concepts was also well developed before A.D. 1000. In subsequent periods, less stress was placed on originality, and there was much emphasis on dexterity of execution and tasteful disposition of familiar motifs.

The basic elements of Japanese art were introduced from China in the fifth century A.D., along with the art of writing. Japanese drawing and painting reveals many affinities with Chinese art, tending to depict religious themes and scenes of court life. Japanese artists placed great emphasis on original and expressive brushwork and unique compositional arrangement, and an element of humor often animates their work. Unique aspects of Japanese drawing are particularly

FIGURE 9–18

Umba Kumba, Groote Eylandt (Northern Territory, Australia).
Bark painting. Red, white, and yellow mineral pigments,
on black, 39¾" x 16¼". *The Smithsonian Institution,
United States National Museum, Washington, D.C.*

evident in the brilliant genre sketches of Hokusai, the outstanding genius of late eighteenth and early nineteenth century Japan.

The exquisite miniatures of Persia and India represent a high level of drawing and painting, both in terms of skills and tastes. The most brilliant development of the art of making pictorial miniatures appeared in the courts of the Mughal emperors of India in the seventeenth century.

In Neolithic cultures the pictorial arts were seldom developed as ends in themselves but remain a part of the ritual activities conducted to insure success in the hunt, in combat with enemies, or to beautify their crafts. Among the pre-Columbian inhabitants of the Americas and among the primitive tribes of Africa and the South Sea Islands, a wealth of pictorial motifs were used in the decoration of household and ceremonial objects such as pipes, textiles, and ceramics. The pictorial symbols, usually highly conventionalized, were frequently drawn with brilliant technical skill and sensitivity to decorative values.

10

THE TWENTIETH CENTURY:
LES FAUVES, CUBISM, AND
ABSTRACTION

The most striking characteristic of twentieth-century drawing is its diversity. Although there has been a consistent movement away from the tradition of pictorial realism toward expressionism, abstraction, and highly personal modes of stylization, a strong vein of disciplined realism still flourishes, not merely as a persistent anachronism from earlier times but as a strong creative force. Drawing serves as a means of jotting down ideas, of making notes and of visualizing compositional ideas; consequently, it has remained more subject to conventional disciplines than painting, sculpture or printmaking but it still reflects the various schools and modes that are currently in the vanguard of artistic expression.

France remained the undisputed center from which new art movements emanated until after World War I in 1918. In France, in the first two decades of the century first a group of expressionists called *Les Fauves* (literally, "the wild beasts," because of their bold colors and free style of painting), later the cubists, and then the surrealists, established the advanced movements in painting for the modern age. A number of what are now considered the twentieth-century old masters achieved their eminence as leaders of these early revolutionary movements: Matisse, Picasso, Gris, Dufy, Modigliani, Léger, Chagall, Miró, Lipschitz, Dali, and others. In Italy an offshoot of cubism, futurism, (Figure 18–16) injected fresh blood into the moribund Italian artistic tradition, and during these same years vigorous unconventional movements dominated by expressionistic tendencies, were initiated by various groups in Germany and Austria.

After World War I (1918), the impulse to experiment, to discard rules and conventions of the past and to move into fresh modes of expression, spread. France ceased to be the center of innovation; Germany became increasingly important, particularly the Bauhaus, in Dessau, with its collaborative school of painters, architects, designers, and other workers in the visual arts. In the twenties the Bauhaus became one of the most dynamic forces in popularizing changing technological and esthetic concepts. New York also grew in importance as a creative center. After 1945, in the years following World War II, the United States and in particular New York, moved into a position of world leadership, and the repudiation of academic concepts of art became worldwide. Travel, circulating exhibitions, books, and periodicals (what Malraux so aptly termed "the museum without walls") almost obliterated the regional and national differences which formerly distinguished the arts of one country or area from another, with the result that today the only significant qualities that differentiate works of art are the differences in viewpoint between the artists as individuals.

The amount of drawing and painting produced since the end of World War II (1945) is prodigious, and its vigor, variety, and quality attest to the vitality of the modern movement. In order to get any comprehensive picture of the kaleidoscopic range of styles in the contemporary scene, some system of classification is necessary. Any such system involves rather arbitrary pigeonholing, which distorts and simplifies the complexity of the artistic impulses. Therefore the various classifications must be viewed as a description of tendencies rather than as definitive modes of operation. The terms that most conveniently describe the extreme tendencies in contemporary painting (and therefore drawing) are *abstraction, expressionism,* and *realism.* These terms are in themselves subject to a wide range of interpretation. Classifying styles as abstract, expressionistic, or realistic, is complicated by the fact that these general terms represent a tendency that is inherent in all art. The tendency to abstract is a tendency to formalize, simplify, and generalize. Expressionism represets a tendency to emphasize, exaggerate, and editorialize. Co-existent in the contemporary scene remains the trend toward visual realism, which is a tendency to analyze, objectify, and particularize. As it is impossible to say where realism ends and abstraction or expressionism begins, no system is valid that does more than classify according to general tendencies and thereby provide a picture of the range and diversity of the contemporary scene.

FIGURE 10–1

Henri Matisse (1869–1954; French).
"Odalisque." Ink on paper, 21⅝" x 29½".
*Courtesy Achenbach Foundation for Graphic Arts,
California Palace of the Legion of Honor, San
Francisco (Gift of Frank Schwabacher, Jr.).*

FIGURE 10–2
Raoul Dufy (1877–1953; French).
"The Artist's Studio."
Brush and ink, 19⅝" x 26".
Collection, The Museum of Modern Art,
New York (Gift of Mr. and Mrs.
Peter A. Rübel). Photo: Sunami.

In the first decade of the twentieth century a number of French painters, encouraged by the original character of postimpressionist art, developed great independence of style, working with highly keyed color, applied with boldness and freedom. Matisse (Figures 10–1, 15–12) and Dufy (Figure 10–2) were leaders of the original group who were known by the derisive epithet *Les Fauves.* The drawings of both Matisse and Dufy (who was influenced by Matisse) reveal the search of these artists for an absolute correspondence between freshness of perception and spontaneity of execution. A conviction that "whatever is useless is consequently harmful" influenced Matisse toward an unlabored simplification of drawing. His theory that "composition is the art of arranging in a decorative manner the diverse elements through which the painter expresses his feelings," encouraged him to compose spontaneously without preliminary planning and with little other than an intuitive feeling for decorative arrangement to restrict or guide his procedures. The casual and unlabored style of drawing that developed from this philosophy delivered another blow toward undermining the traditional emphasis in academic circles upon learning to draw with accuracy and a full rendering of detail. Between 1905 and 1930 the original Fauve group augmented by other artists became the *avant-garde* of the early twentieth-century Parisian art world. Among the notables painting in Paris in these years were Modigliani (Figure 13–11), Chagall (Figure 18–13), Léger (Figure 15–16), and Picasso (Figures 10–4, 5, 6, 13–6).

Modigliani explored a rather narrow stylistic vein that was realized more fully in his drawings than in his paintings which, though charming in color, were essentially linear in conception. As can be seen in his "Portrait of Leon Bakst" (Figure 13–11), his line is elegant and frail, refined to the point of preciosity, but still sufficiently incisive to create a convincing sense of volume. His gift is particularly evident in his portrait drawings, where the small almond-shaped eyes, thin, pinched mouths, and sensitive elongations of the contours of the face create an impression of delicate and precious distinction.

Chagall was born in Russia, but moved to Paris in 1910 and soon became acquainted with the new movements in art and the men who were creating them. Chagall was less interested in describing his immediate visual experience than he was in painting from memory and imagination. Chagall's figures often float free of the laws of gravity; size and space relationships are as arbitrary as in a dream or a child's drawing, and the media are used in a direct naïve manner. All of these qualities are evident in the ink and gouache drawing "Old Musician" (Figure 18–13). The consciously scratchy and crude pen lines and stipplings which appear here create an effect of urgency and inner tension, as far from the technical standards of graphic expression that prevailed before his day as were his themes and modes of drawing. The strong element of fantasy and almost childlike naivete that characterize the work of Chagall colored the emerging Expressionist and Surrealist movements.

Léger came to Paris in 1900, was influenced by the art of Cézanne, and subsequently by Picasso and Braque. He then embarked upon his own bold style, which reflects our mechanized civilization by interrelating, entwining and overlapping a broad variety of forms as though they were cogs in some vast machine. In his earlier works Léger combined details of architecture, machines, cog-wheels and other industrial elements, with human forms as accessory elements. Later the human figure began to dominate his work, but it still appeared as an automaton or puppet. In his pencil, pen and ink and ink wash study for "The Divers" (Figure 15–16), the figures appear devoid of individual significance. The various parts of the anatomy entwine and overlap like the mechanically moving parts of some automotized human machine. Even the line widths in the drawing seem insensitive and impersonal; the dark splashes of wash neither model the forms systematically nor focus attention on parts according to some visible scheme of importance, but instead suggest a grease-implemented, monotonous pattern of movement.

The early twentieth-century revolution initiated a revision of judgment about a large body of what had previously been considered anthropological materials. The esthetic merit of the arts of pre-Columbian America, of Oceana, and of Africa was recognized by the painters and sculptors who were searching for fresh and moving avenues of expression. Negro masks and fetish figures inspired Picasso, Braque, Modigliani, and others to initiate new stylistic distortions in their work, and among the artists who found fresh inspiration in the arts of primitive people was the sculptor Lipschitz. For a period of time Lipschitz created sculptural equivalents of cubist paintings, but later he veered toward the use of organic forms of monumental scale in which the strong simplifications of natural forms are reminiscent of pre-Columbian ceramic and stone figures. Thus primitive art provided him with a pattern for achieving an Expressionist intensity of feeling which is forcefully revealed in a charcoal and wash drawing made as a study for his bronze "Sacrifice" (Figure 10–3). The tendency toward abstraction inherent in expressionism, a tendency which eventually led to abstract expressionism, is very evident in this study. The great priestly figure in the act of piercing the breast of the sacrificial cock, which is clearly evident in the finished bronze, barely emerges from the abstract matrix of this awesome drawing. The direct use of charcoal, wash, and erased lights in the drawing permitted the form to emerge and define itself as the drawing developed, thereby providing the sculptor with a malleable pictorial substitute for clay.

Picasso and Cubism

While Matisse, Dufy and the majority of French artists moved continuously toward a free and lyrical type of expressionism, Picasso, probably the major twentieth-century artist, sought to reconcile expressive intensification with formal values. His earliest drawings and paintings share the expressionist characteristics that dominated the first decade of the century. After this he explored a very sensitive manner, well exemplified by his drawings of a "Seated Figure" (Figure 13–6) and "Head" (Figure 10–4). Picasso then proceeded to move toward more formally structured forms of composition and a more analytical approach to drawing which eventually found expression in the Cubist movement of which he was a leader. The many innovations of style that have marked Picasso's long and productive record have acted as a catalyzer for the

FIGURE 10–4

Pablo Picasso (1881–   ; Spanish-French).
"Head." Brush drawing, 21½" x 16".
San Francisco Museum of Art
(Harriet Lane Levy Bequest).

entire art world during the first half of the century. His beautiful drawing of "The Bathers" (Figure 10–5), done in pencil on white paper, represents a conservative facet of his talents, suggesting a momentary interest in the linear elegance of classical sources. The composition was planned with the same precise formality that characterizes the execution. The bather, seated on a rock at the left, establishes a vertical, which is balanced by the elongated woman arranging her hair on the right. Both vertical figures frame the related central pair of bathers: the reclining woman in an "Ariadne" pose and the standing woman above. The playing couple who move diagonally to the upper right balance the two standing figures that move toward the upper left. Everything feels arranged: the precise unvarying line widths, the curiously elongated figure proportions, the artificial gestures, the glances which do not meet, all these elements reflect Picasso's growing concern with the systematic exploration of the various formal elements with which the artist works. The step toward abstraction is difficult to discern here because the pictorial content hides the underlying concern with formal esthetic values.

"Guernica," one of Picasso's greatest works, was created as a protest against the destruction of the small Spanish town of Guernica. To distill the horror and violence of the bombing into a powerful condemnation of fascism and war Picasso invented a kind of symbolic expressionism, powerful and epigrammatic, in which nightmarish motifs symbolize death, destruction, horror, and pain. In the course of planning the great painting he prepared many drawings of which "Composition Study for Guernica" (Figure 10–6) is one. Despite its complexity and involved symbolism the total drawing retains the vehemence of a scream of pain. The direct quality of the drawing contributes much to its intensity. The bold angularities, the purposeful clumsiness with its implications of brutality, the impassioned execution represent an opposite facet of Picasso's amazing talents from those seen in "The Bathers." As stated before, Picasso's artistic innovations have been as remarkable in their variety as the individual works are powerful in their conception and execution. The combination of these powers has made him one of the most influential of twentieth-century artists.

Marcel Duchamp and Juan Gris were among the painters who joined Picasso in the development of cubism. Marcel Duchamp's "Study for the Virgin —No. 1" (Figure 10–7) in watercolor and pencil represents an early development of the cubist style. Inspired to a considerable degree by the faceted simplifications of form employed by Cézanne, Marcel Duchamp composed this study in terms of flattened planes of form, superimposed on one another, interspersed with symbolic notations of anatomy. Duchamp, one of the most original and inventive twentieth-century artists, invested his work with a strong current of humor and iconoclasm concerning art and life. Thus a kind of abstract pictorial wit remains an essential element in this drawing, which contains at the same time a magnificently composed series of movements which mount up from the lower right to the upper left. Angular and curved lines are juxtaposed with flat, concave and convex surfaces, which in turn are enriched with various textural devices to create a visually entertaining surface. It was through such works that the cubists created a new plastic language with esthetic goals which set aside that concern for relating art to the world of external

FIGURE 10–5

Pablo Picasso (1881–   ; Spanish-French).
"The Bathers." Pencil on white paper, 9½" x 12¼".
Courtesy of the Fogg Art Museum, Harvard University, Cambridge,
Massachusetts (Meta and Paul J. Sachs Collection,

FIGURE 10–6   Pablo Picasso (1881–   ; Spanish-French).
Composition Study for "Guernica," 9 May 1937. Pencil on white paper,
9½" x 17⅞". On extended loan to The Museum of Modern Art,
New York, from the artist, P. Picasso. (Photo: Sunami.)

FIGURE 10–7

Marcel Duchamp (1887–   ; French-American).
"Study for the Virgin, 1912."
Watercolor and pencil on paper, 12½" x 9".
Philadelphia Museum of Art
(Louise and Walter Arensberg Collection).

appearances which had been the chief preoccupation of artists since Renaissance times. Rather than relating fundamentally to the outside world, the cubists and the abstractionists who followed them originated a self-contained world within the boundaries of the canvas in which a sense of order, of visual movement, of interrelationships of the art elements, provide an esthetic experience that is primarily an end in itself rather than a commentary on the world existing outside of the work under scrutiny.

Duchamp's drawing represents an early phase of cubism described as analytical cubism. The later stage of cubism, "synthetic" cubism, is well illustrated by a pencil drawing of a "Seated Harlequin" (Figure 13–2) by Juan Gris, which was made as a study for a painting by the same name. This synthetic phase of cubism witnessed an increase in structural formalism and a concern with what has been described as "simultaneity of vision," that is, the incorporation of more than one aspect of a form in a single canvas. Thus the succession of visual images which one might perceive as one moved around an object, or the object as it might appear if opened, spread out and revealed from the inside, were used to create a pattern full of complex overlappings, ambiguities and visual surprises. The formal composition of the "Seated Harlequin" can be easily followed. A similar Greek fretlike pattern frames the right-hand bottom and left-hand top of the clown. The chair surrounds him with angular and curved lines, while the spiral endings of chair arms, curved costume details and symbolized anatomical forms combine to create a precise, carefully balanced pattern. The element of simultaneity, that is, multiple aspects of the chair, room perspectives, and clown's figure are less easy to identify, for they have been arbitrarily welded together into a visually fascinating, undecipherable whole. The entire drawing interests one visually without involving any sentimental or emotional references to the clown as a human being or to clownishness as a social phenomenon. Even the regular ruled lines, for the most part as precise as though they had been laid out with drafting instruments, contribute to the abstract character of the work.

The first showings of works by the cubists were greeted with derision by critics and public alike, yet the impact of cubism was almost incalculable. In the generally unsettled intellectual and social climate that followed World War I artists found the tradition of visual realism restrictive whereas cubism and the trend toward abstraction provided the sought-after opportunities for original self-expression. Even relatively conservative artists adapted certain aspects of cubism to their personal stylistic needs. Many American painters who went to France in this period, experiencing the exhilarating effects of the new esthetic freedom, returned to America and employed a modified cubism for their interpretations of the American scene.

Preston Dickerson was one of these. "Street in Quebec" (Figure 14–12) is a drawing reinforced with watercolor. It reads both as a piece of American scene reporting and as a cubist composition of planes, angles, and straight lines moving in space. There was a certain literal-mindedness about many American artists that demanded recognizable subject matter, yet these same artists responded to the adventure of a new way of seeing. These two seemingly contradictory views are beautifully reconciled in such a work as "Street in

FIGURE 10–8

Calvin Albert (1918–   ; American).
"Ritual." Charcoal, 29″ x 23″.
Courtesy of The Art Institute of Chicago
(Art Institute purchase fund).

Quebec." The careful framing of the edges of the drawing, the central movement to an increasingly complex series of shifting facets, the sensitively distributed dark accents reveal the same conscious organizing of the pictorial elements to achieve a formal unity as characterized cubism, and it is easy to permit the realism of the work to distract one's attention from its abstract structure. Without the stimulus of cubism, the geometric pattern of the American cityscape might neither have been recognized nor integrated into such a rich pictorial structure.

Abstraction

The initial impetus toward abstraction initiated by cubism in France was reinforced in the twenties by the painters and designers of Central Europe, particularly those associated with the Bauhaus, first in Weimar from its founding in 1919, and after 1929 in Dessau, Germany. After the stimulus of cubism, Paris remained relatively conservative, and in the subsequent innovations of her major artists, particularly Picasso and Matisse, the subject matter remained recognizable no matter how violent the stylistic distortions.

After 1945, the end of World War II, the movement toward abstraction became increasingly important, with America assuming a position of leadership. A charcoal drawing titled "Ritual" (Figure 10–8) by Calvin Albert reveals the manner in which certain elements of cubism provided the catalyzer toward an art in which all association with identifiable subject matter disappeared. Much that is here reminds one of cubism: the sense of faceted planes shifting in space, the repetitions of differentiating textures to relate separate parts and enrich the surfaces. But nothing about the drawing suggests that it was inspired by a visual model. Some hint of an illustrational idea is provided by the dark vertical form at the bottom of the page, which might be interpreted as a priestly figure holding aloft a ritual object. But except for this and the implication of visionary responses to ritual incantations, the drawing lives through the drama inherent in tonal contrasts, vigorous shifting shapes and movements, and its organizational coherence. The drawing is particularly fresh in its sparkling, clear textures: the soft rubbed greys that move from pale smudged tints to velvety blacks, the grainy rough surfaces, the sharp lines made with the pointed end of a stick of charcoal and the bright erased whites.

Though of an earlier date than "Ritual," "Composition No. 4" (Figure 10–9) by Stuart Davis also illustrates the trend toward a bold departure from traditional pictorial conceptions. Stuart Davis was stimulated by synthetic cubism and certain Bauhaus influences. "Composition No. 4" entertains through the vitality and variety of its bold patterns. The essential role of subject matter in a Stuart Davis work, even when it can be identified, is to provide a point of departure for his fascinating shapes and their interrelationships. The uniform heavy line used here imposes a unifying element that relates the varied patterns and provides a machine-age stylistic character to the parts.

Equally dramatic and completely without illustrational or symbolic implications, is the striking "D. 52.2" (Figure 1–19), by Hans Hartung. The bold shapes, striking tonal contrasts, and vigorous movements hold one's attention

FIGURE 10–9

Stuart Davis (1894–   ; American).
"Composition No. 4" (1934). Brush and ink, 21⅜" x 29⅞".
Collection, The Museum of Modern Art, New York
(Gift of Abby Aldrich Rockefeller). Photo: Sunami.

and interest by the vigor of their impact upon the eye. Unlike the Albert drawing that involves one through its complexity, the impact of the Hartung drawing results from its simplicity. Its impact is like some great chord struck by a group of musical instruments, each with its own timbre and tone ranging from deep, rich notes to strident piercing accents, held together by a harmonic relationship more felt than understood. The enigmatic title, like a classification label, helps to remove any literary overtones or auxiliary associations that might encourage the observer to read irrelevant meanings into the drawing.

At first glance the study by Arshile Gorky for "The Plough and the Song" (Figure 10–10) appears to be illustrating some idea, and this suggestion is reinforced by the lyrical implications of the title. The forms appear to be organic in character, their undulating swellings and interpenetrations suggesting the biological processes; the movements up and around the drawing evoke a feeling of continuing action and interaction of movement in time more than in space. Close examination reveals the illusory nature of the symbolism; the forms refuse to be identified and remain as essentially abstract as those in either of the two

PLATE 11

Thomas Rowlandson (1756–1827; English).
"At a Cottage Door." Gray and tan wash with brown ink lines, 7" x 5½".
Collection of the author.

PLATE 12

Pierre Paul Prud'hon (1758–1825; French).
"La Source." Black and white chalk, 21¾₆" x 15⅝₆".
Courtesy of the Sterling and Francine Clark Art Institute, Williamstown, Massachusetts.

previously discussed drawings, their nongeometric and complex character permitting the viewer to read into them meanings from the outside world somewhat more readily than into the simpler geometric kind of abstract forms. As in most abstract act, there is a conscious emphasis upon the flat picture plane, the major forms on the canvas all seeming to float on the flat surface of the paper, the minor forms moving back a bit but only to a formally limited distance.

Enigma often adds a touch of piquancy that provides a counterpoint to the austerity of pure abstract form. "Sawtelle Series" (Figure 10–11) by John Altoon is composed of curious forms that seem derived from organic or anatomical scources. Unlike the Gorky drawing in which precise linear elements dominate, soft cloudlike shapes provide the basic structure here with only an occasional pen line adding an element of definition to help contain the soft floating tones. An occasional cluster of pen lines provides a contrasting texture and thereby avoids a monotonous mush.

Abstract Expressionism

Pure abstraction, art in which there are no symbolic or representational elements, remained predominantly precise in execution and geometric in form until about 1945, at which time the use of freely painted nongeometric elements appeared with increasing frequency. This tendency culminated in the New York school of abstract expressionism or *action painting*, as the most extreme manifestation of the movement was termed. One of the most influential members of the school of action painters was Jackson Pollock, whose drawings and paintings utilized unorthodox qualities of line to build dynamically textured surfaces. "Birthday Card" (Figure 1–4) exploits a wide variety of scribbled, scratched, splashed, and spattered ink marks which play against the wash to create a fascinating agitated surface.

Willem de Kooning works with equal freedom and intensity, but there is frequently a glimmer of figurative elements in his paintings and drawings; consequently, he might be considered as a bridge between the abstract and the more traditional expressionist painters. On close examination, "Two Women III" (Figure 10–12) in crayon on paper, reveals breasts, faces, thighs and other forms that can be identified as anatomical and female. But rather than appearing to have motivated the drawing, they seem almost to have emerged from the vortex of lines of their own volition. Certainly the presence of the vaguely symbolized human elements is not essential to the impact of the work, which involves the viewer through its vehemence. Many of the abstract expressionists commenced working on a paper or canvas with no specific subject or compositional arrangement in mind. A few initial strokes of brush or crayon established directional movements and segmented the picture plane into separate areas. This initial sortie set the stage for subsequent developments: the line movements might be enriched with countermovements, and the separate areas segmented further, emphasized by tonal differences and otherwise estab-

FIGURE 10-10

Arshile Gorky (1904–1948; Turkish-Armenian-American).
Study for "The Plough and the Song." Pencil and crayon,
19" x 25⁵⁄₁₆". Allen Memorial Art Museum, Oberlin
College, Ohio (Friends of Art Fund).

FIGURE 10–11
John Altoon (1925–   ; American).
"Sawtelle Series." Mixed media, 30" x 40".
David Stuart Galleries, Los Angeles (Joseph Hazen Collection).

lished as elements of a unified and complex composition. Although at first
glance such procedure appears casual, impulsive, and lacking in deliberation, it is
in essence very much like the procedure employed by many musicians in
developing a musical composition where a melodic motif that appears spontaneously while whistling, humming, or fingering the piano, is then developed
through manipulations of rhythm, harmony, counterpoint, and other elements
of the musical craft. Psychoanalysis had revealed the rich source of material

stored in the subconscious and available for creative endeavor when it is permitted to rise, undirected and uncensored, to the surface of the conscious mind. The subconscious was exploited as a source for esthetic expression by the surrealists early in the century. At a later date, research into the nature of creativity emphasized the major role played by spontaneous impulses in a wide variety of scientific, inventive and artistic activities. The recognition and frank acceptance of the validity of unpremeditated artistic expression, reinforced by the practice of the action painters, has played a major role in encouraging contemporary draftsmen away from a restrictive dependence upon deliberation and cautious methods of developing works of art.

Summary

Paris was the chief center of radical developments in painting in the first two decades of the twentieth century. Germany became increasingly important between 1920 and 1930, but in 1945 after World War II the United States assumed a position of leadership. The most clearly formulated movements in twentieth-century painting, all of which are reflected in drawing practice, are as follows:

1. EXPRESSIONISM: Expressionist elements were present in the work of *Les Fauves* in France between 1900 and 1910, but expressionism had its most vigorous formulation in Germany between 1910 and 1930.
2. ABSTRACTION: The tendency toward abstraction was initiated by the Cubists in France between 1910 and 1920, developed toward pure geometric abstraction first in Germany and then in the United States between 1920 and 1960 and achieved a unique development in the work of the abstract Expressionists in the United States between 1950 and 1960.
3. SURREALISM: A vigorous movement in Paris between 1920 and 1930.
4. REALISM: A socially oriented school of realists who represented a powerful offshoot of expressionism developed in Germany between 1920 and 1930, and their impact was felt in Mexico and the United States between 1930 and 1950. Realism will be discussed in the following chapters.

The freshness of perception and spontaneity of execution sought by *Les Fauves* received its most effective expression in drawing in the decorative and lyrical linear style of Matisse. Cubism achieved its most brilliant formulation in the drawings and paintings of Picasso, whose successive innovations stimulated a wide range of styles. In the United States the abstract expressionists of the New York school developed an art of bold improvisation in which the preservation and communication of the gesture of drawing played an important role.

11

TWENTIETH-CENTURY
EXPRESSIONISM

The de Kooning drawing "Two Women, III," discussed in the previous chapter, might with equal logic have been included in the section on expressionism. Expressionism, as indicated in the introductory discussion at the beginning of Chapter 9, is an emotionally motivated organization of art elements which provides a means for communicating the individual artist's subjective reality. Objective reality for the expressionists provides the outer stimulus for presenting emotionally intensified content. The primary aim of expressionism is a visual statement of inner feeling. Much precedent exists in the history of art for expressionist theory and practice. The distortion of objective reality to achieve emotional intensity was a basic element in contributing to the power of the greatest masters, most noticeably in men like Michelangelo, Tintoretto, El Greco, and in the nineteenth century, Delacroix,

246

FIGURE 11-2

Emil Nolde (1867–1956; German).
"Landscape with Windmill." Brush and black printer's ink
on tan paper, 17½" x 23¼". The Solomon R. Guggenheim
Museum, New York (Lender: Mrs. Heinz Schultz, Great Neck,
New York) Robert E. Mates Photographer

Van Gogh, and Toulouse-Lautrec—to mention obvious examples. Expressionism as a movement began in Germany in the first decade of the century as a revolt against academic naturalism. Like the French *Fauves*, the insurgents of Germany were encouraged by the unconventional achievements of the postimpressonists to give free reign to emotional agitation, whether joyful, anguished, barbarically violent, or lyrically mystical.

Precedent had already been established in Munich and Vienna by the painters and designers who associated themselves with the *Art Nouveau* movement such as Gustav Klimt. There were elements of expressionism inherent in the drawings and paintings of Klimt even though the works appear decorative and contrived. In his pencil drawing, "The Kiss" (Figure 13–15), there is a premonition of the forthcoming expressionist movement in the way in which the uninhibited sweep of lines and free swirls convey the ecstasy of embrace as much as they describe the contours of the man's robe and its decorative patterning.

The disruptive and anguished aspects of expressionism were first made manifest under the social stress which convulsed Central Europe, particularly Germany before and during the two great World Wars. Oskar Kokoschka was one of the early leaders of the movement. A series of portraits which he painted in Vienna, Switzerland, and, later, Berlin shocked the public, and even his paintings of cities reflected the morbid and turbulent temper of the times. His "Portrait of Olda" (Figure 11–1), executed in blue chalk, conveys a sense of brooding pessimism and inner conflict. The drawing does not describe the external aspects of the sitter's appearance in the normally reassuring manner of most portraits, but instead seems to reveal the inner tensions of personality. It is this haunting quality of insight that distinguished Kokoschka and made him a leader of the youthful expressionist movement.

Emil Nolde, like Kokoschka, participated in the expressionist movement during its formative years, and the solemn, monumental but essentially pessimistic tenor of his drawing and painting did much to influence subsequent developments of expressionism. His "Landscape with Windmills" (Figure 11–2) depicts the landscape of his native Schleswig, but the tone of the drawing suggests with equal force the artist's agitated mood and the somber graceless marshland with its heavy forms and sunless skies.

The art of Paul Klee reveals another dimension of expressionism. His is an art that is less concerned with depicting the world of external appearances than with projecting a vision of his inner world, a world of sensitive nuances of feeling and idea. Essentially symbolic, but of a strangely evocative power, the curious symbols appear to be highly personal or derived from such unexpected sources as the drawings of children, the cryptic symbols of primitive peoples, the rigid and repetitive figures of the deranged. But even more important than the curious symbols and motifs which abound in the art of Klee, is his feeling for the magic of line, color, texture, shape, and the various artistic media. Through his sensitive manipulatons of materials he touches the emotions and evokes bewitching and rare poetic feelings. For instance, in his drawing "Trees Behind Rocks" (Figure 15–20), he explores with unusual originality the contrast between lines drawn with the point and the flat side of a pencil.

Thus, Paul Klee established a new direction for expressionism; in fact, Werner Haftmann, his biographer, has said: "He was the primitive of a new sensibility." The earlier expressionism, characterized by its vehemence, drew its power from the unpremeditated execution of the work and a lack of concern with esthetic refinements. However, even when Paul Klee drew directly from his subject, as when he sketched his beloved cat "Fritzi" (Figure 11–3), the drawing remains sensitive, even whimsical. The slack lines and tender scribbles convey the relaxed mood of the animal and the affectionate amusement of the artist rather than the intense, almost violent, feelings that usually characterized expressionist art. "A Balance-Capriccio" (Figure 11–4) is as dependent technically on Klee's sensitivity to the possibilities of pen and ink as it is original in its whimsical arrangement of charming surprises. The pen point has not been used in the same way on any two surfaces: chevrons, parallel lines, stipplings, crosshatches and a variety of unnamed textural inventions were created which are as playful and amusing as the forms they enliven. Close examination reveals that "Costumed Puppets" (Figure 18–17) is made up of hundreds of flattened lines ending in spirals and the playful ingenuity with which this motif has been used, like a stitch in crocheting, provides a diverting, additional dimension to the charm of the drawing. In each case the image created personifies a concept rather than a physical reality, and the magic of the statement results from the sensitivity with which the art elements were used rather than from vehemence. "Kolo 11" (Figure 11–5) is consciously naïve: the effect is adroitly and amusingly childlike, exploiting awkwardness like some skillful vaudeville performer imitating a toddler's unbalanced movements.

Expressionist Social Commentary

Still another vein of expressionism was established in mid-Europe during the tragic interval between the two World Wars, a vein that might best be described as an art of social commitment. A powerful drawing by Käthe Kollowitz illustrates the essential character of this movement. Motivated by an overwhelming sympathy for the suffering masses of unemployed workers, Käthe Kollowitz pictured the misery of her subjects without any mollifying graces. "Peasant Woman Sharpening a Scythe" (Figure 11–6) is a black-and-white chalk drawing done as a preparatory study for an aquatint etching. The direct quality of the drawing, the generally dark values, the heaviness of form, and the basic compositional emphasis upon the scythe cutting across the figure, combine to project a tone of mordant pessimism. "Self Portrait" (Figure 15–1) is equally revealing.

The social realism of the mid-twenties ranged from the compassion of Käthe Kollwitz to the biting satire of George Grosz. In the art of Grosz popular journalistic caricature joined hands with the great tradition of social satire exemplified by Goya, Hogarth and Daumier to create an art of pungent originality (Figures 11–7, 15–15, 17–4). Other facets of socially conscious expressionism were represented by Max Beckmann and Otto Dix. A silverpoint

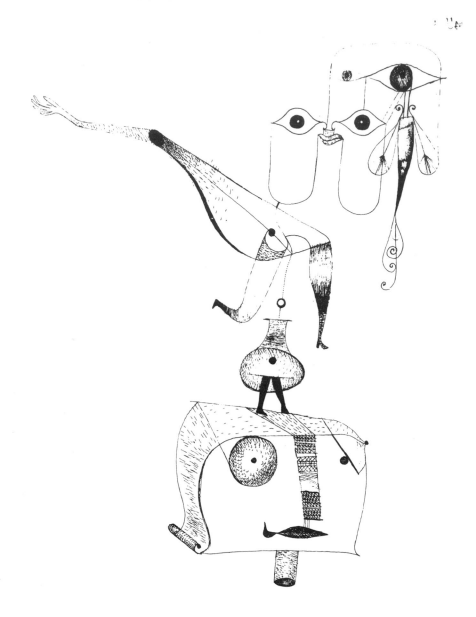

by Otto Dix (Figure 11–8) seems motivated by an almost sadistic insistence upon the ugliness of life. The haggard body, bony hands and arms, and pendant breasts of the old woman, are described with merciless objectivity. No attempt is made to dramatize, sentimentalize, or to establish an esthetic distance between the subject and observer, such as was used by Degas and Toulouse-Lautrec when they described the social rejects who people their work. Both Degas and Toulouse-Lautrec employed compositional arrangements and distinctive modes of drawing which separated the work of art from the bitter or unsavory reality which inspired it. For Dix such devices smack of falsification. An inhuman war and its tragic consequences made Dix and his fellow artists distrust the social and artistic conventions which obscured social injustices and hypocrisies and

FIGURE 11–6

Käthe Kollwitz (1867–1945; German).
"Peasant Woman Sharpening a Scythe."
Black and white chalk, 17⁵⁄₁₆″ x 14⅜″.
Courtesy, Achenbach Foundation for Graphic Arts,
California Palace of the Legion of Honor, San Francisco.

FIGURE 11–7
George Grosz (1893–1959; German-American).
"Workmen and Cripple." Ink, 15⅝" x 11⅜".
Richard Feigen Gallery, Inc., Chicago.

permitted the degradation of large masses of people. Social justice, they felt, could be based only on truth, and if the search for truth revealed pain and ugliness the artist must portray it. There was precedence in German art for this deep respect for fact, and the head of the old woman (Figure 18–8) reminds one of Durer's portrait of his mother. Max Beckmann's "Coffee House" (Figure 13–3) mollifies its realism with sardonic humor. Technically the drawing is more allied to expressionistic goals than the Otto Dix drawing, for the exaggerations of proportion and the spontaneity of execution project the artist's feelings upon the viewer's consciousness with great force.

By the end of the first three decades of the century, expressionism in modern art became firmly established as the counterpoint to formalism. The impact of the early masters of expressionism can be felt in much subsequent drawing and painting. Thus both "Incoming Fisher Fleet" (Figure 11–9) by Lionel Feininger, with its evocative crumbly lines and blurred tones, and "Village in the Storm" (Figure 1–17) by Varujan Boghosian, with its magical, bejeweled, but cryptic symbols, though very personal expressions seem derived from the impulse established by the art of Paul Klee. A "Portrait of Georges Limbour" by the Frenchman Dubuffet (Figure 18–9), carries the portrait of inner psychological stresses, initiated by Kokoschka, to an astonishing level of intensity. A brush drawing by Ben Shahn of "Dr. J. Robert Oppenheimer" intensifies the tradition initiated by the acid caricatures of George Grosz through its expressive exaggerations of proportion and its biting roughness of line (Figure 12–5).

Other facets of contemporary expressionism are not so easily identified with the early masters of expressionism, but instead, seem to relate to the rich artistic culture of past civilizations in which emotional intensity was more highly valued than visual realism. Thus, a study for a stone sculpture of a "Madonna and Child" by Henry Moore (Figure 17–16) derives its sense of monumental generalized form from the simplified sculptures of ancient civilizations, Egyptian, pre-Columbian and Oriental. The curiously elongated and boneless forms seems to relate also to the forms of nature: boulders, worn driftwood, and eroded hills.

In much contemporary expressionism the various rich elements of our cultural traditions are fused by the personal vision of the artist beyond the point where the identification of the probable source is possible, profitable or desirable. Thus, an untitled drawing by Roberto Matta (Figure 11–10) combines curious visceral forms, details that suggest undersea organic life and various cryptic jewel-like symbols that are fascinating because they suggest so much yet cannot be deciphered. These complex forms take the observer to the very border between what can be identified and what remains obscure, thereby creating an imaginative and fanciful art of symbolic ambiguity. Harvey Breverman's "Figure with Tallus VIII" (Figure 14–18) is on the borderline between expressionism and realism. The broad chalk blur from which the head and body of the figure emerges and the contrasting scratchy sharp lines which define details of form and texture seem more effective in evoking the artist's feelings than in reporting the visual facts.

FIGURE 11–8

Otto Dix (1891–   ; German).
"Old Woman in the Nude." Silverpoint on
white grounded paper, 18½" x 22½".
Courtesy, Mrs. Ruth Lilienthal.

FIGURE 11-9

Lionel Feininger (1871–1956; German-American).
"Incoming Fisher Fleet, 1941."
Watercolor and India ink, 11³⁄₁₆" x 19".
Allen Memorial Art Museum, Oberlin College,
Ohio (R. T. Miller, Jr., Fund).

FIGURE 11–10

Roberto Matta ([Echaurren]; 1912–   ; Chilean-French).
Untitled (1938) Crayon and pencil, 12⅝″ x 19½″.
Richard Feigan Gallery, Collection of Mr. and Mrs. Joseph Pulitzer, Jr.

Summary

Expressionism as a consciously formulated movement with the primary aim of giving a forceful visual statement to inner feeling first appeared in Germany before 1910. Much impetus was given to the expressionist movement by the social tensions which convulsed Central Europe between the two world wars. expressionist drawing was free, often almost violent in its direct communication of feeling. Typical early expressionists like Emil Nolde and Oscar Kokoschka consciously avoided the studio subject matter, the sensuous charm, and the emphasis on decorative elements that often characterize the work of their French contemporaries. Expressionist theory and practice were furthered and related to technological change by the Bauhaus artists of the twenties. Paul Klee, one of the most original Bauhaus artists, gave a new direction to expressionism by concerning himself more with the inner world of his imagination than with the social scene. Klee was particularly unorthodox, inventive, and sensitive in his use of media and materials.

In the period following World War I an art of social criticism and commitment appeared as an offshoot of expressionism which produced many strong draftsmen. Käthe Kollwitz, Otto Dix, and George Grosz were among the artists who did much to reinvest documentary drawing with incisive power. Between 1930 and 1960 the drawings of many American artists reflected the various expressionist tendencies initiated in the early decades of the century.

12

SURREALISM AND REALISM
IN THE TWENTIETH CENTURY

Value judgments about modern painting relate to stylistic qualities rather than subject matter. Today this idea needs no defense but in the twenties popular judgment about art was still sufficiently tied to literary elements to justify the publication of a book by C. J. Bulliet entitled *Apples and Madonnas*, which stated that it was quality of vision and execution that gave meaning to works of art rather than iconography; consequently, the apples in a Cézanne still life had greater significance than painted clichés in the form of Renaissance madonnas.

Surrealism

Only one avant-garde movement seemed concerned with extending the subject matter of modern painting and that was surrealism. Many antecedents exist in the history of art for surrealism, but actually it was launched as a consciously formulated movement in Paris and was an outgrowth of Freudian theories about the subconscious mind. Particularly influential in establishing the surrealist movement were Freud's investigations of dream imagery, the discovery of the censoring mechanisms by which the human mind obscures the true significance of dream images, and the use of free association as a method of arriving at the profound symbolic meanings that underlay surface appearances.

In 1924 André Breton published his "Manifesto of Surrealism," in which an absolute directive was given to make a clean sweep of rational systems of art and to substitute for it a reliance upon spontaneous, intuitive and undirected vision. Max Ernst, one of the early surrealists, wrote, "Any conscious, mental control of reason, taste, will, is out of place in a work that deserves to be described as absolutely surrealist." One of the chief principles that developed as surrealism evolved was a dependence upon the unexpected juxtaposition of objects so that familiar associations were upset and things, seen in a new context, acquired new meanings and visual qualities. Free association, automatism, and the other surrealist devices for achieving a direct outpouring of uncensored symbols encouraged qualities of whimsicality, surprise, and a tendency to use fanciful, organic, fearsome, hallucinatory and enigmatic motifs, whether the style of execution be traditional or highly personal. Max Ernst, as a founder of surrealism, employed conventional techniques of painting and drawing, exemplified in his "Maternity, Study for 'Surrealism and Painting'" (Figure 12–1), a drawing in pencil heightened with white chalk on orange paper. In this drawing it is the smooth foetal look and shine of the curious nonbirdlike infant huddled under the protective wing of the mother that provides the note of strangeness. The mysterious dark tone of the drawing and the smooth flowing lines, without accent or variation, by which the forms are defined, create an atmosphere of mystery and unreality.

Salvador Dali is one of the most popular painters in the surrealist group. Very facile, working in an almost baroque technique, he developed elaborate compositions which are full of astonishing assemblages of human and nonhuman forms, such as can be found in his "Composition of Figures of Drawers" (Figure 18–11). Here we see a combination of human bodies and chests of drawers from which emerge enigmatic, organic forms that are highly charged with sexual symbolism. The violent gesticulations, the painful cuttings and dismemberings—all entwining in a great swirling compositional movement—vie at one and the same time to shock, astonish, and entertain. An important factor in the success of this drawing, as in all of Dali's work, is his technical facility. Pencil, brush, and India ink have provided the media for a virtuoso performance. The skill with which the detailed forms have been presented contribute to the convincing quality of this fantastic and grotesque conception. Pavel Tchelitchew remained close to Dali in his technical methods, and his silverpoint "Portrait of

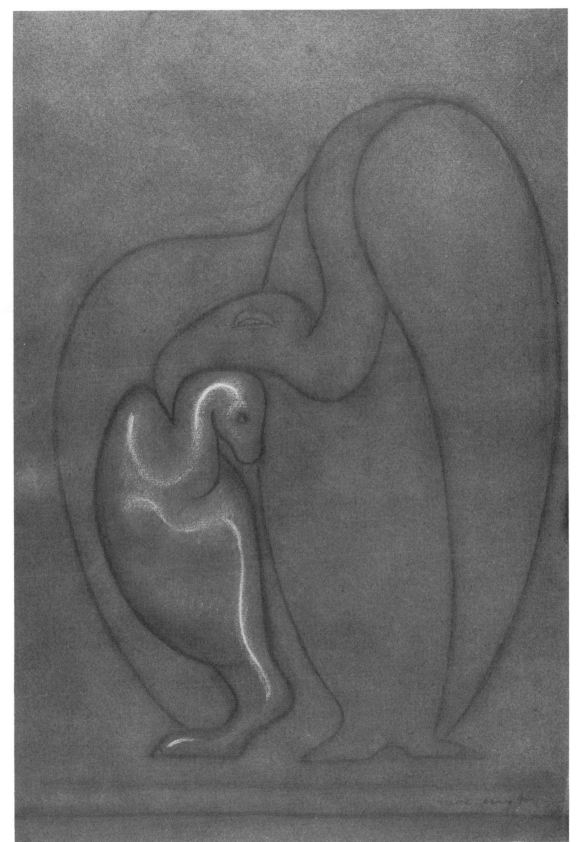

FIGURE 12–2

Joan Miró (1893–   ; Spanish-French).
"Persons Haunted by a Bird." Black chalk with touch of
brown chalk and watercolor, 16¾₁₆″ x 13″.
Courtesy of The Art Institute of Chicago
(Gift of Peter B. Bensinger charitable trust).

Frederick Ashton" (Figure 16–7) reveals the same skillful modeling of forms through flowing clusters of lines which frequently seem to parallel the direction of the surface they describe. Because silverpoint allows for no subsequent changes, it demands a draftsman of great certainty. Its delicacy and precision contribute greatly to the success of this sensitive drawing. Though basically a portrait study, this drawing retains a surrealist taste for the strange and a heightened sense of introspection. The reversed double image, the fixed hypnotic stare, the way in which fringed neckerchief flows into the mass of hair, the gravity of expression, all contribute to an uneasy dreamlike atmosphere.

From his earliest years Joan Miró proclaimed himself an anti-intellectual, and in 1925 he participated in the first exhibition of the surrealists. Even in his early work the qualities that characterize his mature style were evident, a taste for flat pattern, for childlike strange forms, for humor, fantasy, freshness of emotion, sharp visual wit, and great inventiveness. Unlike Dali and other surrealists, Miró did not employ a traditional illustrative technique to make his fantasies convincing. His "Persons Haunted by a Bird" (Figure 12–2) in black and brown chalk combined with watercolor seems both naïve and sophisticated, to have the direct intensity of a child's nightmare and yet to be calculated in its details. Certainly the head in the lower right corner, with its mock-ferocious expression and suggestion of a full figure within a face, and the figure at the left with a face on the body, are amusing rather than horrific. The techniques employed, in contrast to those of Dali and Tchelitchew, are childlike in their lack of finesse. The same qualities distinguish "Figure" (Figure 18–12).

Yves Tanguy employed a disciplined, even traditional, technique in his paintings and drawings to make the strange objects pictured appear convincing. Long stretches of arid flat sea floor or moonscape, often covered with curious bonelike excrescences, fade off into deep emotive space in his most typical works. An untitled drawing (Figure 13–7) seems to be a study for a detail in a more complex composition. In contrast to the Miró, the execution is refined and displays technical finesse. The forms may have been dictated by some undirected inner force, but the delineation of the forms is controlled by the artist's cultivated sensibilities. André Masson also employed a sensitive and controlled technique, although the execution of his drawings seems more spontaneous than that of Tanguy. "Birth of Birds" (Figure 13–8), like much of Masson's work, seems concerned with projecting intuitions concerning the cosmic realm of creation into poetic form. Its sensitive lines, textures, and movements create a lyrical atmosphere that is a decided departure from the dominant trend among surrealists to plumb the more lurid and fearsome depths of the subconscious.

Although surrealism as a movement disappeared in the thirties, its subsequent influence has been important and continuous. It accepted the validity of impulse as opposed to formal intellectual logic, of free association, and dissociation as methods of achieving fresh meanings from familiar images. It revived certain traditional elements of romantic expression, of dream states and heightened sensibilities, of morbid and fantastic imaginings, of the many themes supplied by the unconscious, chance, hallucination, delirium, and even madness. Bosch, Brueghel, Leonardo, Goya, and a host of nineteenth-century Romantics, had drawn upon these psychic sources for inspiration, but never previously had an intellectual rationale existed for the use of such sources of inspiration. The visceral and organic forms popularized by the surrealists can be found in much subsequent expressionist and abstract art (Figures 11–10, 10–11), and the accentuated emotional atmosphere provided a poetic element in much subsequent realistic expression. In drawing, the principle of dissociation, combinations of unlikely objects, stimulated collage in the form of incorporating bits of photography, lettering, parts of old valentines and other evocative fragments into drawings and also encouraged drawing on newspaper and unorthodox materials. By encouraging artists to free their sensibilities from the grip of convention, surrealism like cubism and the earlier and more revolutionary exponents of expressionism released certain dynamic impulses, the full effects of which are still only partially realized.

Twentieth-Century Realism

Because of the startling and unorthodox character of much current artistic expression, it is easy to underestimate the vigor of what can best be termed contemporary realism. The dynamic movements we have been discussing have all colored the character of current realistic drawing. Abstraction increased the concern of the realists with problems of formal structure and style; expressionism stimulated a more freely executed and emotional manner; surrealism activated heightened sensibilities and awarenesses. For the most part the modern realists escape the older boundaries of studio conventions and, by exploring new areas of subject matter and stressing the handwriting of execution as a mainspring of style, they discover fresh inspiration.

Social Commentary

The cartoon, the caricature, and the painting and drawing devoted to social criticism have played an important role in American political and social life. At the inception of the Republic, Paul Revere used his talents as a print-maker to incite the colonists to rebellion. In the late nineteenth century the caricatures of Thomas Nast played a major role in unseating the corrupt Tammany regime from New York's City Hall (Figure 12–3), and pictorial forms of social criticism have played an important part in American politics ever since. In the thirties the disastrous economic depression stimulated American painters to critical efforts similar to those adopted by the German sociorealists of the twenties. One American artist whose work stands on the borderline between propagandistic cartooning and fine art is William Gropper, whose "Farmers' Revolt" (Figure 12–4) reveals elements of pictorial journalism. The bold simplifications of form and the dramatic contrasts of heavily massed blacks against sharp whites provide the simple carrying power so essential for effective competition with the printed

FIGURE 12–3

Thomas Nast (1840–1902; American).
"A Group of Vultures Waiting for the Storm to 'Blow Over'—'Let Us Prey.' " (1871)
Pencil. *New York Public Library.*

FIGURE 12–4

William Gropper (1897   ; American).
"Farmers' Revolt, 1933." Ink, 16″ x 19″.
Collection of Whitney Museum of American Art, New York.

page. The vigorous pattern of opposing lines created by the farmers and their brandished weapons and the lively pattern of grain and symbolic birds of prey create an art that is as handsome as it is lively.

Popular caricature as well as the acid drawings of George Grosz have both contributed to the style of Ben Shahn. His earlier work had a directly agitational vehemence, but in his drawings and paintings from the fifties and sixties, the bite is modified by an increase in esthetic sophistication. His "Portrait of J. Robert Oppenheimer" (Figure 12–5) achieves much of its intensity through the use of a brush line of unusual scratchy vigor, a line that transmits a sense of extreme tension. An atmosphere of urgency and conflict pervades the entire

FIGURE 12–6

Guillermo Meza (1917–   ; Mexican).
"Project for the Exodus." Black and brown chalk, 23½" x 20".
San Francisco Museum of Art.

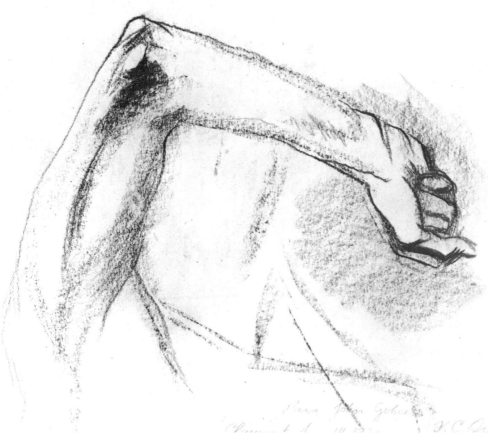

FIGURE 12–7
José Clemente Orozco (1883–1949; Mexican).
"Arm and Hand." Charcoal, 11¾" x 9⅜".
Collection of John Goheen, Stanford, California.

study: the deep-set hypnotic eyes face inwardly, one is uncomfortably aware of the sensitive nostril, no hint of grace softens the hunched posture, the thin arms, and the awkward gestures of the hands. "Farmers' Revolt" exploits the glib surface aspects of cartooning. The "Portrait of J. Robert Oppenheimer" explores the deep psychological perceptions behind caricature.

The work of Peter Blume presents another segment of the art dedicated to social criticism. Blume worked in a disciplined and precise technique similar to that used by the Flemish painters of the Middle Ages, and like the paintings of Flanders, the complex details that make up his paintings must be thoughtfully examined to appreciate the extent of the symbolic references. A pencil drawing of a "Beggar Woman" (Figure 1–9) is a study for a detail of the large painting Blume made as an attack against fascism and Mussolini. The use of the pencil is miraculous in its disciplined sensitivity, evoking a sense of differences in color and texture. The authenticity of the details that crowd the drawing in no way appear to inhibit the originality or creativity of the artist; certainly there is not the slightest hint of academic dryness in the way in which they have been used.

FIGURE 12–8.

George Bellows (1882–1925; American).
"Dance in a Madhouse." Black crayon, pen and ink, red crayon and Chinese white,
18⅞" x 24⅝". Courtesy of The Art Institute of Chicago
(Charles H. and Mary F. S. Worcester Collection).

PLATE 13
Edgar Degas (1834–1917; French).
"Four Studies of a Jockey."
Brush with oil heightened with Chinese white, 17⅝" x 12".
Courtesy of the Art Institute of Chicago
(Mr. and Mrs. L. Coburn Memorial Collection).

PLATE 14

Emperor Hui Tsung (1082–1135; Chinese).
"Ladies Preparing Newly Woven Silk." Detail of Ironing.
Color on silk, 14⁹⁄₁₆" x 57¼". Courtesy, Museum of Fine Arts, Boston.

Fragments of marble statues, a bit of rinceau molding, drums of classical columns, the bricks and arches of ancient Rome, are all piled together in a fascinating jumble around the old beggar woman. The architectural ruins provide a fit setting for the human tragedy.

The second decade of the twentieth century witnessed an agrarian revolution in Mexico which elicited the support of a number of intellectuals and artists. In Paris Diego Rivera was being drawn into the orbit of cubism when he became concerned with the revolution that was taking place in his homeland, and he returned to Mexico. Rivera and a group of his colleagues initiated a vigorous school of mural painting dedicated to changing the lot of the Mexican Indians, both peasants and workers. Part of their program of social reconstruction was educational. Rivera and his co-workers wanted to familiarize the people with their admirable native artistic traditions. In his paintings and drawings of Indian peasants going about their daily activities, he used many of the conventions found in pre-Columbian art, the compact massing of the human figure, the large heads, hands, and feet and a somewhat static and impassive monumentality. In his brush and ink drawing of a "Mother and Child" (Figure 17–8), Diego Rivera has enclosed these forms with heavy brushed outline similar to that employed by the pre-Columbian artists in painting their codices, the illustrated manuscripts in which the Mayans and Aztecs recorded their exploits and other historical data.

A handsome black and brown chalk drawing by Guillermo Meza, "Project for the Exodus" (Figure 12–6), employs curious distortions of facial structure and simplified ovoid forms similar to those one finds in pre-Columbian sculptural and plastic renderings of the human head. Again here, as in the Rivera, there is a conscious striving for that essential dignity of conception which so frequently characterizes the arts of primitive peoples and which gave such grandeur to the prehistoric arts of the Mexican area. The Meza drawing is in black and brown chalk and the earth colors in conjunction with the simple triangular massings of form create an effect of primitive sobriety.

José Clemente Orozco was the most vehement of the Mexican social realists. Contemptuous of academic refinement and equally impatient with the niceties of Parisian sophistication, the urgency of his style was born of a deep dedication to social change. Most of his drawings were executed as studies for the great mural projects he designed to cover the walls of Mexico's public buildings; murals planned to incite the Mexican workers and peasants to social revolution. "Arm and Hand" (Figure 12–7) was one of the many charcoal drawings done in preparation for the murals Orozco executed at Pamona College. Though somewhat restrained for Orozco, this drawing, like all of his work, derives its direct force from both social conviction and esthetic immediacy.

The American Scene

Not all of the realism of the twenties was motivated by a zeal for social reform. Much of it represented a continuation of the tradition initiated by Manet and Degas, the tradition of seeing with a "fresh eye," of perceiving the pictorial potentialities of the familiar environment that had not previously been drawn or painted. In the first two decades of the twenties a group of American

FIGURE 12–9

Edward Hopper (1882–   ; American).
"Study for Manhattan Bridge Loop." Charcoal, 8½" x 11". *Addison Gallery
of American Art, Phillips Academy, Andover, Massachusetts.*

FIGURE 12–10

Andrew Wyeth (1917–   ; American).
"Lightning Rod." Pencil on white paper, 22″ x 14⅞″.
The Solomon R. Guggenheim Museum (Collection
Mr. and Mrs. Philip Hofer, Cambridge, Massachusetts).
Robert E. Mates, Photographer.

artists who called themselves "the eight," and who in turn were frequently castigated as the "ash-can school" by the critics, discovered the face of metropolitan America and treated it with unsentimental vigor. All were effective draftsmen, sometimes more journalists than artists. George Bellows, one of "the eight," drew, painted, and made prints. His "Dance in a Madhouse" (Figure 12–8) is morbid in title rather than visually, for the sad inmates cavort as gaily as any dancers. The grief-stricken wallflower who sits with head in hand is probably no sadder than her more contained "normal" sister who hides her disappointment under a mask of polite indifference. With an unorthodox approach to technique, Bellows combined media as it suited his purpose. Here his velvety darks and flashing lights add to the dramatic effectiveness; at the same time the vigor of direct textures and incisive drawing contribute to the energy and conviction of the study. It is executed in black and red crayon, reinforced with pen and ink and heightened with Chinese white.

In the first two decades of the century Sheeler, Hopper, and a number of other artists who were later to constitute the "American Scene" painters, found stimulus and liberation in the new movements abroad. Hopper, having served his apprenticeship in Paris, experienced the discipline of modern experimental painting. His need to create an art of intense reality out of the familiar world brought him back to America and led him to abandon the rising tide of stylized and abstract painting. Hopper has stated his credo. "Instead of subjectivity a new objectivity, instead of abstraction, a reaffirmation of representation and specific subject matter, instead of internationalism an art based upon the

FIGURE 12–11

Jasper Johns (1930–   ; American). "Numbers." Pencil on paper, 2¾″ x 2¼″. *Leo Castelli, New York. Collection Mr. Ted Carey.*

276

American Scene." Contact with the School of Paris in his formative years inculcated in Hopper a sense of formal order and a taste for geometric patterning that prevented him from exaggerating the picturesque aspects of his chief subject, New York City, its architecture and its quality of light, whether at mid-day, dawn, twilight, or electrically-lighted night.

Two charcoal studies for his "Manhattan Bridge Loop" (Figure 12–9, 14–21) exploit both his formal sense of order and his taste for the newly discovered beauty of geometric patterning. The balance of long diagonals moving in opposing directions provides both stability and movement. Playing against these large movements, there is a counterpoint of rectangles of varying sizes, relieved by minor divergent shapes. Thus the geometry of everyday metropolitan life is revealed, stark, strong, but not grim, for Hopper is essentially optimistic in his acceptance of life. His role is not that of a critic of the social order, but rather that of a reporter.

Charles Sheeler also discovered cubism in Paris and then returned to America to find in American traditional architecture and contemporary indus-

FIGURE 12–13

Richard Diebenkorn (1922–   ; American).
"Reclining Nude." Ink and wash, 17″ x 12⅜″.
San Francisco Museum of Art.

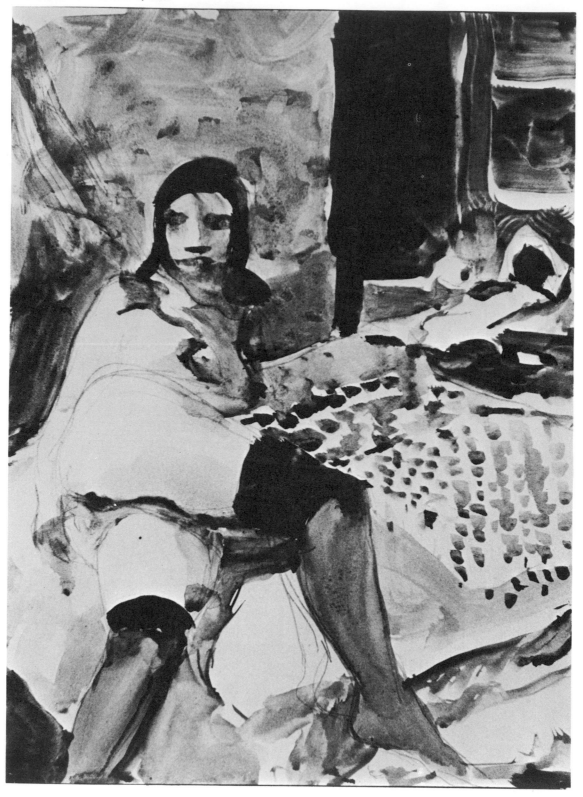

FIGURE 12–14

Wayne Thiebaud (1920–   ; American).
"Standing Figure." Pencil, 8″ x 10″.
Courtesy of the Artist.

trial buildings the clear forms and geometric patternings consonant with cubist tastes and ideals. "Reflections" (Figure 18–21), in black wash, illustrates Sheeler's belief that "a picture should have incorporated within it the structural design implied in abstraction, and be presented in a wholly realistic fashion." The brilliance of the bold contrasts of black, white, and grey has been achieved through striking simplifications, the elimination of much detail, and the technical excellence of the rendering. Equally bold and compelling is the variety in the size of parts, from the broad unbroken areas of shadowed building and sky to the sharp small-scale pattern of the catwalk. Sheeler's disciplined technique and feeling for careful compositional arrangements can also be seen in the beautiful conté drawing, "Feline Felicity" (Figure 1–3).

The same feeling for compositional order, austerely disciplined realism, and outstanding technical performance distinguish the drawings, watercolors, and paintings of Andrew Wyeth. Wyeth's father, N. C. Wyeth, was one of America's most brilliant illustrators at the turn of the century, and Andrew Wyeth had the advantage of a thorough training in both drawing and the craft of painting. Working in a sharp-focus precise technique, his unerring eye catches the surface textures of objects with a feeling for their structure as well as for their sensuous surfaces. In "Lightning Rod" (Figure 12–10), Wyeth used pencil to produce an unusual range of effects, blurred to suggest soft vaguenesses, sharp-edged when describing slivery wood and hard metal edges, in loose patches of strokes to create transparent shadows. But though his technical skills contribute to his effectiveness, it is his sensitivity and insight that make Wyeth a major contemporary artist. His juxtaposition of the worn shingled roof, the lightning rod, and a stretch of sea suggest the endless struggle of man against the elements, the fortitude and loneliness of taciturn New Englanders, and the sweet poetry with which time softens the most rugged structures. All of this is implied with true Colonial sparseness. The roof, the stretch of coast, and the faint indication of horizon line provide both the positive substance for the drawing and the evocative sense of deep space. Wyeth has said, "When you lose the simplicity you lose the drama." Certainly much of the power of "Lightning Rod" results from the fact that the composition is reduced to its absolute essence.

Pop Art

Each of the avant-garde movements that has flourished in the twentieth century has influenced and colored the character of the continuing tradition of realism. The early sixties witnessed a very sophisticated reaction against abstract expressionism and other advanced currents in the bumptious "pop art" (popular art) movement. The pop artists have adopted certain very familiar aspects of our mid-twentieth-century mass culture to use as a basis for their entertaining performances. Jasper Johns retains a sophisticated touch whether he renders such familiar elements of American life as the American flag (his best-known motif) or "Numbers" (Figure 12–11). Here Johns has taken simple stenciled numbers and enriched them by embroidering them with freely improvised pencil textures. Treated with textural variety, the familiar numbers take on unexpected and characterful shapes.

Roy Lichtenstein departed farther from current artistic standards in "Him" (Figure 12–12). He has retained such standardized elements of the mass media as the hero symbol from comic books and the Benday dotted texture used in the cheap reproduction processes by which such books are illustrated. By enlarging and taking these symbols from their familiar setting he makes us aware of their vacuous smartness and slick superficiality. This is a dead-pan kind of commentary which is achieved by the simple device of removing the symbol from its familiar context, changing its scale, and then permitting it to speak for itself. At the opposite end of the spectrum from editorializing through familiar types of expressionist exaggeration, we have here a kind of editorializing through absence of exaggeration which has its own peculiar power.

Though surrealism had less impact upon America than the other major artistic movements of the twentieth century, its subtle flavor has permeated many areas of expression. Thus the surrealist fascination with such morbid themes as death, decay, and fear is reflected in drawings such as "Déchéance Embroyonaire" (Figure 16–18) by Marie-Anne Poniatowski. Executed with exquisite craftsmanship in pencil and conté crayon, the forms are modeled with the greatest sensitivity so that each subtle facet of bony structure is brought into almost sculptural relief. The angular rhythms of the dessicated form are reinforced by subtle linear angularities in the background, created when the corners of the rectangular piece of conté crayon contact the paper. The tiny form of the bird's skeleton has been enlarged into a symbol of the fearsome and haunting fascination of death. Again we witness the power of art to transmute the raw stuff of experience into timeless symbols.

In the early sixties, a few of the most vigorous exponents of abstract expressionism in the San Francisco Bay area reintroduced a strong figurative element in their paintings to create a West Coast school of figurative painters. Richard Diebenkorn and Elmer Bischoff, two of the most influential painters of the group, have revived the human figure as a dominant element in their work, but they have retained the direct vigor of attack that distinguished action painters. "Reclining Nude" by Diebenkorn (Figure 12–13) is in pencil and wash. Composed in vigorous diagonals with bold tonal contrasts, the splotches of coarse wash and the energetic textures reinforce the sharp bite of the unidealized figure. The drama of rapid and exciting execution permeates the entire study. A charcoal figure drawing by Bischoff (Figure 16–3) has a rich tonality, a suggestion of fresh charcoal textures and a strong sense of gesture and form that appears as a continuation of the great tradition of figure drawing. In observing the drawing, one remembers Rembrandt and Degas, among others— not that the drawing is consciously patterned after their example but because it continues the tradition of uncompromising honesty of vision combined with a virtuosity of execution which never develops into showmanship. Wayne Thiebaud has at times been identified as a California pop artist because of his choice of subject matter. Thiebaud was the first to glorify synthetically colored goodies displayed with mechanical regularity to tempt the American youngsters of all ages—the slices of cake or pie arranged in orderly display on cafeteria serving counters or the striped candied apples which enliven the counters of roadside eating stands. He has now turned to the human figure but prefers the beach

FIGURE 12–15

Tsugouharu Foujita (1886–   ; Japanese-French).
"Mexican General." Brush drawing, 15¾" x 12¾".
San Francisco Museum of Art (Gift of Mrs. Juilliard McDonald).

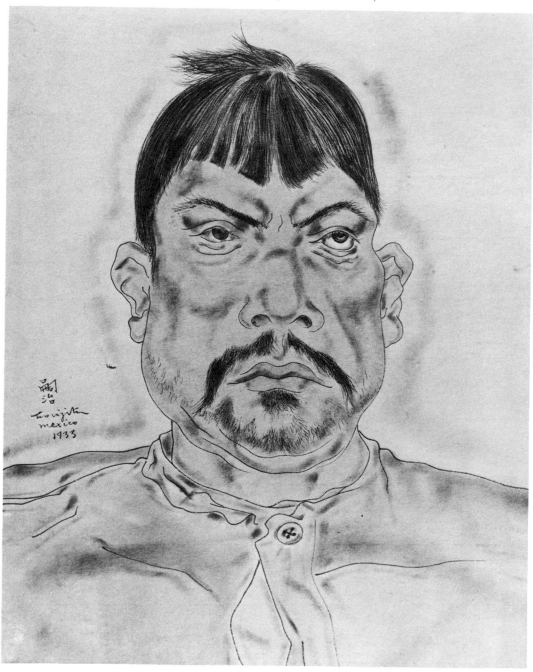

FIGURE 12–16

Rico Lebrun (1900–1964; Italian-American).
"Pippa Zoppa." Brown conté and black ink, 19″ x 25″.
Courtesy of Mrs. Ruth Lilienthal.

girl in a bikini (Figure 12–14, "Standing Figure") to the studio nude. His drawing is light and unlabored as befits the subjects which are depicted, with neither academic idealization nor hostility, but with a quiet appreciation of their modest character and solid grace. Another Californian who continues a traditional vein of figure drawing is Robert Baxter, whose charcoal drawing "I Know Not Why" (Figure 16–4) derives its romanticism not from the manner of execution, but from its symbolic implications and the underlying tone of "diablerie."

Contemporary realism has drawn on the entire history of world art for its stimulus, the personal tastes and proclivities of the artists permitting a wide range of interpretations, no matter what the source of a style. Tsugouharu Foujita employed the magic brush and wash of Oriental tradition to create a memorable portrait of a "Mexican General" (Figure 12–15), in which the elegance of line and tone in no way lessens the suggestion of rude strength of character. Rico Lebrun combined an Oriental calligraphic swirl of line with baroque tonality in his handsome "Pippa Zoppa" (Figure 12–16) and "Seated Clown" (Figure 13–14). Though Lebrun draws upon the past for elements of his style, the multifaceted diversity of tradition proves to be a stimulus rather than a restrictive burden.

Summary   Surrealism was an art movement launched in Paris in the twenties as an outgrowth of psychoanalytic interests. As such, it enlarged the subject matter of painting by encouraging the use of dream symbolism, automatism and other forms of spontaneous outpouring. Some surrealists like Salvador Dali employed traditional academic drawing and painting techniques, whereas others like Joan Miró preferred naïve, even childlike modes of expression. Although surrealism as a movement was short-lived, the surrealist penchant for a heightened imaginative atmosphere and organic forms has influenced much subsequent expression.

Between 1920 and 1950, the United States and Mexico, under the stress of conflict (as had Germany earlier) developed a vivid art of social commentary which received a vigorous expression in drawing. A wide variety of techniques was employed which ranged from graphic satire and caricature as exemplified by Ben Shahn to the disciplined realism of Peter Blume. Between 1920 and 1940 the "American Scene" painters continued the vein of pictorial realism established by "the Eight" in the two previous decades.

The drawings of Edward Hopper, Charles Sheeler, Andrew Wyeth and others are more traditional in character than were those of the men dedicated to social criticism, for they seem content to report rather than to criticize the social scene. After 1960 some West Coast abstractionist painters such as Richard Diebenkorn reintroduced figurative painting, accompanied by much direct fresh figure drawing.

part three

THE ART
ELEMENTS

13

LINE

Whenever an extended mark is made upon a surface, whether with brush, pencil, or pen, a line is created. Although lines do not exist in nature, as we most frequently use them in drawing, to indicate the boundaries of forms, they are one of the oldest conventions in the arts. The first crude scratchings of primitive man revealed to him the effectiveness of marks made upon a surface in isolating the area enclosed within the mark from the surrounding space. He also discovered the magic potency of these enclosed areas in suggesting the forms of the world around him. Many art historians have conjectured about the way the concepts of drawing first appeared. Perhaps primitive man, looking at the crevice patterns of rocks, the stains of water on the walls or ceilings of caves, or studying the grain of wood, suddenly observed the likeness of some familiar form from nature. The addition of a dot or a mark may have completed or strengthened the likeness by providing a missing eye or a tail. The next step would be to dispense with the accidental initial stimulus and, using a burned stick or a finger daubed in mud, provide all the necessary marks to create the desired likeness.

Line, then, is an age-old convention commonly used in drawing to indicate the boundaries of masses. It constitutes the essential element in delineation. The particular quality of a line and its consequent expressive effect depends upon three main factors: the nature of the person making the line, the instrument producing it, and the surface receiving it. The interaction of these three factors determines whether a line will be firm or wavering, even in width or of varying widths, smooth or crumbly edged, dark, pale, or graduated from dark to pale, straight, crooked, angular, curved, graceful, contorted or possessed of other qualities. As stated before, the beginner learning to draw soon discovers he is assuming command over a most potent tool. Every mark one makes, whether a thoughtful line or a careless scribble, will inevitably convey something of the maker to the sensitive observer. Not that this implies the need for self-consciousness or cautious and methodical procedures—but like every good workman, the artist must be conscious of his tools, their potentials, and use them with maximum effectiveness.

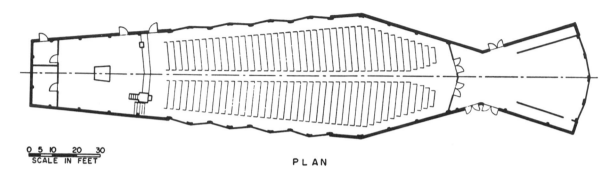

0 5 10 20 30
SCALE IN FEET

P L A N

FIGURE 13–1

Wallace K. Harrison and Max Abramovitz, Architects (American). Floor Plan, First Presbyterian Church, Stamford, Connecticut. Pen and ink, 9¾" x 2¼".

Types of Line—the Mechanical Line

In making a diagram, chart, or plan a line is usually desired which is impersonal and intrudes itself as little as possible on the observer's attention. The function of such a line is to convey information without editorial comment (Figure 13–1), and such drawings are usually made with mechanical drawing instruments on very smooth paper so that a minimum of the artist's physical and emotional constitution is transmitted through the drawing. Drawings of great beauty can be made using these impersonal, cold lines, and the beauty of the drawing depends upon the refined relationship between the weight of the lines, the size of the surrounding spaces and the general sense of orderliness, control, precision, and mechanical exactitude that permeates the entire drawing. It is indeed a classical and rational kind of beauty, closely related to the beauty found in the geometric abstraction of artists like Stuart Davis (Figure 10–9) or the cubist study by Juan Gris (Figure 13–2).

Few artists, however, strive for this impersonal and formal type of expression. Most drawings are rendered with more freedom and spontaneity and

FIGURE 13–2

Juan Gris (1887–1927; Spanish-French). "Seated Harlequin." Pencil on buff paper, 12″ x 9¾″.
The Solomon R. Guggenheim Museum (Private Collection). Robert E. Mates, Photographer.

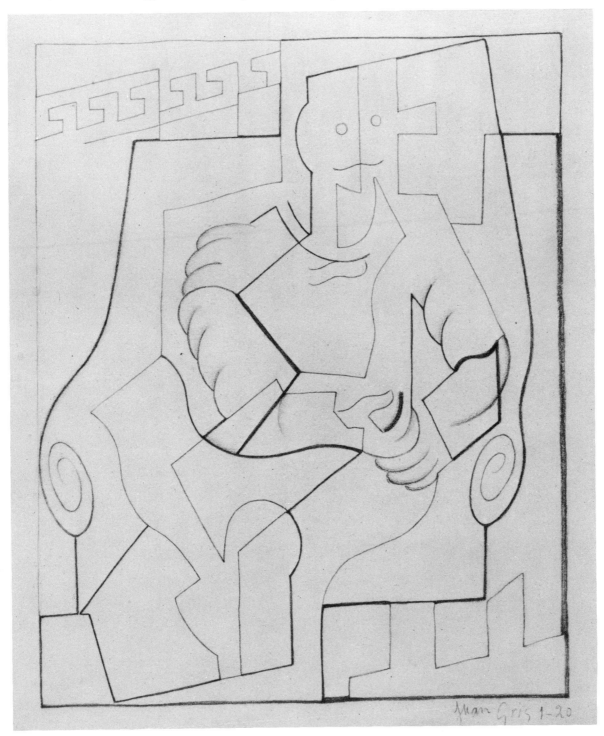

FIGURE 13–3

Max Beckmann (1884–1950; German).
"Coffee House." Pencil,
11¼" x 8¾".
Richard Feigen Gallery, Chicago.

FIGURE 13–4

Hokusai (1760–1849; Japanese).
Kakemono "The Old Woodcutter."
Ink and brush, 11⁷⁄₁₀" x 21⁹⁄₁₀".
Stanford University Museum (Ikeda Collection).

the artist's personal touch provides the life-giving ingredients to the work, making each person's drawings different from those of every other. The vigor or delicacy of an artist's touch, the resistance set up by the rough or smooth paper to the medium of his choice, his response to the soft messiness of chalk, the fluidity of wash, the ease with which pencil can be manipulated, all of these factors are related to the artist's innermost physical and psychological characteristics and all of them color his style of drawing. Some individuals sing while drawing, others are tense and grit their teeth; each emotional state is transmitted through the work to the observer in the same way that speech transmits the speaker's personality. Even when we are not sufficiently analytical about art to describe our reactions to a drawing in words, we react emotionally to the same factors. The more conversant we are with a mode of pictorial expression, the more sensitive are our intuitive responses.

FIGURE 13–5

Gaston Lachaise (1882–1935; French-American).
"Standing Nude." Pencil, 17¾" x 11¾".
Collection of Whitney Museum of American Art, New York.

Types of Line—the Spontaneous Line

At the opposite end of the spectrum from the impersonal and mechanical ink line is the completely spontaneous unformalized line used in the pencil drawing "Coffee House," by the German Expressionist Max Beckmann (Figure 13–3). The very fact that the sketch is on the back of a menu contributes to the impromptu effect. For the most part, this drawing does not appear to involve disciplined observation. The profile of the woman on the right seems to have been sharply observed, and it might have well been the initial step that sparked the drawing, with the remainder of the sketch improvised around the incisive profile to establish the atmosphere of movement and animation that characterized the coffee house. The complete absence of a feeling of constraint in making the drawing contributes much to its vivacity. The way in which the arm of the seated woman shows through the child's head at the bottom of the page, with no attempt made to obscure the underlying arm, the bodyless head of a waiter resting upon the shoulder of the left-hand woman, the freely scribbled, rough-textured lines of shading, the unidentifiable forms with which the drawing abounds, all communicate vividly the atmosphere in which the drawing was made and the hearty and untrammeled act of making it. Done in the mid-twenties by a German expressionist, it was the vitality of such works that inspired the American "action painters" thirty years later consciously to create a style from an unpremeditated approach by making an organizational principle from the act of drawing (Figure 10–12). The contrast between the styleless spontaneity of Beckman and the style of spontaneity exemplified by de Kooning throws much light on the way in which artistic movements evolve.

Types of Line—the Virtuoso Line

In marked contrast to both the formal rendering done with mechanical drawing instruments and the cafe sketch by Max Beckmann, with its complete absence of technical niceties, is a brush drawing by the master of the calligraphic line, Hokusai (Figure 13–4). Here a tradition of conscious concern with every brush stroke and a life devoted to a disciplined handling of tools and materials created a drawing of formidable skill, taste, and control. The line is equally admirable for its descriptive powers and for its purely esthetic character. The narrow twigs, the striated texture of bark, the round blobs of leaves, the rough clothes, the smooth shining axe are all described deftly, vividly, and beautifully, and though each line fulfills its descriptive function admirably, the sensuous beauty is captivating. Only close study reveals their full variety: the contrast between pale gray lines in the tree and in parts of the fisherman's costume and the rich blacks elsewhere; the crisp delicacy of the man's profile; the crinkly softness of his shoes and trousers; and the shaggy boldness of other lines in his clothing and in the bundles of reeds—altogether they run the full gamut of linear variety.

FIGURE 13–6

Pablo Picasso (1881–   ; Spanish-French).
"Seated Figure." Pen drawing, 16 x 11¼".
San Francisco Museum of Art (Harriet Lane Levy Bequest).

So far we have observed three very different kinds of drawings distinguished by very different qualities of line: the first, controlled, mechanical and impersonal; the second, rough, spontaneous, yet vital; the third, displaying great taste, esthetic refinement, and virtuosity in the handling of tools and materials. In each drawing the interplay between the artist's temperament, tradition, his materials and tools, and his own personal esthetics work together to create a unique style. The Hokusai drawing would not have been the same if he had used pen and ink or pencil, the floor plan if the draftsman had been satisfied to convey information with no visual distinction, the Otto Dix drawing if he were concerned with conventions of craftsmanship or propriety of performance. It is not possible, nor would it serve any purpose, to try to evaluate the role of each separate factor involved in every work, for art is the result of a synthesis that is more than the sum total of its separate parts. Thus, in the following discussion of line, our concern will be less to analyze the mechanics of production (media, equipment, the artist's mode of procedure, and so on), but rather to observe briefly the essential character of the line and evaluate its expressive power.

No artist has done more to explore the potentialities of line than Paul Klee. Among the hundreds of drawings from his hand, many appear to be essentially exercises in line—straight, curved, thick, thin, smooth or jagged. Whatever its quality the line has always been used so that its particular character contributes to the essential mood and idea of a particular drawing.

"Fritzi" (Figure 11–3) is a most casual pencil sketch of a relaxed cat. The slack lines, seemingly scribbled, suggest an intimate, comfortable domestic moment. Such a complete absence of esthetic rigor is rare in Klee and makes this drawing surprising as well as delightful.

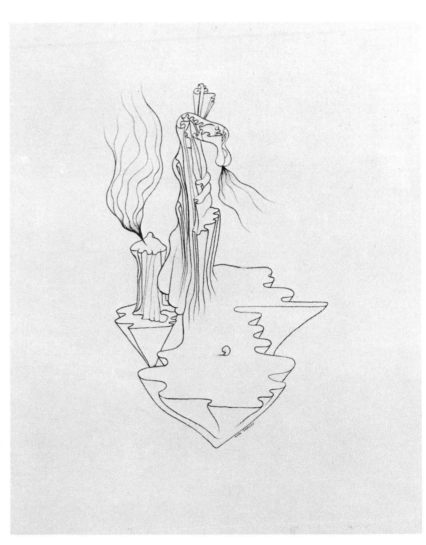

FIGURE 13–7

Yves Tanguy (1900–1955; French-American). Title unknown. Ink, 9½" x 7". *Richard Feigen Gallery, Chicago.*

La naissance des oiseaux.

FIGURE 13–8
André Masson (1896–   ; French).
"Birth of Birds." Pen and ink, 16½″ x 12⅜″.
Collection, The Museum of Modern Art, New York (Purchase).

FIGURE 13-9

Jean-Auguste Dominique Ingres (1780–1867; French).
Detail from "A Study for the Dead Body of Acron."
Lead pencil on paper. *The Metropolitan Museum of Art*
(*Rogers Fund, 1919*). See Figure 1–10.

"A Balance-Capriccio" (Figure 11–4) employs thin and fragile ink lines to reinforce the sense of delicate and precarious equilibrium. Appropriately enough, an air of artifice dominates the execution. The tense exactitude here is in direct opposition to the almost scribbled "Fritzi." "Kolo 11" (Figure 11–5) was done in brush and ink. Here an awkward crudity of line works with the naïve perspective to create a childlike, playful interpretation of a Mediterranean memory. In no two drawings does Klee seem to repeat himself (Figures 15–20, 18–17), and his inventiveness is always balanced by his esthetic sensitivity.

In the drawings discussed thus far in this chapter we see line used less to describe the outside world than to provide a sensitive projection of the artist's inner world. Thus the line not only describes, but also creates, for it brings into being an element that did not previously completely exist, even in the artist's imagination. It is only in the act of putting the imagined into pictorial form that full esthetic realization can occur.

Functions of Line—the Contour Line

One of the principal uses of line is to define contours. The contour line moving vigorously to delineate the edges of solid forms is well illustrated in "Standing Nude" by Gaston Lachaise (Figure 13–5). The pencil recorded the rapid movements of the artist's eye as it followed the edges of the form, providing the simplest possible description of that form. Only when major masses project toward us (the hair bun and the buttocks), or away (the

FIGURE 13–10
Peter Paul Rubens (1577–1640; Flemish).
Study for the Figure of Christ for "The Raising of the Cross."
Black crayon heightened with white chalk on buff paper.
Courtesy of the Fogg Art Museum,
Harvard University, Cambridge, Massachusetts (Meta and Paul J. Sachs Collection).

suspended breast and left hand), is there a break in the continuous flowing line. Despite the ostensibly noncommittal character of the line, the drawing has wit and verve. The line plunges boldly around the forms, moving in big sweeps but stopping occasionally to describe the saucy wiggle of curls, the awkward weight of breast, or the elegant taper of leg into tiny feet. These changes of pace and scale all reflect the light-hearted zest with which the drawing was executed.

Picasso is the master of the contour line, and in his hands it reveals an astonishing variety. A very simple, small nude figure in pen and ink is emotive because of its simple sincerity (Figure 13–6). Unlike the Lachaise drawing, the pen moves slowly and searchingly, feeling the relationship between each undulation of edge and the inner changes of surface. The raised foreleg and foot are masterly, as is the foreshortened thigh that comes directly toward us to culminate in the solid form of the knee, which is described almost entirely by a change in angle, a slight overlapping of edges, and an increased firmness of line. The pen is used without any flourish, and this too contributes to the endearing modesty of statement. A striking contrast is provided by the elaborate and involved pencil study titled "The Bathers" (Figure 10–5). Executed in Biarritz in the summer of 1918, this drawing represents the culmination and integration of many trends which Picasso had initiated previous to that date. A taste for neoclassic effects, for the involved linear arabesques that provide a sense of conscious artifice, for rhythmically flowing curves, and for rather formal interrelationships between parts, give the drawing a studied elegance in sharp contrast to the unpretentious sensitivity of the earlier nude.

Contour Lines of Unvarying Width

Many modern artists share Picasso's concern with formal esthetic values, and a number of men have preferred to use an unemotional line of unvarying width to achieve an art that is elegant and controlled and without passion. Such is the simple untitled drawing in pen and ink by the Surrealist, Yves Tanguy (Figure 13–7). The strange imaginary forms of his creation are presented with cool detachment as a scientist might present the curious rocks, mollusks, and plants of a remote undersea world. This same air of detachment characterizes a pencil and crayon drawing made by Arshile Gorky as a study for his painting "The Plough and the Song" (Figure 10–10). Though the line here has more variety than in the Tanguy drawing, the variations in width and darkness appear calculated to provide an effect of differing color or to create compositional stresses rather than an impulsive response to visual perceptions or the physical act of drawing. As in the Tanguy drawing, the even line tends to bring all of the drawing up to the flat picture plane, and this also adds an element of esthetic formalism which minimizes the illustrational or pictorial emphasis.

Contour Lines of Varying Width

The effectiveness of the even, unaccented line in creating an atmosphere of elegance and detached formality has just been stressed. By way of contrast, let us

FIGURE 13–11

Amedeo Modigliani (1884–1920; Italian-French).
"Portrait of Leon Bakst." Pencil, 22½″ x 16½″.
Courtesy of Wadsworth Atheneum, Hartford, Connecticut.

look at a pen and ink drawing by André Masson titled "Birth of Birds" (Figure 13–8). Here too we have elegance and even detachment, but the drawing thoughtfully exploits a wide range of linear resources: the smooth flowing line of even width, the line that moves from thin to thick, the rough textured line, the stippled line, the contorted, and many combinations and modifications of these. Thus a complex conception is implemented by an unusual variety of visual fare, for the birth of birds involves many aspects: the airy flight through space, the ecstatic soaring and dippings of pursuit and mating, the microscopic mysteries of fertilization, the organic swellings of gestation, and, above all else, the lyric exaltation we find in contemplating the idea of birth.

Functions of Line—the Delineating Edge

The great Renaissance tradition of draftsmanship demanded a discipline of line kept captive to the observant eye no less exacting than the discipline of line serving the esthetic imagination. During Renaissance times, the delineating edge, which is essentially a contour line reinforced by modeling, became an essential element in the great tradition of draftsmanship. It was primarily from such High Renaissance masters as Raphael that the great draftsman Ingres drew inspiration. A detail from the study by Ingres for the "Dead Body of Acron" (Figure 13–9) reveals a delineating edge under the complete control of an unerring eye. The thicknesses and thinnesses, the precision or softness of edge exists only in response to the eye as it perceives the form. Thus where the bone of the elbow pushes hard against the skin, the line is firm, to become softer and less defined when it is describing the softer and rounder fleshy parts. When the flesh presses heavily against the ground the line thins out, where the small of the back arches away from the ground and casts a small shadow, the heavier molded dark describes the shadow. The beauty of the drawing to a large extent rests upon the exquisite perfection with which the line performs its assigned task. It is an example of functional beauty, a tribute to Ingres' mastery of his craft, an example of line completely under control of the eye.

The same functional clarity distinguishes the line quality on Meryon's "Le Pompe de Notre Dame" (Figure 7–9), but here the line assumes the additional function of clarifying structure. It has a slightly arbitrary schematic role for it must simplify to minimize confusion, eliminate minor fluctuations of surface to convey a sense of basic form that is not evident on the surface. Here we see line, not only in the service of the eye but equally in the service of the mind, for defining structure involves an intellectual analysis of what is beneath.

Degas commenced his career as an artist as an admirer of Ingres, and like Ingres he remained a master of the delineating edge. However, in "The Gentleman Rider" (Figure 16–9) Degas ceased to model the edge by means of a fused tone but instead employed a cluster of coalescing lines to create an animated tone halfway between the modeled edge used by Ingres and the shattered contour line of Cézanne. Here Degas' use of the pencil shows that even when line remains the obedient servant of the eye it can have an independent life with a free and relaxed relationship between the moving pencil and the roving eye. The precise lapel caught Degas' attention, and he defined it neatly with a single stroke of the pencil. The front of the coat was sketched with a loose cluster of lines. The roundness of the upper thigh was seen both as a congregation of small wrinkles and a rounded, not sharply defined top plane. The entire drawing is filled with fascinating variations of perceptions and responses to these perceptions.

Acting in the service of the eye, the delineating edge becomes the servant of the entire artistic personality, for the eye, mind, hand, and the emotional structure of the mature artist function in unison. Ingres, Meryon and Degas—all three reflect the discipline of French tradition. Restraint was more admired than enthusiasm, and the imagination was kept in check by a respect for fact. A study by Rubens of a figure of Christ for his painting of "The Raising of the Cross" (Figure 13–10) provides an exuberant contrast. Here, too, the line carries the chief descriptive function, reinforced as in the Ingres drawing by delicate modeling. But the vigor of Rubens' personality and his baroque enthusiasm for movement permeates the entire drawing. Each roundness of form is stressed by the overlapping contour lines, each rounded muscle given its full volume. A sense of swelling life flows through the entire form, infusing it with a rhythmic energy. Ingres viewed his model as fact. Rubens, by contrast, took the body of his model as a point of departure to project his enthusiasms and ideals. The eye looked, the hand followed, but the imagination carried both eye and hand far beyond the fact to the grand forms that existed in the artist's mind.

Two more drawings in which there is a sensitive concentration on outline to describe the contours of form can enlarge our appreciation of the range and variety of perception encompassed by this basic kind of delineation. A drawing of a "Head" by Picasso (Figure 10–4) employs a small pointed brush and ink to create a slow-moving, searching line which breaks continuously as it follows the edges of the form. This hesitant tremulous edge has the ring of sincerity, much as a deeply felt, inarticulate search for words may convey sincere feeling more effectively than brilliant rhetoric. The line seems particularly appropriate for conveying the sad, almost morbid beauty of the subject.

A pencil portrait of "Leon Bakst" by Modigliani (Figure 13–11) reveals another kind of sensitivity. The line quality ranges from being sharp and precise, as when it defines the small sharp eyes, the nostrils, ears and upper lip, to a pale soft tone as in the chin and the edge of the forehead. The play of hard and soft, of sharp and vague, describes not so much the physical characteristics of the surfaces (though this factor influences the quality of line) but more the qualities of personality that distinguished the sitter. The small pale Slavic eyes set obliquely in the head were given importance beyond their size by their sharp definition. The uplifted nostril and drooping moustache create an asymmetrical face that is tense, sensitive but controlled. The small features accentuate the broad forehead with its thin crown of hair. The body and hands seem drawn with a knife-edged line, pure but curiously insensitive as compared to the head. Again, the implication is of a surface formality and propriety that is in opposition to the sensitive artist hiding behind the sharp eyes and disdainful mouth. The elegance, purity and variety of line made it possible for Modigliani

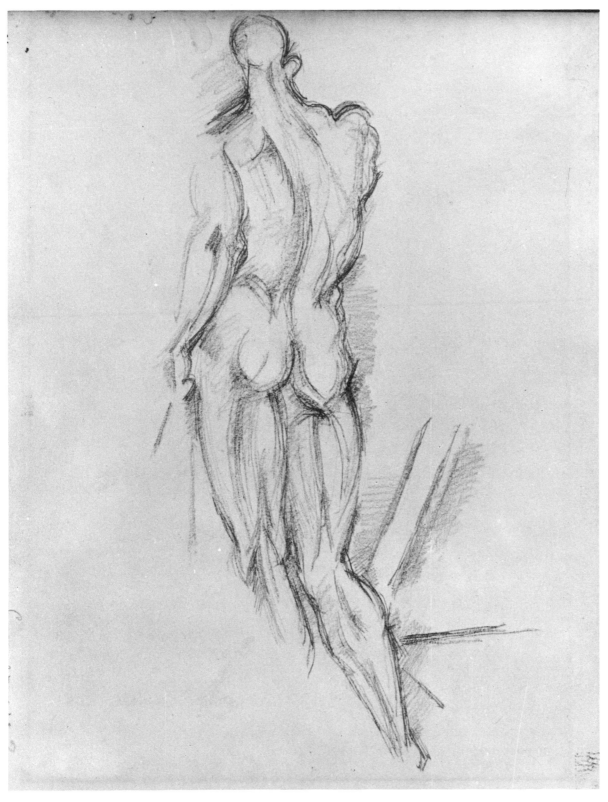

FIGURE 13–12

Paul Cézanne (1839–1906; French).
"Study after Houdon's Écorché." Lead pencil on paper, 8¼″ x 10¾″.
*The Metropolitan Museum of Art, Maria DeWitt Jesup Fund, 1951,
from the Museum of Modern Art, Lizzie P. Bliss Collection.*

FIGURE 13–13

Hokusai (1760–1849; Japanese). Detail from "The Mochi Makers."
Ink drawing on Japanese paper. See Figure 9–9.
The Metropolitan Museum of Art, New York (*Gift in memory of Charles Stewart Smith, 1914*).

to express the paradox of the sensitive artist in the sophisticated world of the theatre.

Functions of Line—the Fragmented Line

Cézanne saw too much for facile drawing and for a simple statement. His hand stubbornly following his eye refused to accept the convention that was fundamental to Renaissance pictorial concepts, that one saw the world from a fixed eye position. Instead, Cézanne insisted on looking while drawing, as one

PLATE 15
School of Jahangir, Mughal (early seventeenth century; Indian). "The World of Animals." Brush drawing in pale tints, mounted on an album leaf with illuminated border, papers 13⁵⁄₁₆" x 8⁹⁄₁₆", painting 9³⁄₁₆" x 4¹¹⁄₁₆". *Courtesy of the Smithsonian Institution, Freer Gallery of Art, Washington, D. C.*

PLATE 16

Claude Lorrain ([Gellée]; 1600–1682; French).
"The Tiber Above Rome." Brush and bistre, 7⅓" x 10¾".
Courtesy the Trustees of the British Museum, London.

looks in everyday life, with a head-on-a-swivel neck which moves to either side and up and down to view a subject more fully. Thus the contours change, the planes along the edges of forms slide alternately into and out of view, and visual ambiguity, complexity and fluidity replaces the visual fixedness of earlier conventions. One need only glance at "A Study after Houdon's Écorché" (Figure 13–12) to see how his assault upon the convention of the continuous delineating line opened new vistas for twentieth-century draftsmen.

Functions of Line—the Calligraphic Line

In all of the drawings we have analyzed, commencing with the study by Ingres for the "Dead Body of Acron," the act of making the line seems to have been held firmly in check and subordinate to the act of seeing. A tradition of linear calligraphy is equally ancient and equally worth investigation by the student of drawing. The calligraphic line reveals with particular force the gesture by which it was created. It follows that tools, media and receptive ground play a dominant role in establishing the character of calligraphic drawing. The calligraphic line is most easily identified by its bold variations in width, moving from thick to thin according to the pressure on the brush or pen. It has been most fully developed in Japanese and Chinese brush drawing, for here the brilliance of brush work is a key factor in determining artistic excellence (Figure 13–13). Unlike Hokusai, many minor Oriental painters used their drawing and painting almost exclusively as a medium for the display of virtuosity in handling the brush. The West has never placed quite so high a premium on virtuosity for its own sake. Instead, the vivacity and expressive force of the calligraphic line has been kept more in the service of a general pictorial purpose. A splendid example of such combined purposes is offered by Rico Lebrun's "Seated Clown" (Figure 13–14). Sketched and partially modeled first in chalk, the underdrawing has been reinforced with a bold play of brushed ink lines. The ink lines have an exuberance and vitality about them that is exhilarating to observe. The flourish of line by which the contour of the collar is established is worthy of study, as is the heavy sweeping line of the back of the clown which defines the form, establishes the weighty quality of the heavy figure, and at the same time moves with exuberant vigor that makes it a joy to behold, irrespective of its descriptive function. The contrasts of rich curved lines, of angular, of thin and thick, all play together to create a drawing that is equally exciting as a visual record and as an esthetic performance.

Probably no one has combined to as great a degree as Rembrandt a disciplined exposition of what his eye saw and a love of line as a beautiful thing in itself. His "Winter Landscape" (Figure 5–13) displays the virtuosity of performance of an Oriental master, yet unlike the Oriental calligraphy, it is not based on an established convention of brush performance. It is as personal as handwriting. The bold, almost harsh shadow of the low wall accents the graceful sweep of lines in the bare tree at the far right. The lines that define the distant trees and buildings contrast in both scale and texture with those that establish the front plane. Their graduations are exquisite, ranging from firm darks to the

most delicate stippled tones. In the far distance they barely touch the paper. In each line one can feel the artist's hand, tense or relaxed, manipulating the reed pen, pushing it stubbornly, making a sweeping gesture, or barely touching the paper as a musician might barely touch the keys when making a pianissimo glissando.

The Lyric Line

To capture the fresh lyric impulse has been one of the aims of many modern artists, particularly among that group known as *Les Fauves*, who painted in France in the first two decades of this century. One of the devices employed with great effectiveness by Raoul Dufy was the use of a casual calligraphic line in which the variations of width appear to be the result of his relaxed and effortless execution. Through his deft and unlabored manner he communicated his delight in the sensuous beauty of his environment as in his sketch of "The Artist's Studio" (Figure 10–2) in brush and ink. From the little balcony that leads to the second-story sleeping quarters of the typical French atelier, he looked down on the room which was undoubtedly very dear to him. Madame Dufy sat comfortably reading the newspaper, the dog (or cat) slept on the chair beside her, near by an unoccupied swivel chair flourished its curves. The paintings on the wall, the brushes on his work table, even the mansard roof seen from the window, were all viewed with a gush of warm affection, and the drawing exudes this delight in a comfortable milieu. Individual parts might even be criticized as badly drawn (Madame's feet, for example, or the legs of the work table), but such carelessly indicated details are irrelevant to the effect of the whole and may even contribute to its air of relaxed, pleasurable notation. At no time does the artist's activity seem impeded by self-criticism, and so in no area of the drawing does one feel the tension that comes with restraint.

The Emphatic Line

Spontaneous execution that would preserve the lyric impulse was equally dear to Van Gogh, but the temperament of Dufy and Van Gogh and the milieu in which they worked were very different. Raoul Dufy worked in Paris, the city in which sensuous beauty and pleasure seem to be the core of life, and he performed naturally in this worldly atmosphere, recording its charming surface with pleasure-giving ease. Van Gogh fled from the pleasure-loving city. A glance at "The Bridge at L'Anglois" (Figure 15–2) reveals the tension under which he worked. At heart he was a moralist, dedicated to uplifting mankind. The beauty of the landscape was for him, unconsciously, a symbol of the goodness of God. The vitality of the landscape, of growth, of the light, overwhelmed him. He was torn by the intensity of his feelings, by his sense of aloneness. He never seemed able to reconcile all the conflicting elements that go to make up life. Such a man would inevitably choose the unwieldy reed pen that bites into the surface of the paper to make his harsh bristling marks. There is not a relaxed and easy stroke in

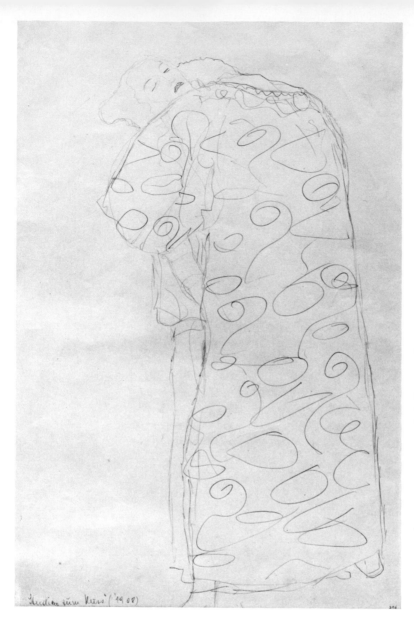

Studien zum Kuss ('1908)

the entire drawing except for the few lines he drew when he recorded the
graceful swirl of the water as it reflected the dark gap of the bridge. And just as
the lack of tension gives the Dufy drawing its quality, here the tension creates
the work of art, since it communicates the essence of the dedicated man who
produced it.

Three more drawings that live by their emphatic variety of line are well
worth studying. Emil Nolde was one of the German expressionists strongly
influenced by the art of Van Gogh. During much of his life he worked in the
coastal marshlands of northern Germany, in country not too unlike that in
which Van Gogh was reared. Like Van Gogh, the vitality of nature and his own
intense feelings were the catalyzers for much of his artistic expression. For his
"Landscape with Windmill" (Figure 11–2) he chose a bristle brush and
printer's ink, since the stiff bristle brush and the viscous heavy ink provide a
grainy texture and an intransigent stroke that by their very resistance set up a

physical conflict which contributed to the expression of the emotional conflict motivating his art. The great awkward shapes that give the drawing its power grow inevitably from these clumsy tools. It is an art that scorns the facile, for the artist has learned that ease and grace of performance too often enable the artist to glide across the surface of appearances, never penetrating deeply either into his own feelings or into the nature of the world about him.

Not all boldness is the result of the direct expression of intense feelings. A brush and ink study by Diego Rivera of "Mother and Child" (Figure 17–8) has consciously employed a heavy line to create an effect of primitive momumentality. The large head and feet of the woman recall the pictorial conventions of pre-Columbian Mexican art, while the almost square format of the drawing and the heavy lines with their varied thicknesses, remind one of the painted hieroglyphics of the Mayan and Mexican codices. The calculated shapes and the conscious manipulations of line widths create an art that is static and formal. Its simplicities, like those of Gauguin and the many modern artists who seek inspiration in the arts of earlier cultures, are essentially sophisticated.

The Flowing Line

A few more categories of line should be compared and analyzed to make our survey complete: the flowing line, the crabbed line, the meandering line, and the encompassing line. The desire of the group of painters who worked in France in the first two decades of this century to create a lyric art characterized by a joyous spontaneity has already been mentioned. Henri Matisse is the artist who has most fully explored the resources of this vein through the use of a linear arabesque, a flowing line of even width in which the decorative potential is strongly felt. An "Odalisque" (Figure 10–1), done in pen and ink, has the airy lightness and fresh charm of a bouquet of spring flowers. The lines move effortlessly, for Matisse purposely avoided guiding the pen too tightly, since restricting the line movements would result in a directed, more incisive and therefore more tense quality of drawing than he desired. The flowered spread, the geometric patterns of tiles, and the flowing forms of the figure were all executed in the same unaccented line, thereby giving equal importance to all of the elements of the composition. An equal lack of emphasis provides the dominant tone in the pencil study for "The Kiss" (Figure 13–15), by the Austrian art nouveau painter, Gustav Klimt. The Klimt drawing compares interestingly with the Matisse; though the main lines of the figure and the pattern of the man's robe were executed with an abandon equal to that of the Matisse drawing, the features of the woman's head stand out in striking contrast to the rest of the drawing. Though barely indicated, they have been placed with precision, and the features created with short tense strokes. The contour lines of the face can scarcely be seen. The result is astonishingly expressive, for against the play of flowing patterned arabesques, untrammeled as the ecstatic pleasure of the kiss, is juxtaposed the few tense touches that make up the face to evoke the poignant anguish which in human affairs seems the counterpart of joy.

FIGURE 13–16
Édouard Vuillard (1868–1940; French). "Portrait of Madame Vuillard." Pencil, 8⅛" x 4⅝". *Yale University Art Gallery, New Haven, Connecticut.*

The Crabbed Line

George Grosz was the most powerful satirist working in Germany during the tragic inflationary years of the twenties. It was during these years, when a disrupted economy and a chaotic political system enabled Hitler and the Nazis to come into power, that George Grosz recorded the conflicted social order with his vitriolic pen. An ink drawing of "Workmen and Cripple" (Figure 11–7) reveals his original and powerful manner. Every stroke of the pen appears charged with tension; in the entire drawing there is not one flowing, relaxed line. The line movements are short, contorted, crabbed, as thwarted in their movements as the lives led by the subjects Grosz described. His eye is constantly stopped in its movements by the wrinkles and creases of clothing, by the wrinkled skins and scratchy hair of embittered faces, by the tight closed fists. If the Matisse "Odalisque" is a song of joy, the Grosz is a cry of pain.

The crabbed and crooked line need not always be at the service of social protest or used to describe human anguish; in "Incoming Fisher Fleet" (Figure 11–9), a watercolor and ink drawing by Lionel Feininger, the blur of watercolor laid into a wet ground is reinforced by an irregular jiggly edged pen line that tends to fuse with the soft-spreading atmospheric tone. Thus an all-pervasive mistiness of effect is achieved, the ink line neither confines nor defines but simply reinforces the blurred forms of boats, waves, and pilings. The very irregularity of the line movement, moving as irrationally as it does in all directions, adds an element of whimsy, almost of fantasy, which takes the work beyond illustration into the realm of imaginative evocation.

The Meandering Line

Édouard Vuillard has left us a pencil portrait of his mother, "Madame Vuillard" (Figure 13–16), in which the meandering, irregular movements of line contribute to atmospheric evocation, providing a linear equivalent to the broken brushwork of the Impressionist painters. Vuillard might best be described as an intimist, an artist particularly sensitive to the total atmosphere of room interiors. He painted the overfurnished, heavily patterned apartments of early twentieth-century Paris, when individuals seemed almost prisoners of their environment, owned and shaped by their possessions, confined by upholstered ease, enervated by the surplus of decorative patterning that surrounded them. Madame Vuillard was drawn as part of the decor, hardly separate from the chair that supports her or the room that encloses her. The crinkled, gathered and frilled fabrics of her costume evoke the patterns and pleats of draperies, curtains, and carpets. But just as Madame Vuillard dominates the tremulous, shadowy interior of her apartment, so does her face emerge from the drawing. The untextured plane of the side of the face, framed as it were by the ruchings on the cap, the texture of aged neck, and the frill of the neckerchief, contributes its visual weight to reinforce the slightly firmer line of lip and chin as the dominant accent among the generally crumbly textures. Had the general texture of the drawing been firmer, it would not have been possible to establish the character of Madame Vuillard with such a delicate and tenuous touch.

The Encompassing Line

Much of our attention in this chapter on line has been directed toward line as it functions in describing the edges of forms. Before concluding our discussion of line, let us glance briefly at a pencil drawing by the French sculptor Maillol of "Two Nudes" (Figure 13–17). The drawing commenced as an exploratory swirling mass of lines. From this matrix of moving lines, Maillol gradually defined the figures, and in areas such as the breasts of the bather at the lower left, the circular lines move over the full form rather than define the edges. Encompassing the form through continuous movements of line across the surface can be seen in seventeenth-century Italy (Figure 4–10), but in earlier drawing there is a less candid pleasure in the swirl for its own sake. In contemporary drawing classes the development of a drawing through the use of such circular line movements is frequently employed to make students aware of the full volume of surfaces, since beginning students find it difficult to perceive and define those aspects of form which cannot be seen at the edges and therefore described by contour lines.

Summary

Line as used by artists to denote the boundaries of masses is the oldest artistic convention. Lines vary tremendously in character, and each type of line has its expressive potential. Three extremes of line quality are (1) impersonal lines of unvarying width made with mechanical drawing instruments, (2) lines produced impulsively with no thought of quality, and (3) the virtuoso line glorified by Hokusai which was consciously controlled for decorative and expressive purposes. No modern artist has used varied types of lines with greater esthetic sensitivity than Paul Klee.

The contour line represents one of the simplest types of boundary line, and according to expressive purpose it can range from a contour line of unvarying width to one with great variety of width and texture. Reinforced by light modeling, the contour line expands and becomes the delineating edge. In the hands of such master draftsmen as Ingres, Degas, and Rubens a full sense of form is communicated by the delineating edge in the service of the eye. With Cézanne the fragmented line provides a vehicle for describing the ambiguous and complex character of visual experience.

The character of the calligraphic line is determined by the gesture which produced it in interplay with the instrument, media, and surface upon which it is inscribed. The calligraphic line reached a virtuoso development in China and Japan. Rembrandt more than any other draftsman combines the richness of Oriental calligraphy with the descriptive power of Western drawing. A number of kinds of line deserve special notice, namely the lyric line, the emphatic line, the flowing line, the crabbed line, the meandering line and the encompassing line.

FIGURE 13–17

Aristide Maillol (1861–1944; French).
"Two Nudes." Pencil on paper, 8⅛″ x 8¾″.
Achenbach Foundation for Graphic Arts,
California Palace of the Legion of Honor, San Francisco.

14

FORM AND VALUE

Value

Value, form, and space are so interrelated that it seems logical to discuss them in one chapter. The term *value* is used to denote relationships of light and dark; white is the lightest possible value and black the darkest, with the range of intermediate values forming grays (Figure 14–1). Pure black, white, and gray seldom occur in the external world, for almost every surface has some degree of local coloration which in turn is influenced by the color of the source of illumination. However, every colored surface also has a degree of lightness or darkness and in the typical drawing the artist records a relative degree of darkness and lightness (value), rather than whether a surface is primarily red, blue, yellow, and so on. Thus a red apple placed against a white wall would be drawn as a medium-dark object against a light background. The extreme of lightness occurs when we see facets of a white or extremely light object catching very bright illumination. The opposite in the light-to-dark spectrum occurs when we see areas of a dark or black object receiving little or no illumination.

Form

Every object has a specific three-dimensional character which constitutes its *form*. The simplest forms are spheres, cubes, and pyramids. The character of a more complex form, such as a human head, cannot be fully conveyed by

FIGURE 14–1

Value Chart.

a simple word like sphere or cube since words cannot convey its full three-dimensional complexity. Most forms seen in the world about us are characterized by many deviations from a simple geometric base and even when seen under brilliant illumination the exact interrelationship of parts, that is the degree to which parts project, indent or depart from a geometric basis is not easy to perceive or comprehend.

The contours of an object, as we have seen in the previous chapter, can be described by means of line and through such contour lines we get much information about the form of an object. But objects usually have aspects of form which are not described fully by contours. This relates particularly to the projections and indentations on the surface of a form which face the observer and therefore are foreshortened. We are made aware of these aspects of form by light and shadow. As light flows across the surface of a three-dimensional form it catches on projecting surfaces and illuminates them, while recessed areas which are hidden from the direct rays of light fall into shadow. Thus a continuous change of values is created which reveals the form to our eyes. Value relationships as they reveal form are most easily seen in a white object, with clearly defined planes illuminated from above and to one side by a strong light. Thus, if a white polygon is placed under a bright light, one can easily see the way in which the form is revealed, since the angular edges which divide the planes of the polygon will create sharp changes of value (Figure 14–2).

Perspective and Space Systems

Space is best described as the distance between forms. Without forms to serve as points of reference which relate objects in space, spatial intervals cannot be perceived.

In the Renaissance, certain systems were developed to describe the external world, its forms and spaces upon a two-dimensional picture plane. One of these systems, linear perspective, to quote the *Oxford Universal Dictionary*, "is the

FIGURE 14–2
Faceted Form under Illumination.

art of delineating solid objects upon a plane surface so as to produce the same impression of relative positions and magnitudes, or of distance, as the actual objects do when viewed from a particular point." The simpler principles of perspective are familiar to all of us. First, objects appear to diminish in size as they become more distant. Second, objects close to the observer overlap and obscure more distant objects when they are in the same trajectory of vision (hence the successive overlapping of forms in a drawing creates the illusion of a succession of forms in front and in back of one another). Third, and this is a corollary of the first point, parallel lines (and by this we mean the edges of a continuous plane of regular width, such as a wall, road, or the frequently used railroad track) appear to converge as they become more distant from the observer. This convergence, if uninterrupted, continues until the converging lines meet and the point at which they meet (or disappear) is on the horizon line, where the actual curve of the earth obscures what is beyond. These three aspects of linear perspective: (1) diminishing sizes, (2) overlapping forms, and (3) converging lines can be seen in a perspective drawing by an eighteenth-century Italian, Gaetano Gondolfo (Figure 14–3).

While these fundamentals of perspective arc disarmingly simple, the corollaries are extrmely complex. A rigorous and exact science of perspective was developed in fifteenth-century Italy (Figure 14–4) which has grown and been elaborated upon since. In fact, today's perspective theory often goes far beyond the artist's needs, moving into theories of spatial projection more closely allied to solid geometry and the demands of engineering and science.

Tiered Space   Systems of perspective existed in various cultures before the Italian Renaissance. The ancient Egyptians suggested space by placing levels of action one above another, each on its own ground line. The lowest band of action in a composition was read as the frontal plane, the highest as the most distant (Figure 2–5). This constituted a system of perspective that had both intellectual logic and to a degree conformed to visual experience, inasmuch as commencing with the ground in the forefront, one's eyes move up as one looks into the distance. This kind of "tiered" perspective has also been used by other cultures and periods. We see it in medieval drawing (Figure 14–5), in Oriental drawing (Figure 14–6), and it has been used by contemporary artists as a means of suggesting space, yet maintaining the sense of picture plane. Obviously, once a system has been widely used and is familiar and accepted, it functions for the initiates.

Isometric Perspective and Modern Space Concepts

Isometric perspective has been used by Oriental artists from very early times (Figure 14–6). It is still frequently used by architectural draftsmen, industrial designers, and others, particularly when the exact measurements of surfaces going into depth have to be indicated. In isometric perspective the parallel lines going into the depth of the drawing do not converge, that is, objects do not get smaller as they recede into space. To quote again from the *Oxford Universal*

FIGURE 14–3

Gaetano Gandolfi (1734–1803; Italian).
"Figures and Animals in Deep Architectural View."
Sepia pen and ink and grey wash and pencil, 21″ x 29″.
Los Angeles County Museum (Museum Purchase).

FIGURE 14-4

Leonardo da Vinci (1452–1519; Italian).
Perspective Study for "Adoration of the Magi."
Silverpoint, then pen and bistre,
heightened with white on prepared ground, 6½" x 11½".
The Uffizi Gallery, Florence (Alinari-Art Reference Bureau).

Dictionary, isometric perspective is a "method of projection or perspective in which the plane of projection is equally inclined to the three principal axes of the object, so that all dimensions parallel to the axes are represented in their actual proportions, used in drawing figures of machines, etc." The effect of isometric perspective is to provide a kind of bird's-eye view of objects and areas depicted, since the lack of convergence creates the illusion of a very high eye-level. The impressionists found the patterns created by the isometric perspective employed in Japanese prints very delightful. They frequently practiced a modified version of Oriental isometric perspective in their paintings, and Cézanne went further in his modifications of conventional uses of perspective, tipping up the receding planes of forms to make the observer more fully aware of the spatial intervals involved in a drawing. Cézanne also rather consciously limited the implied depth in his works, thereby enabling himself to eliminate ambiguity of spatial relationships between the objects in his drawings. These departures from conventional perspective practices also had a certain shock value. They made the observer more sharply aware of space-and-form relationships because they did not conform to familiar conventions, inducing the observer to see with a fresh eye, even when irritated with what seemed violations of "correct" practices.

Many modern painters and draftsmen employ concepts of pictorial space which they feel maintain the validity of the picture plane. Rather than try to create "illusory depth" and volume, they have accept the flatness of the canvas or paper as an esthetic entity. Thus, overlappings of form provide one fundamental way of creating pictorial space without violating the flatness of the picture plane, as can be seen in the Hartung drawing discussed in the first chapter (Figure 1–19). "Tiered" space such as was used in many early cultures has been reintroduced. Varying degrees of value contrast are also used to convey modern space concepts. Most important in painting is the use of the advancing and receding characteristics of pure color, but this is not of prime importance in a discussion of drawing.

Aerial Perspective

Linear perspective represents only one phase of perspective, and in most drawings and paintings which have a considerable degree of spatial complexity, the illusion of depth created by linear perspective is reinforced by aerial perspective. Aerial perspective is based upon two observations. The first is that air is not completely transparent and, therefore, that a thin but with distance an ever-increasing layer of the obscuring atmosphere gradually interpolates itself between the seen objects and the viewer. Second, as objects go into the far distance and become smaller, the eye gradually fails to perceive individual forms and the separate facets of light and dark that make up individual forms. These blend together, cancel out one another, leaving a general prevailing middle value which, in turn, is further obscured by the intervening layer of light-colored air to become a medium-light value. These two factors create the illusion of aerial perspective, the principle of which is that contrasts of value diminish as objects recede into the distance; the lights become less light, the darks less dark, until all value contrasts merge into a medium-light uniform tone (Figure 14–7). (Color

FIGURE 14–5

Göttingen Manuscript (probably fifteenth-century;
German). "Apostles Sitting in Stocks."
Red, brown and green color on parchment, 12″ x 8⅜″.
Göttingen, University Library.

FIGURE 14–6

Hanging Scroll (Kamakura period, c. 1300; Japanese).
"Kumano Mandala: The Three Sacred Shrines."
Color on silk, 52¾″ x 24⅜″.
The Cleveland Museum of Art (John L. Severance Fund).

FIGURE 14-7

John Constable (1776–1837; English).
Detail of "Poplars by a Stream."
Pencil. *Henry E. Huntington Library and Art Gallery,
San Marino, California.* See Figure 7–14.

contrasts also diminish and gradually assume the bluish color of the air, but this too is more a concern of the painter than of the draftsman.)

Chiaroscuro and Form

In addition to the systematic use of linear and aerial perspective to establish the major relationships of forms in deep space, the Renaissance artists also developed a methodical use of changes in value to describe the way light and shadow model three-dimensional forms. Observation of the central figure in the chalk study for the "Wedding Feast of Cupid and Psyche" (Figure 14–8), reveals the typical broad chiaroscuro of the High Renaissance, with its clearly defined areas of light, shadow, reflected light (light cast back into the shade area by surrounding surfaces which illuminates the movement of form within the shadow), and cast shadow. Cast shadow is the shadow thrown by a solid object upon a nearby plane (in this case the shadow cast by the arm against the side of the body, commencing at the armpit and continuing down the thigh). By his systematic use of chiaroscuro, Raphael described the full complexity of the body form in a most convincing manner.

When an object is shiny, a fifth element helps to describe form, the highlight. The highlight is a clearly defined reflection of the source of light which occurs on the crest of a smooth or shiny surface, and accents the sense of volume sharply. Another area that escapes the untrained eye but becomes a part of the value system used to describe form is the "core" of darkness that establishes the division between the "light" and "shade." This core of darkness which lies between the light and the reflected light and separates the fundamental planes of the form can be clearly seen in the Raphael drawing running down the arm from shoulder muscle to armpit, down the back from shoulder blade to hip and is defined with great clarity in the rounded form of the buttock and the full cylinder of the thigh. To summarize, the repertoire of elements used systematically from Renaissance to modern times to describe form as it is revealed by light and shadow are (1) light, (2) highlight, (3) shadow, (4) core of shadow, (5) reflected light, and (6) cast shadow (Figure 14–9). In this system, if it can be so called, the highlight was kept almost white and the

FIGURE 14–8

Raphael (Raffaello Santi, 1483–1520; Italian) or Giulio Romano (1492–1546). Detail of "The Wedding Feast of Cupid and Psyche." Red chalk. The Royal Library, Windsor Castle, England. *Reproduced by gracious permission of Her Majesty Queen Elizabeth II.* See Figure 3–16.

most recessed areas in the shade and the cast shadow were closest to black. These conventions for conveying form, beautifully shown, though without highlights, in Lorenzo di Credi's "Allegory for Astronomy" (Figure 14–10), subsequently provided the basis for the brilliant personal styles of rendering form employed by most baroque artists permitting as wide a range of style as exists between Rubens, Rembrandt, Tiepolo, Goya, and Boucher, to name but a few.

Schematic Form

It was Cézanne, more than any painter, who violated the conventional perspective system developed in the Renaissance so that he could introduce new observations as to the nature of both natural and pictorial space. He also employed other fresh innovations to convey his perceptions about form in drawing and painting. A study by Cézanne from Houdon's "Écorché" (Figure 13–12) reveals none of the conventional means we have just discussed for suggesting form. Instead of chiaroscuro, this drawing conveys the sense of three-dimensional solidity through rather arbitrary indications of structure. The complex anatomical forms of the human figure were translated into semigeometrical equivalents, the buttocks becoming partial spheres, the thighs tapered cylinders, and the hollow between the tendons behind the knee became triangles. Other artists before Cézanne had employed an almost diagrammatic indication of structure to convey a sense of solid form. In the fascinating pencil study made by Charles Meryon for his etching of "Le Stryge" (Figure 14–11), the drawing of the gargoyle clearly displays a tendency to see the form in planes and to convey this by stressing the way the chiaroscuro reveals these planes. Cézanne went farther and initiated a concept which rejected the use of chiaroscuro and conveyed a sense of form purely through schematic indications of these structurally simplified planes.

The various developments that subsequently grew from Cézanne's methods have already been touched on in Chapter 5. "Street in Quebec" by Preston Dickinson (Figure 14–12) retains Cézanne's tendency to limit space distort perspective, and facet form, but he reinforces Cézanne's innovations with elements of conventional chiaroscuro; one might say that he incorporates Cézanne's innovations into more traditional concepts. The opposite is the case in Duchamp's "Study for the Virgin" (Figure 10–7). Here the sense of form is intellectual, schematic, and consciously relates to a flat surface rather than to the three-dimensional external world, and in this sense is "pure," rather than imitative. Such an approach, which freed artists from their concern with describing the real world about them, encouraged painters to be inventive in their disposition of art elements rather than imitative of natural phenomena, and thus opened up endless new vistas.

There are a number of devices that create visual illusions and many artists enjoy playing with them, thereby entertaining the spectator. One such device is the use of spaced lines arranged regularly to create graduated values and placed in a context that suggests familiar forms. Skillfully done, this can create a remarkable sense of space and three-dimensional solidity. Hardy Hanson is the author of an unusually intriguing and evocative drawing titled "Landscape of the Ancients" (Figure 14–13) in which the wavering horizontal lines suggest undulating hills with illuminated swells and shadowy valleys. Vertical lines play against the horizontals and the verticals in turn create projecting and receding columnar forms of considerable magnitude. In "Landscape of the Ancients" the vibrato character of the lines adds an element related to aerial perspective and as a consequence the dark grays between the buttresses recede far into the distance.

We have just seen how the changes of value across a surface suggest the flow of light over the surface and reveal its planes, projections, and hollows. "Two

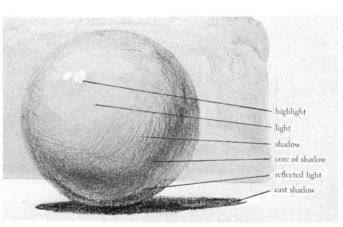

FIGURE 14-9
Sphere Illustrating Light and Shadow System.

highlight
light
shadow
core of shadow
reflected light
cast shadow

FIGURE 14–10

Lorenzo di Credi (1459–1537; Italian).
"Allegory for Astronomy." Drawn in black
chalk continued with brush and sepia,
heightened with white, 15½" x 10¼".
The Uffizi Gallery, Florence
(Alinari-Art Reference Bureau).

Soldiers Playing Checkers" by Gérôme through its careful modulations of dark and light, conveys very precise information about the shape and space relationships of the people and objects shown in the picture (Figure 14-14). Though the Gérôme drawing conveys form and space with clarity it neither elicits emotion nor does it project a powerful sense of volume and deep space. As a consequence it seems inconsequential even though it is brilliant technically. A detail from Michelangelo's "The Archers" (Figure 14-15) provides an instructive contrast. Both because of the grand idealizations of the human figure, the rhythmic repetitions of compositional line movements, and the effects of aerial perspective conveyed by the diminishing contrasts of dark and light which occur as the eye moves into depth, the Michelangelo drawing radiates a monumental sense of volume and space, as powerful in its implications of plastic grandeur as are his idealized bodies. It was consonant with High Renaissance ideals to create an esthetic world which in its physical splendor and magnitude could convey the potential for moral and social order within mankind, a magnitude echoed by the vast hierarchical structure of the church and symbolized architectually, above all else, by the vastness of St. Peter's in Rome.

FIGURE 14–11

Charles Meryon (1821–1868; French).
"Le Stryge (The Chimera and the Tower of St. Jacques)."
Pencil, 7⅞" x 5⅞".
*Courtesy of the Sterling and Francine Clark
Art Institute, Williamstown, Massachussetts.*

FIGURE 14–12

Preston Dickinson
(1891–1930; American).
"Street in Quebec."
Water color, 18¹⁵⁄₁₆" x 13¾".
In The Brooklyn Museum Collection.

Pattern

Flat, unmodulated surfaces carry as pattern, rather than as form. We see the shape of the area, are conscious of its silhouette, but the sense of volume is minimized. As the sense of space and form disappear, the decorative character of pattern becomes more evident, one's attention concentrates on shape relationships rather than on seeing the implied three-dimensional complexities. This can be observed in the facsimile of a rock painting, "A Fight Apparently for the Possession of a Bull," from Khargur Tahl, in the Libyan Desert (Figure 2–4),

FIGURE 14–13
Hardy Hanson (1932–   ; American). "Landscape of the Ancients." (1963) Ink drawing, 3¾" x 5½". *Rex Evans Gallery, Los Angeles, California.*

which is the pictorial opposite of the Michelangelo. There is almost no sense of solidity or volume in the forms and only a slight sense of space. Because, as has been previously noted, we tend to read down in a picture as close and up as distant, and because in this particular drawing the upper right-hand figure appears smaller than the others, there is a slight feeling of the foreground being closer to the observer than the distance. When areas overlap, a very limited sense of front and behind is conveyed.

When areas of flat value are bounded by outlines, rather than being silhouettes, a greater feeling of volume and space result. Thus, in the Beardsley pen-and-ink sketch "J'ai Baise ta Bouche, Jokanaan" (Figure 8–12), the overlappings of form are more repeated and complex than in the Libyan rock painting, and the outlines which separate areas from one another increase the sense of "front" and "back." Also, the occasional modulations in the width of outlines, as in the folds of Salome's robe, suggest form. The sense of form is nonetheless not sufficiently great to overwhelm the flat-patterned decorative appeal.

Like the Beardsley illustrations for Salome, "The Doorbell" by Matt Kahn (Figure 14–16) achieves much of its effectiveness from its decorative, flat-patterned character. Unlike the *art-nouveau*, turn-of-the-century illustration where flat patterning results from the elimination of form and space, "The Doorbell" uses the flatness of its surfaces positively. The picture plane is utilized as a means of achieving the maximum vigor of all of its parts. Thus, as one's eye moves across the surface, the energy of the various shapes results from the conscious manipulations of tone to create contrasts of the maximum brilliance. Where line is used it is not employed as outline (to separate the boundaries of three-dimensional masses) but instead, as linear entities which contrast with broader areas of black, white, or gray, or as sharp edges which contrast with soft-edged grays. Thus the flat character of this drawing consciously derives from the contemporary tendency to compose pictorial space independently of older concepts of perspective and aerial space. Much of this was implied by the Beardsley drawing, but the full implications of it were not realized.

Contrasts of Value

The same drawing, "The Doorbell," provides an excellent vehicle for launching into a more detailed discussion of value, somewhat independent of its role in relation to form and space. In Chapter 1, *value* was defined as "the range of possible darkness and lightness that exists between black and white, black representing the greatest possible degree of darkness, white the maximum light." One of the remarkable aspects of "The Doorbell" is its brilliance of

FIGURE 14-14

Jean-Leon Gérôme (1824–1904; French). "Two Soldiers Playing Checkers."
Black and red chalk, heightened with white, 7¾" x 10¹³⁄₁₆".
Courtesy of the Sterling and Francine Clark Art Institute, Williamstown, Massachussetts.

FIGURE 14–15
Michelangelo Buonarroti (1475–1564; Italian).
Detail of "Archers Shooting at Mark."
Red chalk. The Royal Library, Windsor Castle, England.
Reproduced by gracious permission of Her Majesty Queen Elizabeth II. (See Figure 3–14.)

whiteness, blackness, and grayness. One senses that the artist, perhaps after repeated interruptions, had a heightened sensitivity to the impact of the jangling sound of a doorbell—of its sharpness, its unexpectedness, its insistent energy—and he translated this awareness into the most percussive value pattern he could invent.

If sharp contrasts of value provide the basis for achieving emphasis and create energetic and percussive effects, close value relationships in which contrasts are minimized are used to create effects of quiet, of soothing restfulness, or of introspection and restraint. Almost a complete opposite of "Doorbell" in terms of value relationships is "Maternity, Study for 'Surrealism and Painting'" by Max Ernst (Figure 12–1). Here there is not one sharp contrast or accent to disturb the prevailing sense of quietude. A general gray tone pervades the entire study; a feeling of a submerged, soundless, lightless world is created, with only the phosphorescent glow of the embryonic baby-bird form radiating beyond the sheltered gloom. The effect is much like that of a musical composition in which all sound is rendered pianissimo and there is little change of tempo. Though very different in subject, the same feeling of hushed quiet pervades Whistler's "Venetian Canal" (Figure 16–17). Executed in pastel

328 / THE ART ELEMENTS

on gray paper, the soft crumbly lines and tones create no strident accents. A generally light value prevails through most of the sketch, the paler tones of the sky filter down on the buildings relieved only by the soft-edged smudges of dark. The same all-prevailing sense of quietude characterizes "Rembrandt's Studio" (Figure 14–17), and here also, no sharp contrasts of value disturb the generally prevailing grayness.

Darkness is in general synonymous with night in our thinking and feeling, night with its mystery and its overtones of fright. Perhaps an inevitable hangover from childhood is the fear of the dark, the frightening and impenetrable void that surrounds a child at night during moments of wakefulness, peopled with his fears and without the reassuring familiar contacts of daytime. Whatever the basis for the fearful mystery of darkness, artists have always been aware of its potential. No one has used value relationships more skillfully to establish a persuasive tone in his drawings and paintings than the French nineteenth-century Romantic, Odilon Redon. His "Human Rock (Idole)" (Figure 1–15), like the magic image created by a poetic figure of speech, depends upon the power of darkness to evoke mystery and fear. Strangely dreamlike, the almost unrelieved dark has, at first glance, little form. Upon closer examination a curious landscape is revealed. Against a low-lit sky a rocky cliff assumes the shape of a great head. What little light exists glitters on a jeweled headdress, an eye can barely be perceived staring into space. The great head merges into the landscape and in the foreground we perceive a dark pool of water, the faint line

Dark Values

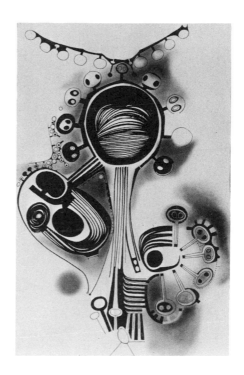

FIGURE 14–16

Matt Kahn (1928– ; American).
"The Doorbell."
Ink and charcoal, 14″ x 23″.
Collection of the Artist.

FIGURE 14–17

Rembrandt van Rijn
(1606–1669; Dutch).
"Rembrandt's Studio."
Wash, brush and pen, 8⅛″ x 7½″.
By courtesy of the Ashmolean Museum, Oxford.

of shore and a few low bushes. The same subject illuminated in the full light of day would probably appear ludicrous; certainly it would lose its strange magic. The evocative power of the ambiguous has been mentioned in the opening chapter, and darkness is a potent factor in creating ambiguity. Hervey Breverman's "Figure with Tallus VIII" (Figure 14–18) utilizes this particular potential of darkness with great effectiveness. The shawled praying figure stands silhouetted against the light. One's eye moves from the quiet explicit hand through the less clearly defined forms of the prayer shawl to the shadowed head in which the features can barely be distinguished. A sense of the rapt involvement of ritual, of the mystery of religious practice, is implied, not through specific illustrational elements but rather through the vague, amorphous, cloudy darkness which is intensified as attention moves up to culminate in the head.

An interesting contrast to "Figure with Tallus VIII" and "Human Rock" is provided by Courbet's "Self-Portrait" (Figure 7–13). This too is dependent for its effect upon the generally prevailing tone of dark, but in the Courbet drawing the light falls upon and reveals the major forms, and even the strongest darks are easily read as shadowed parts of the body or costume. In the two previous drawings the dark helps to obscure form, while in the Courbet it helps to define it. Thus, the prevailing atmosphere of the Courbet is logical rather than mysterious, and the strong dark with contrasting lights becomes the means for dramatic emphasis and through it the entire drawing is charged with a strong emotional tone.

Light Values

If black suggests night, darkness, mystery and fear, certainly white at the opposite end of the value scale is associated with illumination, clarity, and also suggests a rational and optimistic attitude toward life. Words like radiant, bright, clear, and shining all seem related to white, particularly when we think of white, not as the lightness of a flat piece of paper but rather as the reflection of intense illumination. Tiepolo's "Rest on the Flight into Egypt" (Figure 17–11) conveys this sense of dazzling illumination, of an all-pervasive light that dilutes the middle values and in which only the deepest recesses can hold their darks. As a result the effect of the drawing is buoyant and happy, so much so that the treatment can seem superficial or sentimental in relation to the subject and its eventual tragedy. If dramatic darks and bold contrasts characterized drawing and painting in the Baroque seventeenth century and the Romantic nineteenth century, light values were utilized to their fullest in the Rococo modes of the mid-eighteenth century. A "Reclining Nude" (Figure 14–19) by Boucher achieves remarkable solidity of form without any extended area of shadow. Though more conventional in technique and in the full development of its three-dimensional form than the dazzling Tiepolo drawing, Boucher retained the clear light tone preferred by the Italian master. The systematic use of white chalk hatchings with darker accents of red against the blonde tan of the paper created a remarkable solidity of form without any extended areas of dark. The erotic beauty of the figure, frank and without mystery, bathed in light, suggests the worldly atmosphere of a pleasure-loving aristocracy.

FIGURE 14–18
Hervey Breverman (1934–   ; American).
"Figure with Tallis VIII."
Charcoal, 31″ x 23¼″.
Ball State College Art Gallery,
Muncie, Indiana (Courtesy of
Mr. and Mrs. Martin D. Schwartz).

FIGURE 14-19

François Boucher (1703–1770; French).
"Reclining Nude." Red chalk, 12⁷⁄₁₆″ x 16⅜″.
Courtesy of the Fogg Art Museum, Harvard University Cambridge, Massachusetts
(Meta and Paul J. Sachs Collection).

Value Contrasts and Pictorial Emphasis

Contrasts of value provide one of the most effective means for accenting and emphasizing areas in a composition, and are used to reinforce the linear and spatial elements in building up a composition. Thus, by manipulating the degrees of lightness and darkness of the various parts, one can focus the viewer's attention upon parts of a composition according to their degrees of importance. This kind of pictorial emphasis was particularly important in narrative painting, where the demands of the story necessitated a clear organization of parts. An excellent example of this type of composition is provided by Sir David Wilkie's "Arrival of the Rich Relation" (Figure 17–6). The importance of the group of figures in toto was established by placing them as a light mass in front of the dark background. The most important single figure is the rich relation, whose white face and body was singled out by placing it in front of the darkest shadow and surmounting it by the light umbrella. Second in importance is the welcoming hostess. She and her surrounding entourage form a light mass, with her hair and features sharply accented as darks. The gentlemen extending a helping hand, the excited boy, and the two dogs, take their respective places as the tertiary elements in the composition. Because it all reads naturalistically, it is easy to overlook the skill and logic with which value relationships have been established. The use of value contrasts as focusing agents is also brilliantly displayed in van Ostade's "Peasants Dancing" (Figure 14–20) and in the study attributed to Caravaggio (Figure 4–1). The plan of the van Ostade is very simple. The two dancers are almost in silhouette against the flood of light that comes in through the open door, illuminating the group of watching fellow revelers. From the large L-shaped area of illumination, the values taper off to a medium gray at the top of the drawing and to darker grays in the lower corners. An overturned bench and wine jug at the lower left serve as a foil to keep the dark forms of the dancers from being too obvious. One can hardly conceive of a simpler value scheme, but the humor of the figures, the charm of the interior, and the spirited rendering make the drawing warm and alive. The Caravaggio study is more complex, with the two front-plane figures accented by the strongest darks, with the woman's head to the left of the seated man providing the culminating focus of the entire composition. This is achieved by framing the light mass with its bright notation of features against two strong darks and by making the head the culminating point for the flood of light that starts at the lower right-hand corner of the drawing and flows diagonally up in one big movement to the startled face. The potency of bold contrasts of value in creating a sense of drama is very evident in this same study. The use of large, almost unmodulated areas of contrasting values creates a theatrical atmosphere, just as the breadth and directness of rendering suggest that the execution of the drawing was impetuous and unhesitant, with the description of surface qualities being sacrificed to the impact of the whole. By contrast, the van Ostade suggests a tender and affectionate concern on the part of the artist with the surface subtleties of values and textures he is describing.

The effectiveness of increasing value contrasts to intensify the dramatic impact of a subject is also vividly illustrated by comparing two drawings by Edward Hopper, done as studies for his painting of the "Manhattan Bridge Loop" (Figures 12–9 and 14–21). The first study, probably relatively uncomposed and factual in both value and placement of parts, has a sketchy naturalism. There was no attempt made to do more than record the forms. The second drawing has a value pattern similar to that of the final painting. The darks have been intensified all through the sketch, thereby eliminating details of window pattern, moldings, and so on on the shadow side of the building. This adds to the importance of the illuminated façades of the three principal

FIGURE 14–20

Adriaen van Ostade (1610–1684; Dutch).
"Peasants Dancing." Black chalk, pen and brush with brown ink, 8⅜" x 6⅜".
Teyler Museum, Haarlem. Teylers Stichting Fotoverkoop.

FIGURE 14–21

Edward Hopper (1882–   ; American).
"Study for Manhattan Bridge Loop." Charcoal, 6" x 11".
Addison Gallery of American Art, Phillips Academy, Andover, Massachusetts.

buildings, and dramatizes the front sides of the structural-steel bridge support in the foreground. The impact of the drawing is intensified, a sense of the endless, vast, drab and yet mysterious life of a great city is suggested, the straight reporting gives way to the work of art. A final illustration of the dramatic power of contrast of dark and light is provided by the master of value relationships, Goya, in his drawing of "Sainted Culottes" (Figure 14–22). The starkness of the tonal contrasts creates a work with an unforgettable impact, yet its impact does not make it obvious. The shadowed face, with only the tip of the nose catching the light, is powerful in its evocative mystery: one is free to read into it any features one desires.

Summary

The term *value* describes relationships of light and dark, white being the lightest possible value, black the darkest, with grays providing the intermediary steps in the value scale. Every object has a three-dimensional form, and the flow of light across an object creates a range of values which reveal that form, since illuminated surfaces that catch the light become lightest in value while recessed areas that fall into shadow become darkest. Space is the distance between forms.

Linear perspective is a system devised in Renaissance times for projecting an illusion of form and space on a flat picture plane. Three basic elements of perspective which relate to the perception of depth in space are (1) diminishing sizes, (2) overlapping forms, and (3) lines converging to vanishing points. Other systems than linear perspective for suggesting space in pictorial terms are tiered space and isometric perspective. Aerial perspective describes the diminishing contrasts in value that occur as objects recede into the distance. In addition to the systematic use of perspective, Renaissance artists developed a methodical use of chiaroscuro (changes in value) to describe form. The chief elements in this system are light, shadow, reflected light, and cast shadow. Two additional refinements of the system, the highlight and the core of the shadow, can also be identified.

Many contemporary artists, following the suggestions inherent in Cézanne's work, use schematic and diagrammatic indications of space which preserve the identity of the picture plane in preference to the illusion of depth preferred by Renaissance and Baroque tradition. Flat unmodulated areas of value carry as pattern rather than as form and as the sense of form is diminished the decorative character of patterning is intensified. Bold contrasts of dark and light create dynamic and dramatic effects, close relationships of value suggest quiet and restraint. Dominantly dark values suggest mystery, night, and have pessimistic overtones, dominantly light value schemes relate to daytime, illumination, and create a mood of euphoria. Contrasts of dark and light provide a familiar compositional device to focus attention on certain areas.

FIGURE 14–22

Francisco Goya (1746–1828; Spanish).
"Sainted Culottes."
Wash, brush and ink, approximately 5″ x 8″.
Museo del Prado, Madrid.

15

TEXTURE

Three factors determine the textural character of a drawing. First, in those works concerned with picturing objects there is the surface quality of the objects represented. Second, there are the textures inherent in the artist's materials: coarse chalk on rough paper (Figure 15–1) as contrasted to fine pencil on smooth paper (Figure 15–5). Third, there is the suggestion of roughness or smoothness that results from the artist's manner of work. The Van Gogh drawing "The Bridge at L'Anglois" (Figure 15–2) has a rough scratchy look that is neither inherent in the subject nor in the medium of pen and ink but rather results from Van Gogh's intense and impetuous way of working. An interesting comparison is offered by "Head of a Man" (Figure 15–3) by Alphonse Legros in which the drawing reveals little difference between the textures of skin, hair, eyeball, and so on, but the dominant texture in the drawing is established by the artist's controlled and orderly procedures. The textural differences between the Van Gogh and Legros drawings are essentially the result of differences in artistic personality.

FIGURE 15–1

Käthe Kollwitz (1867–1945; German). "Head of a Woman."
Black chalk with touches of white and pale tan chalk, 16″ x 12⅝″.
Courtesy of The Art Institute of Chicago (Herman Waldeck Memorial Fund).

FIGURE 15–2

Vincent van Gogh (1853–1890; Dutch-French).
"The Bridge at L'Anglois." China ink, 9½" x 12½".
Los Angeles County Museum of Art
(*The Mr. and Mrs. George Gard De Sylva Fund*).

A fine example of a drawing which derives its textural interest primarily
from the effectiveness with which the surface qualities of its subject matter are
described can be seen in the "Portrait of Docteur Robin" by Ingres (Figure
16–8). One is made very aware of the various qualities of the surfaces
represented in the drawing; the solid smoothness of skin, the soft fibrous
character of the sitter's wavy hair, the feltlike mat surface of the material of the
topcoat, and the roughness of distant tiled roofs. In the early nineteenth century
a number of artists developed a pen-and-ink technique in which the chief
discipline was directed toward describing surface textures. In "Weinberg,
Olevano" (Figure 7–6), Heinrich Reinhold was most concerned with describing
the roughness of weathered wood, the soft grassy slopes, the rich masses of
foliage and the general surface feel of the out-of-doors.

The second factor that was mentioned as contributing to esthetically effective texture in drawing is the actual texture of the artist's materials. The graininess or smoothness of paper, charcoal, pencil or chalk, the stiffness or softness of brush, the flexibility or rigidity of pen; these are all factors that contribute textural character and so provide visual richness and interest or the lack of these qualities. Had the "Self Portrait" by Käthe Kollwitz been done with pencil on smooth paper it would inevitably have had a different character.

The third factor mentioned as determining the textural character of a work of art is the personality (artistic) of the artist. This is the most significant of the three determinants because the artist's temperament determines what is drawn, what aspect of the subject will be stressed, and what materials will be used. It is the artist's deftness of finger, the impetuosity or deliberation with which he works, his tastes, and his esthetic beliefs which transmute both materials and subject. The freedom or caution with which the medium is applied to paper, the degree to which hands and body are relaxed, all of these expressions of inner tension or harmonious calm as well as his intellectual convictions and esthetic tastes work together to form an artist's mature style; and each artist's style had its textural character.

FIGURE 15–3

Alphonse Legros (1837–1911; French). "Head of a Man." Silverpoint, 8¾" x 7". *The Metropolitan Museum of Art, New York (Gift of the Artist, 1892).*

Perception of Multiple Units as Texture

Modern students of the psychology of perception have observed that we see similar things as making up a unit. Thus, when we look at a tree, we are not aware of the hundreds of leaves that make up the tree, but rather fuse them into a single visual entity. Although in the physical act of seeing the cornea of the eye records all the leaves that make up the tree, the mind tends to group these many leaves into units and to identify such units as wholes—in other words, a cluster of leaves becomes a tree. Even elements which we ordinarily do not see as part of a larger configuration, such as people or automobiles, when seen in large numbers are seen as a unit; witness the way in which the people in a stadium or the cars parked around the stadium during a football game are seen as a tonal mass that fills a certain area.

At the same time, when observing objects we remain aware that a process of fusion has taken place and though we see a tonal mass when we look at leaves on a tree or people in a football stadium we see it as having a certain textural character. In rendering a surface, an artist tends to suggest something of that textural character by wiggling the hand, stippling, making lines, splotches, or using any other measures that appropriately suggest the proper surface quality. In reading the drawing, the same process is at work as occurred when the artist observed his subject. Thus, in viewing a drawing, we see groups of related lines, dots, or splotches as values which suggest forms having a certain surface character. For instance, densely packed parallel lines create the effect of a smooth surface, as can be seen in the hair and shimmering satin in Degas' pencil study for the "Portrait of Julie Burtin" (Figure 15–5) or in the hilly forms in Hanson's "Landscape of the Ancients" (Figure 14–13). By contrast, in "Rocky Landscape, Death Valley" the boldly rendered irregular bumpy lines suggest the chaotic surface of scattered rocks on the desert.

Tones built up through carefully placed lines or dots of even width, such as are frequently used in engraving or in certain kinds of pen and ink drawings, provide an almost mechanically smooth tone which can be most effective in conveying accurate description of form. This technique has been carried to a remarkable level of effectiveness by scientific illustrators, who desire an objective description of the facts of appearance uncolored by an awareness of the artist's personality or the nature of the materials being used. Such an objective rendering of fact can be seen in a detail of "Prionotus Ruscarius" by Chloe Lesley Starks (Figure 15–6). Here one is made visually aware of the surface form and texture of the fish, but the observer remains unaware of the artist or media. It is only when seen greatly enlarged that the remarkably textural aspect of this drawing is evident and that one begins to sense the performance of the artist and the nature of the media used in the drawing.

FIGURE 15–5

Edgar Degas (1834–1917; French). "Study for a Portrait of Madame Julie Burtin." Pencil, 14¼" x 10¾". *Courtesy of the Fogg Art Museum, Harvard University, Cambridge, Massachusetts (Meta and Paul J. Sachs Collection).*

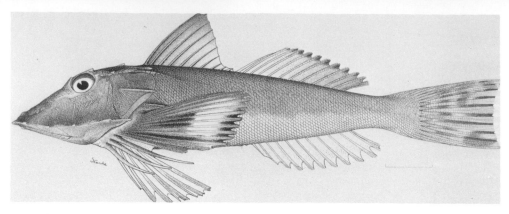

FIGURE 15–6

Chloe Lesley Starks
(1866–1952; American).
"Prionatus Ruscarius."
Ink, 3½" x 7". Detail (below).
*Collection of Mrs. Willis Rich,
Menlo Park, California.*

The Disciplined Texture

As stated before, media do much to determine the textural character of a drawing. The pen and ink and smooth paper used by Chloe Lesley Starks in "Prionotus Ruscarius" leaves no rough burr on the edges of lines or dots, and so contributes greatly to the desired smoothness of texture and impersonality of handling. Coarse chalk or charcoal on rough paper provides a heavy graininess of surface which precludes a fine finish and encourages a direct impetuous manner. Each medium also has a tradition and certain conventions which influence its use.

The sixteenth-century techniques for using those drawing media which produce clean-cut lines without any softening of edges or blurring of tones, pen and ink and silverpoint for instance, were strongly influenced by the technical demands of wood-cutting and engraving; in fact, the use of these media originated largely in the making of preliminary studies which would later be turned into prints. Because pen and ink and silverpoint produced sharp, clean-cut lines of even width such as were incised by gravers and wood-cutting tools, drawings made in these media could easily be engraved in wood or metal by skilled technicians. Therefore, the conventions of engraving had a decided influence upon the drawing techniques used in Northern Europe in the late Middle Ages and early Renaissance times. The skill and resourcefulness of German and Flemish draftsmen in using such intractable media as pen and ink and silverpoint in a flexible way can be observed in the drawings of many men; and particularly admirable is the way in which rich and varied textural qualities were achieved through the use of a wide variety of graphic devices. Two master drawings provide an excellent example of this skill. A copy of Hugo van der Goes' "Lamentation," attributed to Pieter Brueghel (Figure 15–7), executed in brown ink over a stylus preparation, reveals the resourcefulness with which the rigidity of pen and ink was overcome by using stippling, cross-hatching, sets of

344

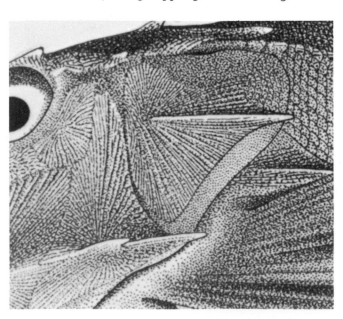

parallel lines either straight or curved, and combinations of these various devices, to describe a wide variety of forms and surfaces and to create a pictorial texture of great richness.

Albrecht Dürer is equally impressive as an artist and as a technician; certainly his skill and inventiveness with the engraver's tools have never been surpassed. Much of his experience as an engraver is reflected in the powerful way he described the texture of old age in his compelling "Portrait of a Ninety-Three-Year-Old Man" (Figure 15–8). Executed in India ink and opaque white on a greyish-violet paper, the clusters of curved lines of varying length move in all directions to describe swirling hair, bushy brows, crinkled skin, swellings, hollows, and many other aspects of surface and form. Aside from the remarkable force of the drawing as a study of character, it remains overwhelming as a pure example of technical virtuosity. The certainty with which the lines move together or change direction, the changes in length and width of line, the brilliant use of the middle value ground so that it serves as a continuous support

FIGURE 15–7

Pieter Brueghel, the Elder (1525/30–1569; Flemish) or Hugo van der Goes (1440?–1483). "The Lamentation." Pen and brown ink over stylus preparation, 5½" x 7¼". *Albertina, Vienna.*

for both the light and dark lines, provide an inspiring source of study for the student of textures. Both drawings share one common trait; they employ a disciplined technique to describe a series of highly differentiated textured surfaces.

The Uniform Texture

These two drawings can be profitably contrasted with another type of drawing in which a very disciplined technique is used to create a surface in which there is almost no differentiation of textures and the interest of the drawing is to a large extent the result of the style established by maintaining a uniform texture throughout. Seurat made many drawings of this type (Figures 8–11, 16–20) and his influence is strongly felt in Theophile van Rysselberghe's drawing of "Marie van der Velde at the Piano" (Figure 15–9). The conté crayon has been applied in short sharp lines, some straight, some slightly curved, which range in value from rather light crumbly to dark sharp-edged lines. These lines build together to create a uniform texture in values ranging from very dark to almost white of great surface vitality. Much of the distinction of the drawing comes from the fact that the manner of rendering creates its own texture and the artist does not attempt to describe the surface quality of the objects he pictures. In this respect it functions in accordance with the precepts of the Impressionists who were more concerned with the texture of the painting than with the texture of the objects painted and who consequently made the method of applying media an important stylistic, even abstract element in picture making.

The Freely Rendered Texture

An interesting contrast to a consciously controlled and maintained texture like that used by Van Rysselberghe is the texture of "Bank of a Pond" by Rudolph Bresdin (Figure 15–10). Bresdin's pen and ink lines are freely sketched, with unstilted movements that seem to follow the artist's eye and hand in all directions. Clusters of almost parallel straight lines, radial groupings of straight and circular lines, irregular concentric clusters of lines, and many other combinations can be seen in this drawing, each particular kind of line scheme suggesting a surface direction or a surface quality, while single lines define contours or separate areas from one another. Unlike the Dürer drawing,

FIGURE 15–9

Théophile van Rysselberghe (1862–1926; Belgian).
"Maria van der Velde at the Piano."
Conté crayon, 12½" x 14⅛".
Courtesy of The Art Institute of Chicago (John H. Wrenn Fund Income).

which is consistent throughout in the way in which the sets of parallel lines follow surface directions, or the Van Rysselberghe drawing in which one consistent texture is maintained throughout the drawing irrespective of the nature of the surface being described, the Bresdin drawing shows no set scheme for applying pen lines. Its stylistic unity is maintained by the consistency with which a variety of visual perceptions were translated into freely executed scribbles, all of about the same degree of openness and density.

FIGURE 15–10

Rodolphe Bresdin (1822–1885; French). "Bank of a Pond." Pen and India ink, 6⁷⁄₁₆″ x 6¹¹⁄₁₆″. *Courtesy of The Art Institute of Chicago (Gift of the Print and Drawing Club).*

FIGURE 15–11

Honoré Daumier (1808–1879; French).
"A Clown." Charcoal and
water color, 14⅜" x 10".
The Metropolitan Museum of Art, New York
(Rogers Fund, 1927).

FIGURE 15–12

Henri Matisse (1869–1954; French).
"Figure Study." Pen and ink, 10⅜" x 8".
Collection, The Museum of Modern Art,
New York (Gift of Edward Steichen).

Texture as the Gesture of Rendering

As we said before, it is the interaction of man and medium which establishes the textural character of each artist's work; we might more wisely say, the "textural personality" or even the "textural handwriting," for the characterizing texture of each artist's work is a most subtle blend of elements, easier to recognize than to analyze and translate into words. Daumier, for instance, frequently drew with swirling lines which interlace and overlap in what at first glance seems a completely random and accidental way (Figure 15–11). Further analysis reveals that Daumier's sense of the dynamics of movement interplaying with his sense of form enabled him to relate these tangles of line so that they assemble into readable images that are both solid and pulsing with life. The free movements with which he drew had a basis in both his physical and emotional exuberance. Work undoubtedly excited him. From this physical and emotional matrix a dynamic texture was created that was shaped by his eye and mind into the forms suited to his needs. An artist like Daumier would select media which encouraged free and rapid movements; chalk, charcoal, and wash served him well, and he used them with assurance and vigor. The academic refinements of his day bored him or he would have used them. His lithographs provide ample evidence that had smoothness of finish been his goal, he could have competed with the foremost academicians of his day, but in the drawings he did for his own pleasure he cast aside all artificial restraints and gave expression to the innermost demands of his nature.

In his early years Matisse produced many drawings and paintings which were characterized by an Expressionist urgency. One of his early "Figure Studies" (Figure 15–12) done before 1910 reveals an agitated angularity in the rhythm of the pen strokes that is difficult to reconcile with the decorative urbanity of his later manner. A coarse pen has been applied in intense, sharp jabs to create a dynamic surface that radiates energy and youthful turbulence. The suggestions of tension and conflict suggested here is far removed from the exuberance of the Daumier drawing with its rich flowing vigor.

Both the drawing by Daumier and that by Matisse have one thing in common: each represents the direct unpremeditated performance by an artist in a rapidly executed work in which vigor of expression is valued above refinement of execution. By way of contrast, let us turn our attention to a detail from the Li Ch'eng "Buddhist Temple Amid Clearing Mountain Peaks" (Figure 15–13). The painting was executed in ink upon silk, and the smooth, luminous, and absorbent ground of the silk contributes an initial refinement of surface that influences the subsequent execution. In this grand landscape one sees a high level of technical proficiency in manipulating the brush and ink in interaction with an old and highly developed esthetic tradition in which specific ways of depicting trees, rocks, waterfalls, temples and all the other elements of a picture have evolved over a long period of time. The artist is a dispassionate but very sensitive instrument through which the elaborate conventions of Chinese culture are transmitted, elaborated, and further refined. And unlike Daumier and Van Gogh, the artist seems not to be close to his subject physically or

FIGURE 15–13. Li Ch'eng (Ying-ch'iu c.940–967; Chinese). Detail of "Buddhist Temple Amid Clearing Mountain Peaks." Ink and slight color on silk, *Courtesy of the Nelson Gallery, Atkins Museum (Nelson Fund), Kansas City, Mo.* (See Figure 9–1.)

emotionally, but rather to regard it from a remote pinnacle of philosophic detachment. Van Gogh seems to feel each surface he describes in physical terms; he empathizes with each roughness, smoothness, as well as each movement under the surface. Li Ch'eng seems too emotionally remote from the surfaces to feel them; instead, he sees each surface as a beautiful pattern, rich, varied, and complex, and his hand is the obedient servant of his mind. The texture becomes a texture pattern, a texture pattern which seems to transmute the harshness of reality into visual harmony.

Media and Texture

Charcoal became popular during the Renaissance for making large studies for mural projects. Except among late nineteenth-century academicians, who took a perverse delight in making the media perform as a colorless servant, charcoal has been popular primarily because of the freedom it permits, since it enables an artist to work without undue concern over niceties of technique, encouraging him to make fresh vigorous drawings uninhibited by cautious procedures. "Seated Figure" by Elmer Bischoff (Figure 16–3) falls into this category. The medium is used with directness and vigor, and the result is as fresh as colloquial speech. The rich heavy grain that results when compressed charcoal is used on rough paper creates a vibrant alive surface which is only modulated in a few spots where the charcoal has been blurred with the fingers to describe the soft roundness of the body. A very different kind of pleasure results from observing a work where there has been a conscious exploration of the textural potentialities of charcoal as a medium. Calvin Albert's "Ritual" (Figure 15–14) is at first glance deceptive, for the direct quality of the surface textures suggests less calculation than is revealed by closer examination. With careful study of the detail of the drawing, one can discern a full and conscious exploitation of the potentialities of charcoal. Various roughnesses of grainy surface, smooth gradations, sharp lines, blurred tones, and clean erasures create a visual texture-banquet of pleasing variety. The full drawing (Figure 10–8) reveals the thoughtful distribution of these elements throughout the composition.

Even a medium which we think of as intractable such as ink, can be used in sufficiently varied ways to provide for textural variety and interest. William Gropper's "Farmers' Revolt" (Figure 12–4), though formalized into an almost

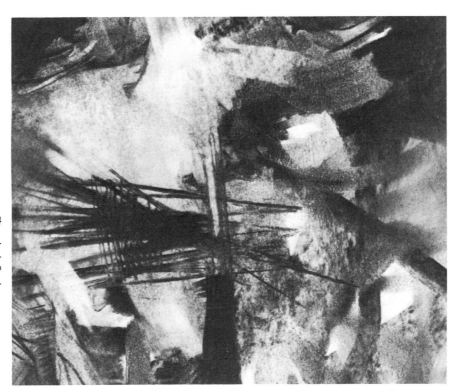

FIGURE 15–14

Calvin Albert (1918– ; American). Detail of "Ritual." Charcoal. Courtesy of The Art Institute of Chicago (Art Institute Purchase Fund). (See Figure 10–8.)

FIGURE 15–15

George Grosz (1893–1959; German-American). "The Survivor." Pen and India ink, 19" x 25".
Courtesy of The Art Institute of Chicago (Gift of the Print and Drawing Club).

Fernand Léger (1881–1955; French). Study for "The Divers." Pencil, pen and ink, and ink wash, 12″ x 17⅔″. Courtesy of The Art Institute of Chicago (Gift of Tiffany and Margaret Blake).

FIGURE 15–17
Bartholomeus Breenbergh (1599–1659; Dutch).
"Roman Ruins." Pen, brown ink and brown wash,
10½″ x 7⅝″.
The Metropolitan Museum of Art, New York (Rogers Fund, 1960).

posterlike simplicity, shows solid values, dry-brushed gradations, sprayed texture, white scratched-out lines, cross-hatchings and various combinations of these elements. "The Survivor" (Figure 15–15) by George Grosz is frankly sketchy and without the formalistic restraints that distinguish the Gropper drawing. However, the inventive turn of George Grosz is equal to the demands of his sensitive eye. Ragged lines, smooth lines, sets of parallel straight lines, groups of curved lines, cross-hatching, dry bush, and ink patterns made by pressing a textured material wet with ink against the paper, are a few of the devices he has employed to create a surface of enviable variety and vitality.

Media are frequently combined to increase the textural effects in a work of art, for variety is a basic principle in the arts, essential for the creation of interest, contrast and emphasis. Just as a cook, in preparing a salad, dessert or an entire meal, contrasts the crisp and the smooth, the hard and the soft, the tangy and the bland, so an artist finds a work of art monotonous which maintains a uniform texture throughout. In a "Study of Trees" by Claude Lorrain (Figure 6–8), the crisp lines of pen and ink contrast with the soft blurred splotches of

FIGURE 15–18

Duane Wakeham (1931–   ; American). "Trees and Foliage." Colored inks, wash, sponge and pen, 9½" x 11". *Courtesy of Richard Sutherland.*

FIGURE 15–19

Domenico Mundo (–1806; Italian).
"Study for Bacchus and Ariadne."
Wash, gouache and ink, 12″ x 18″.
Collection of Dr. Robert Prentice.

wash, like crust and custard in a dessert, to produce a drawing with great surface variety which also suggests something of the range of nature's surfaces from rough to smooth and hard to soft. In Fernand Léger's study for "The Divers" (Figure 15–16), pencil, pen and ink, and ink wash again provide for contrasting textures. In this drawing the hard ink lines are cross-hatched or scribbled in free patterns, the washes are fluid and soft, and the pencil hatchings provide a transition between the two. Unlike the Claude Lorrain drawing, which suggests nature's textures, the Léger textures are designed to be regularly repeated as pattern elements in the composition, with little relation to the surface qualities of the objects depicted in the drawings.

Bartholomeus Breenberg's drawing, "Roman Ruins" (Figure 15–17), also in pen, ink and wash, used the pen textures more extensively than either of the two previously noted drawings and with more variety to describe brick, stone, grass, broken plaster, and shrubbery. In many areas Breenberg has permitted the pen lines to touch the washed areas while the wash is still wet, thereby providing a transitional texture which fuses the wash and the dry lines into a unit. Duane Wakeham has used pen lines, brushed textures and sponged stipplings to exploit the transparency of colored inks in his animated and charming drawing of "Trees and Foliage" (Figure 15–18). The textures and lines move in eccentric and circuitous ways with angular, curved and crinkled lines reinforcing the softer brush marks and unpredictable sponged stipplings. The varied textures create an illusion of the endless complexity, variety and movement of nature's arboreal surfaces without attempting to duplicate the involved leaf and branch patterns in a literal manner.

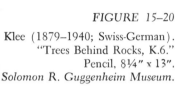

FIGURE 15–20
Klee (1879–1940; Swiss-German).
"Trees Behind Rocks, K.6."
Pencil, 8¼" x 13".
Solomon R. Guggenheim Museum.

Among the most interesting of textures are those created by age. The eroded oft-repainted walls of ancient buildings, the flaked and worn surfaces of old paintings, the patina on bronzes which have been buried for centuries, all have rich and interesting surfaces that cannot be rivaled for complexity and subtlety. In the same way many old drawings, enriched by discoloration, foxing (the brownish-yellow spots that appear on paper), the flaking of paint and the rubbing of soft lines have a surface complexity that adds greatly to their interest. Dominico Mundo, a painter who worked in Naples in the late eighteenth, early nineteenth centuries has left us a "Study for Bacchus and Ariadne" (Figure 15–19), executed in wash, gouache, and ink. The drawing was executed in soft painterly lines and roughly brushed areas of gray. Occasional short jagged accents have been added in ink. The original drawing must have had a rich complexity of surface, crumbly and rough in feeling with no clear simple system evident in the application of the media. The animated surfaces thus created have been augmented by time, the crumbly gouache having flaked off in places to add an element of ambiguity to the already irresolute manner.

Much of the genius of Paul Klee lay in his ingenuity in exploiting the textural qualities of various media and materials to evoke a poetic image or create a sensuously pleasing surface. In "Trees Behind Rocks" (Figure 15–20) he has created a number of contrasting textures through his sensitive application of pencil. Pencil lines which are for the most part sharp-edged but which occasionally fade into a softer tone define the rocky facets with a Cubistlike pattern. A contrasting visual obligato has been created by using the flat side of the lead to produce a variety of soft-textured patterns, no two of which are alike. Surfaces of still another character are suggested by the longer wavy lines used in the trees and the short scattered flakes of tone in the sky. Each effect is lovely in itself and at the same time evokes the poetry of landscape surfaces.

Summary   Texture refers to the tactile qualities, the suggestions of roughness or smoothness, inherent in a drawing. Three primary factors determine the textural character of a drawing: (1) the surface qualities of the subject, (2) the media and materials used in the rendering, and (3) the personality of the artist.

Studies of perception have revealed that we see similar things as making up a larger unit; that is, though the eye sees the many leaves of a tree, except where special interest directs attention to the individual leaves, the mind identifies the multitude of leaves as a single tree. As we represent such a form in drawing we suggest the multiple elements that make up the form as a texture and in reading the drawing we tend to reverse the procedure and read the drawn texture as multiple units. In certain very controlled and systematic styles of rendering both the sense of the media and of the act of drawing remain anonymous, and in viewing the drawing one is primarily aware of the form described and of its surface quality. Such a control of the descriptive function is most effectively displayed in scientific drawings and in the rendering of certain old masters, particularly men like Dürer who were trained in the exacting techniques of engraving. By contrast certain modern artists are less interested in describing the textures of the objects depicted in their work and stress the texture that develops from the manner of rendering as an important stylistic element: the texture of rendering becomes the handwriting of each artist. Such textures vary from those which are uniform throughout and contribute an abstract character to the work, to those which communicate the impetuous manner of the drawing act (as in the work of Daumier and Van Gogh), to the conscious manipulation of media and materials for visual richness such as one finds in the great Oriental masters.

Media play an important role in determining the textural character of a drawing, charcoal contributing to a coarse bold texture, pen and ink to richly varied linear textures, and wash to painterly fluid textures. Combinations of pen, wash, and other media provide for rich textural variety; pencil too permits a wide range of textural effects.

part four

DRAWING MEDIA

16

MEDIA AND MATERIALS
THE DRY MEDIA

T he media in which an artist executes a work and the surface upon which he draws or paints contribute significantly to the esthetic character of the finished work. A feeling for media, sensitivity to their intrinsic beauty and expressive potential, a delight in manipulating them, are part of the make-up of most artists. Today most of what an artist needs is purchased ready for use but in earlier times before such materials were standardized and factory made, artists carefully prepared or supervised the preparation of their own grounds and materials. In the Renaissance high standards of production were maintained by the guilds. Young apprentices were carefully trained in all aspects of the craft to insure the fine quality and durability of everything that went into making a work of art. As they surfaced the papers upon which drawings were to be made the papers were tinted with subtle colors. They also prepared chalks, inks, and other materials to suit their masters' personal tastes. Many of the drawings made as studies for painting projects were enhanced far beyond utilitarian purposes so that they became desirable objects of beauty in their own right. They were carefully finished, the forms were heightened with tempera and often colored accents were added to further enrich the study. Since pleasure in the craft is an important component of the artistic temperament, the joyful savoring of the particular qualities of each material that the artist uses and each surface upon which he works contributes to the total effectiveness with which he functions. Enjoying the velvety blackness of India ink or compressed charcoal, the pale silvery gray of hard pencil, the grainy vigor of dry-brushed tempera, adds to the pleasure of using the various media and this pleasure is reflected in a fuller and more sensitive exploitation of the potentialities of each medium.

The media used in drawing divide rather naturally into the dry and the wet, those that are essentially graphic and those that are painterly in character. The dry range from chalk and charcoal, easily applied, rather coarse granular materials which are usually shaped in sticks for ease of application, to pencil and silverpoint, where a smooth-grained texture and fine point make possible more precise detailed effects. The wet media reveal a similar variety. Wash executed with water and a large brush provides for extreme freedom and breadth of handling, whereas pen and ink permits an exacting control by building tones and textures line by line and dot by dot. No medium, of course, is limited to one particular use. Smoothly finished, detailed drawings can be made with charcoal and chalk if these materials are handled with precision and care. Pencil though well adapted to precise and delicate drawing can be used freely for sketchy spontaneous effects. In the same way the usual roles of wash and pen and ink can be reversed. Though each medium has its potentialities and limitations the artists temperament remains the most influential factor in determining how media will be used.

Charcoal

Charcoal is an extremely friable material which readily leaves a mark when rubbed against any but a very smooth surface. Since it adheres to any soft or slightly rough paper, it is well adapted to making large drawings, and because the marks made by the charcoal are not deeply imbedded in the surface of the paper they are easy to erase—in fact, a large drawing can be eradicated in just a few seconds by a broad swipe of the chamois. When used in an open sketchy fashion, charcoal demands little technical skill.

Though there is ample evidence that charcoal has been used for drawing since the cavemen first rubbed soot and burned sticks against the walls and ceilings of their caves, the oldest extant charcoal drawings come from the early Renaissance. In fourteenth- and fifteenth-century Italy the complex nature and large scale of the frescoes and mural paintings which were produced in numbers necessitated the making of extensive preparatory drawings and preliminary studies. These were usually executed in charcoal or chalk. Then as now, the ease with which tentative lines could be put down and subsequently erased, and the fact that the same piece of charcoal could with equal ease be used for line drawing or turned on its side to produce broad tonal masses, made it particularly useful for the rapid visualization of large-scale projects, both in the initial and in the later developmental stage.

For these same reasons charcoal remains an excellent material for beginning students in drawing. It is particularly important that beginners form habits of exploring a number of approaches to compositional problems, and when sketching, to draw and redraw a subject many times and from varied points of view. The beginner, because of timidity and lack of experience, hesitates to abandon a drawing to explore other possibilities, often being afraid that a subsequent drawing might be even less satisfactory than what he has in hand. Media such as charcoal and procedures such as quick sketching, because they encourage the habit of exploration, do much to contribute to the flexibility of thinking so valuable to the artist. The disadvantages of charcoal are first that it is dirty and second, because it erases easily careless movements of the hand or arm across a drawing can almost eradicate it. Consequently charcoal drawings have to be "fixed" (sprayed with fixatif) to preserve them.

The two most widely used types of charcoal are stick charcoal and compressed. Stick charcoal is made by heating sticks of wood about one-fourth inch in diameter in closed chambers or kilns until the organic materials have been evaporated and only dry carbon remains. Woods of even texture such as willow, bass, and beech, free from knots, straight and of even width, make the finest charcoal. Stick charcoal comes in sticks of varying thickness, the finest quality called *vine charcoal* usually coming in very thin sticks of an even, soft texture. Manufacturers package charcoal in four degrees of hardness: very soft, soft, medium, and hard. Compressed charcoal (also called *Siberian charcoal*) is made by grinding the charcoal into powder and compressing it into chalklike sticks about one-fourth of an inch in diameter. Compressed charcoal is also packaged and labeled according to hardness ranging from 00, the softest and blackest, through 0 to 5, which contains the most binder and is consequently the palest and hardest. In general, compressed charcoal produces less easily erased lines and tones than stick and is most effective for very large-scale quick sketches or when rich darks are desired. Because it is less friable than stick charcoal and is in many ways very similar to chalk, it is less well adapted to beginners' needs than the regular stick charcoal.

Charcoal pencils are made by compressing charcoal into thin sticks and sheathing them in paper or wood. Charcoal pencils are also packaged and labeled according to their degree of softness or hardness, usually coming in 6B (extra soft) 4B (soft), 2B (medium) and HB (hard). The chief virtue of the charcoal pencil is that it is clean and can be handled like a pencil, but this also constitutes its chief liability for it does not have the flexibility of stick charcoal inasmuch as only the point can be used effectively.

Charcoal can be used on many kinds of drawing paper. Newsprint suffices for quick sketches and studies that do not demand erasing or the careful building up of smooth tones. Manila paper and many kinds of coarse drawing paper are also acceptable grounds for quick sketches with either stick, compressed or charcoal pencils. Regular charcoal paper is best for sustained studies.

This is a hard-surfaced paper with a pronounced tooth that will take repeated erasures and rubbing and not lose its grain. Many of the fine imported charcoal papers come in handsome toned colors, and such papers are well adapted to the making of studies accented with white or light pale colored chalks. Cheap charcoal papers are soft and lack tooth and so do not hold the flaky charcoal; consequently it is difficult to get extended areas of rich dark tones on such papers. Compressed charcoal can be used effectively on relatively smooth bond papers to produce rich darks, but these materials demand certainty and consequently are not for beginners.

In drawing with charcoal the chamois acts as an eraser and is used to wipe out lines and tones that are not satisfactory. The kneaded eraser can be used to erase small areas, to clean away smudges and to pick out small light accents. Stumps or tortillons are pencil-shaped rolls of soft paper which are used to rub the charcoal into the paper to produce even tones of gray. Charcoal drawings can be "fixed" by spraying them with fixatif (shellac or a transparent plastic material dissolved in solvent), and artists who use charcoal to make elaborate studies with carefully graduated values often fix the drawing in its successive stages of development so that the initial steps do not get lost through smudging. It was in the nineteenth-century European academies that elaborate techniques were formulated for using charcoal to make fully developed, detailed studies. By carefully pointing the charcoal stick with sandpaper and gradually developing a full tonal drawing through repeated rubbings and fixings, very fine gradations of value were achieved, ranging from almost solid blacks to sharp whites. The following group of selected master drawings in charcoal reveal some of the ways in which the medium can be used effectively.

Master Drawings in Charcoal

Millet made many charcoal drawings of peasants, farm scenes, and the landscape as studies for his paintings. "Man with a Barrow" (Figure 16–1) illustrates the unforced simplicity of his style. The contour lines are strong and expressive of the inner form and are reinforced with simple planes of shadow. The shadow is kept to a rather neutral gray tone and the granular texture of the soft charcoal on medium rough paper is maintained throughout. There is no artifice in the style of the drawing; even the direction of the lines from which the grays are built seems to follow no general principle, conforming at times to the natural upper right to lower left movements of the hand, while at other times the lines of shading appear to follow the contours they are describing. The unpretentious but sensitive use of the medium contributes to the grave honesty of effect that constitutes the particular charm of Millet's drawings.

"Groupe de Danseuses Vues en Buste" by Degas (Figure 16–2) presents a more free and energetic style than the Millet sketch. The contours were for the most part established with open sketchy strokes rather than consolidated into a single defining line, and an air of casual animation is produced by such devices as the rapidly sketched zigzag used to define the raised arm and hand at the upper right. The linear open texture of the shadowed faces is consistent with the light sketchy tone that predominates throughout the drawing, and it also contributes to an effect of strong illumination for it suggests transparent shadows full of reflected light. Much of the beauty of the study comes from the fact that the act of drawing is clearly evident; there is no feeling that the technique is hidden from the viewer. It is candidly a drawing, not a simulation of a segment of reality.

A "Seated Nude" by Elmer Bischoff (Figure 16-3) to an even greater degree than the Degas drawing just discussed, achieves much of its vitality from boldness of handling. This drawing exploits both the velvety darks and the vigorous textures that can be made with very soft charcoal on rough paper. In a few places the charcoal has been smudged to describe the soft roundness of the model's body, but even the smudged areas have been handled in a casual way consistent with the rest of the drawing. By avoiding extensive areas of middle-value gray and keeping the drawing primarily black and white, an effect of bold illumination and strong shadows has been created.

Jacques Lipschitz has made many of his studies for sculptural projects with charcoal, for the medium has an almost plastic malleability. The rich masses of dark can be pushed around with thumb and fingers, smeared, erased, added to, or graduated in value. His study for "Sacrifice" (Figure 10-3) feels modeled rather than drawn, which makes it particularly appropriate for the initial visualization of a sculptural project. The background was given a quick free wash of gray watercolor to isolate the sculptural form. An initial gray tone was spread over the entire page, bold outlines of the main masses were established, some of these were modified by rubbing, and then an eraser was used to cut into the grays and darks and leave bold light strokes. The erasures have a vigorous texture that in places suggests the faceted surface of the bronze in which the eventual sculpture would be cast.

The usefulness of charcoal in making freely executed quick sketches has been amply illustrated, but the medium is also well adapted to sustained and fully developed drawings. In "I Know Not Why" (Figure 16-4) by Robert Baxter, a complex composition with three closely related figures and an enigmatic supplementary decor has been built into a rich tonal study with carefully graduated values, which include large amounts of middle darks. A minimum of blurred tone is present; for the most part the individual lines from which the full-bodied darks have been built up can be distinguished, providing a pleasing granular texture that keeps the drawing from appearing slick. The individual lines in most parts of the drawing have a strong directional emphasis that contributes solidity and helps model the form, frequently separating similar values which are placed next to one another. The drawing was done with compressed charcoal and no fixatif was applied until after the drawing was completed, since according to the artist, premature fixing and subsequent working on a surface provokes a gritty texture and makes it impossible to get the velvety darks that are most desirable. Baxter is a lithographer and the discipline of building rich value patterns through a sustained accumulation of lithographic crayon or pencil lines has colored his use of charcoal.

Alexander Wyant was an American nineteenth-century landscape painter who was strongly influenced by the drawing methods of the French Barbizon school of painters and draftsmen. His "Landscape" (Figure 7-15) combines smoothly rubbed tones with a variety of lines, from soft to clearly defined, to create a drawing with unusual surface textures. The soft sky was produced by rubbing charcoal into the paper, then erasing areas to create the white clouds. The textures of foliage, branches, trunk and earth have been suggested by lines blurred to varying degrees by the thumb or a stump with the entire drawing drawn into final focus by clean very sharp, dark accents.

FIGURE 16–2

Edgar Degas (1834–1917; French).
"Groupe de Danseuses Vues en Buste."
Charcoal, 28″ x 19½″. *Allen Memorial Art Museum,*
Oberlin College, Ohio (Friends of Art Fund).

FIGURE 16–3
Elmer Bischoff (1916– ; American).
"Seated Figure."
Charcoal, 15" x 18".
Courtesy of the Artist.

The Classical acadamies trained artists in the use of charcoal to build a smoothly finished, elegant drawing. Pierre-Paul Prud'hon has left us a handsome example of this disciplined approach in his "Head of a Woman (Marguerite)" (Figure 16–5). In making such drawings the charcoal stick was carefully pointed by rubbing it on sandpaper, and then even gray values were built up with lightly applied parallel lines. (A faint residue of these lines can still be seen in some areas which were not fully developed, as in the neck.) Each set of parallel lines was then rubbed with a paper stump, reinforced with another set of lines, and this procedure was repeated until tones of the desired smoothness were established. When areas became dirty or smudged they were cleaned off with an

FIGURE 16–5
Pierre-Paul Prud'hon (1758–1823; French).
"Head of a Woman (Marguerite)." Charcoal, 14" x 11".
Courtesy of The Art Institute of Chicago
(The Simeon D. Williams Collection).

eraser. (Bread crumbs were used for erasing before rubber erasers were discovered.) Highlights were frequently applied with chalk to complete the drawing. A drawing such as this may have been sprayed with fixatif many times to hold the darks and prevent them from blurring. The fresh linear accents in the hair provide a beautiful foil for the smoothly rubbed flesh tones.

Pencil and Silverpoint

Since the pencil evolved from the silverpoint and there is a close resemblance between silverpoint and drawings done with a very hard pencil, these two media will be discussed together.

The pencil is probably the most familiar tool in our culture inasmuch as children use pencils from their earliest years, if not for drawing certainly for writing. Pencil remains a very important drawing medium useful in a wide variety of situations despite the fact that habits contracted in school while learning to write, do arithmetic, and so on, frequently mitigate against the free and expressive use of the medium.

A glance through the catalogue of any art supply house reveals an astonishing variety of pencils. Graphite, carbon, charcoal, wax, conté, lithographic (grease), and a wide range of colored pencils (either soluble or insoluble),

FIGURE 16–7
Pavel Tchelitchew (1898–1957; Russian-American).
"Portrait of Frederick Ashton."
Silverpoint on prepared paper, 18″ x 12⅛″.
Courtesy of the Fogg Art Museum, Harvard University.

all can be used for drawing; each has its particular character making it useful for certain effects. The full range of pencils becomes further evident when we realize that graphite pencils, the most familiar type, are manufactured in hexagonal, round, and flat shapes, with many companies producing them in seventeen degrees of hardness ranging from 6B, the softest, to 9H, the hardest.

The common lead pencil is misnamed, for it is made of graphite, a crystalline form of carbon having a greasy texture. Graphite is mixed with varying amounts of clay to determine hardness, the more clay being present, the

FIGURE 16–8

Jean-Auguste Dominique Ingres (1780–1867; French). "Portrait of Docteur Robin." Pencil, 11″ x 8¾″. *Courtesy of The Art Institute of Chicago (Gift of Emily Crane Chadbourne)*.

FIGURE 16–9

Edgar Degas (1834–1917; French).
"A Gentleman Rider."
Pencil with touch of Chinese white,
17⅛″ x 10½″. *Courtesy of The Art Institute
of Chicago (The Charles Deering Collection).*

harder the lead. All pencils, whether made of graphite, carbon, charcoal, dry, waxy or greasy chalks or various colored pigments, have certain common qualities. The narrow lead is sheathed in wood or rolled paper, and this coming to a point whether sharp or blunt, contributes to an essentially linear handling. Even when a very soft pencil is used to build broad value patterns, as in the Constable "Poplars by a Stream" (Figure 7–14), the areas of dark are built up of groups of massed lines. Because pencils of medium hardness are clean and make a light line they are frequently used for preliminary sketching, laying out compositions, and planning lettering, designs or diagrams, since the light lines can easily be erased or can be obscured by subsequent layers of paint or ink.

Thus, although the pencil is one of the most important tools used by artists, it is most widely used as an auxiliary tool rather than for producing finished works of art. Pencil is also frequently used to form a counterpoint to another medium, such as wash, watercolor, or pen and ink. In the "Rock Quarry" by Caspar Friedrick (Figure 16–6), pencil lines are used with great effectiveness for structural reinforcement of the washes.

Silverpoint

The metal point stylus was the historic precursor of the pencil. Already known to the Romans, metal points of silver, gold, or lead, mounted on a stylus, werc extensively used during the Middle Ages for writing, bookkeeping, and drawing. Silver was the favored material for metal point, since the point wears very slowly and makes a fine even light grey line which soon becomes brownish through oxidation. Silverpoint leaves no mark upon ordinary paper; consequently papers had to be specially prepared for use with silverpoint. Bone dust or some other fine abrasive material was mixed in a thin glue size and used to coat smooth paper or parchment. Color was frequently added to the size to produce a

FIGURE 16–10

Théodore Géricault (1791–1824; French).
"Studies of a Cat." Pencil, 14⅛" x 13¼".
*Courtesy of the Fogg Art Museum,
Harvard University, Cambridge, Massachusetts
(Grenville Lindall Winthrop Collection).*

FIGURE 16–11

Louis Michel Eilshemius (1864–1941; American).
"Old Saw Mill." Pencil drawing, 4½" x 6".
Amherst College.

pale tinted paper, and upon completion of the silverpoint drawing white tempera was often used to build highlights, accenting the plasticity of the fine silverpoint and creating clear, precise effects that though delicate are firm. Silverpoint produces clean isolated lines which have almost no variation in width or gradations of value. Because erasures are not possible, the medium requires great skill. The lines do not smudge, and values can only be built up through groups of parallel or cross-hatched lines. This contributes to a tight, calculated effect which, if handled without sensitive variations, can appear mechanical. An excellent example of the traditional use of silverpoint can be seen in Rogier van der Weyden's "Devils in Hell" (Figure 5–4). In this drawing silverpoint has been used with sufficient variety to do away with any suggestion of mechanical regularity and the vigor of the design and the grotesque and imaginative content are made more plausible by the lucid and controlled style of rendering.

Silverpoint still appeals to artists who love finely drawn lines and careful detail. Modern drawings in silverpoint usually stress the potential for controlled elegance inherent in the medium. Pavel Tchelitchew's "Portrait of Frederick Ashton" (Figure 16–7) achieves this quality of elegance and at the same time provides a series of entertaining surprises. First, one is amazed at the freedom with which the long flowing lines appear to have been put down, for once down silverpoint cannot be erased or changed. While many artists would appear to be intimidated by this intractable medium, Tchelitchew groups his long clusters of almost parallel lines to build solid forms and, as can be seen in the darker head, adds cross-hatching to provide a sense of darker color. Although the forms have clarity and precision, there is nothing constricted or mechanical about this lyrical work. The contrast in value between the two identical heads, giving the darker one a brooding and conflicted character; the fascinating way in which the two images deny an upside-downside format; the intriguing ambiguity of the form created by the flamelike lines that continue from the hair—all of these elements add the fascination of enigma to a technical *tour de force*.

Pencil

Lead point, placed in a stylus and later sheathed in wood, had one decided advantage over silverpoint; it did not require a special abrasive-coated paper. Around 1400 Cenninni describes such a pencil with a lead containing two parts of lead to one of tin, which gave a smooth regular line of not much strength. Such a lead was sometimes used to lay out a composition which would subsequently be rendered in pen, brush, or black and red chalk since the lead left only a light mark on the unprimed paper.

Baroque artists had little use for a stylus or pencil of this character. The freedom of their style, the large scale of their work, their love of rich value contrasts and painterly textures rendered the pale narrow line almost useless. Consequently, not until the middle of the seventeenth century, when the graphite pencil began to replace the lead stylus as a writing instrument, do we find it praised as a medium for drawing. The early drawing pencils were soft and smudgy, but at the end of the eighteenth century the Frenchman Conté developed the process of mixing viscous graphite with clay to create leads of varying degrees of hardness, and thus produced the serviceable tool that we know and use today.

Master Drawings in Pencil

Because of the narrow lead, the gray color, and the shiny character of graphite, the graphite pencil is best suited to a cool, reticent style of drawing. Ingres remains one of the undisputed masters of pencil used for the objective rendering of visual perceptions, and his "Portrait of Docteur Robin" (Figure 16–8) bears testimony to that mastery. The drawing remains essentially a line drawing reinforced with delicate modeling and finely rendered details. Very wisely Ingres did not try to develop extended areas of dark throughout the drawing, but concentrated his few dark accents in the spatially restricted but crucial area of the head. Here the values are developed fully, with exquisitely modeled forms built up through middle value grays which have been accented with very small areas of deep black, probably executed with a sharply pointed soft lead. The entire drawing breathes an atmosphere of control, intelligence, and taste. The discipline necessary to achieve this technically brilliant performance has in no way inhibited the sensitivity of the artist but instead has permitted the finest nuances of perception to find expression.

Degas, too, frequently displays this combination of the reticent, detached observer whose unerring eye prefers a medium which will contribute a minimum of emotional coloration to his sketch. His pencil sketch of "A Gentleman Rider" (Figure 16–9) reveals this sharp eye and obedient hand moving together to record the exact direction of each contour and by varying degrees of incisiveness to describe the bulk and weight of the various volumes. The frankly sketchy and linear quality of the drawing in no way demands that the pencil do more than it does easily. The drawing is casual, unforced and, as compared to the Ingres, unfinished, but as in the Ingres drawing, the artist finds in pencil a medium particularly adapted to his observant, unimpassioned point of view.

The two drawings we have just observed give almost no indication of the color or surface texture of their subjects. A page of "Studies of a Cat" by Géricault (Figure 16–10) conveys a richer sense of form, texture, and color without forcing the medium. By using a softer pencil and keeping the scale of the sketches small, the soft texture of fur, the pattern of broken stripes and the vigorous anatomy of the animal have all been described with vivacity. Particularly telling is the way the variations in thickness of the contour lines help to convey a sense of the swelling muscular forms in contrast to sharp bony parts of the cat.

One seldom sees clearly defined pencil lines used with greater sensitivity to build areas of gray than in "The Old Saw Mill" (Figure 16–11) by Louis Eilshemius. Large areas of background foliage have been covered with an upper-right to lower-left diagonal stroke and by varying the weight of the lines, shadows and lights have been clearly separated. By deviating from the predominantly diagonal movement used in the background, contrasting textures have been suggested, as in the broad boards of the saw mill, the deep grass in the foreground, some small trees at the left, and so on. By confining the darks to small areas and stressing the linear character of pencil, the drawing has been kept light, airy, and unforced in feeling.

Though pencil, and particularly graphite pencil, is not well adapted to the making of rich tonal studies, if a sufficiently soft lead is used upon a fairly rough paper, small studies can be very effective. In Constable's "Poplars by a Stream" (Figure 7–14), which is only 4¾ inches by 7½ inches, the typically linear character of pencil is almost obliterated and replaced by rich tonal masses of a granular quality. By bearing on the soft pencil with varying degrees of pressure, a sequence of grays was produced, the palest in the cloudy sky, the darkest in the heavily accented forms in the front plane.

Pencil seems best adapted to sketchy and informal renderings rather than to formalized and abstract modes of expression. However, Juan Gris, a cubist, in his "Seated Harlequin" (Figure 13–2) used pencils of different hardness to produce lines of varying darkness and thickness in a highly controlled formal manner. By shading one side of some of the lines he added an element of hard and soft to the changes in darkness and width. This drawing might well have been executed with the aid of a French curve and ruler.

Another cubist, Albert Gliezes, has sensed the potentialities of pencil for a rather formal value study in his "Port" (Figure 16–12). Pencils of varying

hardness have been used to produce lines of different darkness, and the lines have been applied with systematic consistency to build rather typically cubist gradations from light to dark. Except in the clearly defined contours the lines have been kept short, giving the entire drawing a somewhat staccato rhythm that reinforces the rather dense pattern to communicate a sense of action at curious variance with the static and monumental nature of the composition. By thus formalizing the pattern Gliezes achieves the cubist goal of transposing commonplace experience into a semi-abstract and emotionally remote pattern. As in the previously discussed drawing by Elshemius, Albert Gliezes recognizes the linear character of pencil and thus creates a bold tonal pattern, yet does not force the medium.

Chalk, like charcoal, is an ancient material which can be found in the cave paintings from the Old Stone Age in France and Spain. In prehistoric and Neolitic times, man discovered natural deposits of richly pigmented earths, pieces of which could be used for drawing and coloring. Natural carbons provided black, iron oxides reds, ochres dull yellows, umbers produced a range of browns, and chalk and talc produced whites. These materials used either directly as they came from the earth, or ground into a fine powder, mixed with an adhesive material and shaped into rounded or rectangular sticks, came into common usage in fifteenth-century Italy and have remained popular drawing materials ever since. The most frequently used chalks in Renaissance times were

Chalks, Pastels and Crayons

FIGURE 16–13

Hans Holbein, the Younger
(1497–1543; German).
"A Kneeling Nobleman."
Colored chalk, 15⁹⁄₁₆″ x 10¹³⁄₁₆″.
Kupferstichkabinett, Basel.

FIGURE 16–14
Jakob Jordaens
(1593–1678; Flemish).
"Two Bacchic Revelers."
Black, white, and red chalk,
13%₁₆" x 8¾".
Albertina, Vienna.

FIGURE 16–15

Rembrandt van Rijn (1606–1669; Dutch).
"Elephant." Black chalk, 9¹³⁄₁₆" x 14".
Albertina, Vienna.

the beautiful red oxides which were often combined with black and highlighted with white on a tinted paper to produce studies of great plastic strength. The use of colored chalks continued to be popular throughout the seventeenth and eighteenth centuries and was used with great effectiveness in the large-scale drawings made by Rubens, Van Dyck, and other Baroque masters (Figures 13–10, 6–3, 6–10).

Types of Chalk

The term *chalk* covers a wide variety of materials which range from coarse to fine and from dry to greasy. It is impossible to establish the point at which chalk becomes crayon or pastel, and the dividing line between chalk and compressed charcoal is equally tenuous.

Since the early nineteenth century the manufacture of chalk has been standardized to insure regularity in the sizes of the sticks, the degrees of softness and hardness, in color range and intensity, and the dryness or oiliness. Most familiar are the regular blackboard chalks, which are inexpensive and come in bright but not necessarily permanent colors, are without any oily binder and consequently are very dry, dust off easily, and are only usable for projects of a crude or temporary nature.

Pastels

Pastels represent a high quality, dry (non-oily) chalk of very fine even texture which come in a wide range of hues, each hue in turn being available in graduated sequences from full intensity to tints and shades of each color. Soft pastels (so-called French pastels) usually come made up in sets. A fairly elaborate set of pastels will contain over two hundred separate sticks of color. Such pastels are made from dry pigment mixed with an aqueous binder and are usually cylindrical in form. Soft pastels are nonadhesive and consequently must be used on a paper with a decided tooth and subsequently fixed to achieve permanency. Semihard pastels are made with some oil added to the binder and this makes the pastel adhere to paper more readily than do the soft chalks. Semihard pastels are usually made in rectangular sticks; the oily texture and smooth sides make them less crumbly than ordinary pastels, the flat sides provide for rapid coverage of broad areas, and the sharp corners make them effective for detailing and accenting. Hard pastels do not ordinarily come in as great a color range as the more traditional soft pastels, can be used on almost any type of drawing paper, and do not require fixing.

Wax Crayons

At the opposite end of the scale from the blackboard chalks and pastels in hardness are wax crayons such as children use in elementary school. These are made with wax or paraffin as a binder, are hard to apply and do not dust off easily on hands or clothes. This means that they produce sharply defined lines and are not easy to blend into fused tones. Inasmuch as wax crayons are made largely for use by children and must be inexpensive, little care is given to permanence of color; therefore most of them fade too readily to be used for serious purposes. They also lack the blending qualities that most artists prefer in a chalk.

Conté Crayon

In between the dry blackboard chalks, the very soft-expensive pastels, and the inflexible wax crayons, there exists a wide variety of chalks made expressly for drawing, one of the most popular of which is conté crayon. Conté is a semi-hard chalk of fine texture with sufficient oily material in the binder so that it adheres readily to smooth paper and does not dust off easily. Conté, which comes in stick about one-fourth inch square and about three inches in length, is manufactured in three degrees of hardness: No. 1 hard, No. 2 medium, and No. 3 soft. It is usually available in four colors: white, black, sepia, and sanguine (a Venetian red, and the most popular of conté colors). Where a more greasy high-quality chalk is desired, lithographic crayons provide a wide variety of hardness and softness which make possible varying degrees of light and dark values or fine and coarse textures. In addition a variety of chalks similar to

FIGURE 16–16
Gian Battista Piazzeta (1683–1754; Italian).
Black and white chalk
on gray paper, 20½" x 15⅜".
"The Drummer." *Museo Correr, Venice*
Photo: the Smithsonian Institution, Washington, D. C.

conté crayons in texture but manufactured in soft greys, tans, browns, and yellows is also generally available for sketching purposes.

The virtues of chalk as a drawing medium are similar to those of charcoal, but since chalks come in a wide range of formats, hardnesses, degrees of adhesiveness and of color, they suffice for a broader scope of artistic purposes than does charcoal. On the other hand, almost no chalk can be erased as readily as stick charcoal, so chalk tends to be used by experienced artists to build up finished drawings rather than as a learning medium for beginners. Thus as artists discover their particular preference as to texture, color effects, and ways of working, they frequently settle on certain chalks for the execution of favorite kinds of drawings. One can imagine Charles Sheeler deriving great pleasure from working with the reliably even-textured smooth conté crayon when he drew "Feline Felicity" (Figure 1–3), and this deliberate choice of medium and method of work could only result from a long apprenticeship.

Master Drawings in Chalk

Ever since the Renaissance master artists have turned to chalk to make studies for paintings as well as drawings for their own pleasure, and a superabundance of magnificent chalk drawings is still in existence. A few must suffice here to show the versatility of this medium. The many studies Holbein made for portraits provide ample evidence of the mastery with which he used the various drawing media. However, not all of his drawings were done as studies for paintings. From his hands comes a wondrous colored chalk-sketch of "A Kneeling Nobelman" (Figure 16–13) made from a statue of Jean du Berry now in Bourges Cathedral. Although chalk is most frequently used for bold, broadly executed studies, Holbein's incisive and sure touch enabled him to use the chalk with both precision and freedom; without ever forcing the granular chalk into a smooth texture, he recorded every nuance of form and surface texture in the face. To finish the drawing he defined the body forms only to the degree necessary to support his primary focus of interest, the head. The viewer appreciates not being distracted by overly developed irrelevant details.

A very traditional Baroque handling of chalk is illustrated by Jacob Jordaens in his black, red, and white chalk drawing of "Two Bacchic Revelers" (Figure 16–14). The red chalk has been applied in loose diagonal and cross-hatched patterns to build a solid sense of form. In some areas such as in the lower back of the right-hand figure, the initial strokes of chalk have been gently smudged and then reinforced by the addition of more precisely defined lines. Black chalk has been added to strengthen the darks to provide accents and the rich dark of the black accents gives the red tones a luminous brilliance. As a finishing touch a soft tone of white has been applied to heads, shoulders, and the back of the foreground figure, and the sweeping arc of white from upper left to lower right provides a beautiful unifying movement to the two figures. Although the drawing is executed in an unstilted style, the treatment throughout is uniform and conforms to the generally accepted mode of drawing practiced in seventeenth-

century Flanders. Rembrandt has provided us with a more personal style of drawing in his study of an "Elephant" (Figure 16–15). The drawing appears to have been executed in two kinds of black chalk, a thinner stick which made a lighter line and a thick very soft chalk. The lighter lines move easily in all directions, frequently describing the voluminous forms of the elephant by seeming to encircle the volumes. To this sculpturally defined mass the very dark lines have been added in bold strokes that suggest the deep folds of the elephant's skin and the heavy sagging forms. The drawing has an admirable virility, its strength deriving from the certainty and exuberance with which this great draftsman drew a fascinating animal.

Both the drawing by Jordaens and that by Rembrandt employ the chalk in a linear-draftsman manner. Piazetta's beautiful "The Drummer" (Figure 16–16) relies on broadly massed value relations for its essentially painterly qualities. Black and white chalk has been used on a medium gray paper. The black chalk was applied in broad lines or with the side of the stick, but even where there is evidence of a linear application, the lines have been blurred by rubbing or subsequent layers of chalk laid on in various directions. To this soft rich tonal matrix, masses of dark have been added, but the darks have been made translucent by adding sharp black lines as accents into the heaviest shadows. As a final touch the softly textured whites were applied in broken patterns that seem almost to shimmer as they reflect light back into the shadowy face of the drummer boy. Piazetta was famous for his heads in black and white chalk, most of which were done independently of painting projects.

A Master Drawing in Pastel

In the last drawing Piazetta utilized the effectiveness of chalk to build broad tonal patterns. In a charming sketch of a "Venetian Canal" (Figure 16–17), Whistler exploited pastel as a medium for tonal rather than linear effects and at the same time utilized its soft crumbly texture most effectively. Using the side of the pastel to cover broad areas in a granular and uneven texture, he created soft blurred value patterns which he occasionally strengthened with a sharp line, but the lines were not used with sufficient frequency to dominate the drawing. The effect seems particularly appropriate for evoking the old weathered surfaces of Venetian buildings seen in the soft light of a gray day. Many of Whistler's drawings were done as studies for his etchings and both the drawings and the etchings reflect a thoughtful mood of nostalgic contemplation. The absence of strong contrasts, of sharply defined forms and of vigorously applied strokes of chalk, all contribute to the tone of quiet revery.

Master Drawings in Conté Crayon

Pastel, as used by Whistler in the "Venetian Canal," depends for its effectiveness upon the crumbly texture of soft pastel. Almost at the opposite end of the spectrum of chalk textures is conté crayon, which, being very fine, slightly

FIGURE 16–18

Marie-Anne Poniatowska (1931–   ; French-American).
"Déchéance Embryonaire." Conté crayon and pencil, 28" x 34".
Rex Evans Gallery, Los Angeles, Calif.

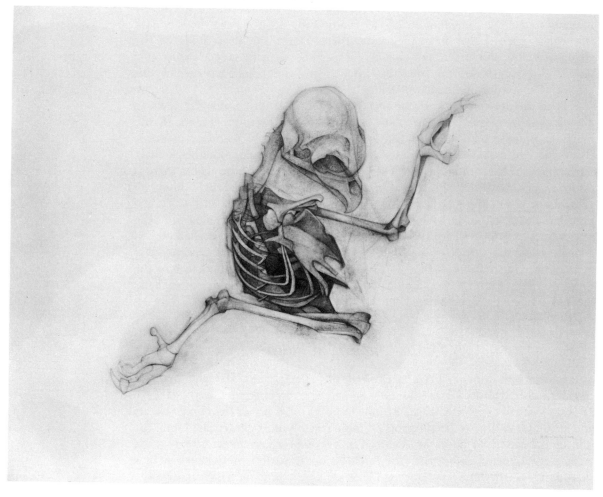

greasy and firmly compressed, can be applied in beautifully controlled, very smooth tones, particularly when it is used on somewhat smooth paper. Sheeler's miracle of craftsmanship in conté has already been referred to (Figure 1–3). Marie-Anne Poniatowska has made an exquisite conté crayon drawing of great firmness and delicacy in her drawing of the skeleton of a dead bird entitled "Déchéance Embryonaire" (Figure 16–18). The drawing has been purposely kept rather pale in color. The conté was applied in very delicate gradations of tone, the surfaces having been built up through repeated applications of thin layers of crayon, and the edges of the delicately modeled contours were strengthened with pencil lines. Much of the beauty of the drawing results from the almost paradoxical contrast between the exquisite technique and the macabre overtones of the subject.

Mature students in life drawing frequently enjoy the rich color and vigorous contrasts of value that can be built up in conté crayon. Since the chalk is sufficiently greasy so that it does not rub off readily and yet soft enough to provide for smooth gradations of dark and light, it is particularly well adapted to fully developed drawings such as Victor Arnautoff's "Study of a Model" (Figure 16–19) in sanguine and black conté crayon. The drawing was first fully modeled in red crayon and the black was then added to reinforce the strongest darks. Most of the drawing was done with the side of the crayon, which was applied with a motion that followed the surface of the form. The sense of directional movements achieved in this way can be seen to best advantage in the thighs. The modeling was frequently reinforced by swipes of the kneaded eraser which lifted out lights almost in the way white chalk marks function. The result is a life study of unusual force and solidity.

Most of the drawings we have observed in conté crayon have been done on fairly smooth paper to produce a fine-grained gradation of light and dark. Seurat selected a vigorously grained paper for the drawing of a "Seated Boy with Straw Hat" (Figure 16–20) made as a study for his famous painting of "Bathers." As the painting was to be executed in the Neopointillist method of applying equidistant evenly-sized and shaped dots of color, Seurat carried out the study in a manner relevant to the eventual execution of the painting. A soft conté was used and applied to the grainy paper in such a way that no directional stroke is evident. By a very even pressure on the chalk the grain of the paper was filled according to the degree of desired darkness, so that only in the darkest passages does the white grain of paper completely disappear. The even texture of the conté crayon as it is used here, without variations of size in the grain or of direction in stroke, contributes a somewhat impersonal surface to the drawing that in combination with the simplified and generalized form, creates an abstract and monumental quality to the drawing.

Scratchboard

Scratchboard is essentially an engraved drawing process involving the use of light lines incised on a dark ground to expose an underlying white surface. A specially prepared ground is necessary which is made by covering illustration board or heavy smooth-surfaced paper with a coating of fine white gesso or chalk. This white ground is usually covered with india ink and the ink surface is then scratched to expose the white ground underneath. The effect is similar to wood or metal engraving. In the twentieth century scratchboard drawing has been largely used for advertising illustration where a suggestion of precise high-quality craftsmanship is desired. Scratchboard is practical for commercial illustration since drawings made this way can be reproduced by line cuts (the least expensive type of reproduction). Because most scratchboard drawings employ white lines against a black background they stand out effectively on the page of the average magazine or newspaper where the text is composed of black letters upon a white ground.

Scratchboard came into use in France in the last half of the nineteenth

FIGURE 16–19

Victor Arnautoff (1896–   ; Russian-American). "Study of a Model."
Red and black conté crayon, 19" x 25".
Department of Art and Architecture, Stanford University, Calif.

century in making drawings for photochemical reproduction. Unlike most artists working in scratchboard when Monet set out to draw "Two Men Fishing" (Figure 8–1) he did not cover the board with solid areas of black. Instead he drew freely on the prepared cardboard with black crayon. The sharp light lines were then scratched through to expose the white undercoat below.

Scratchboard effects can be achieved without special materials by covering a white cardboard or heavy paper with a thick layer of wax crayon and then scratching through the layer of crayon with a sharp needle or pointed knife blade to expose the white paper underneath. This technique is often used to provide students with an engraving type of experience using light lines on a dark ground.

Summary

The medium in which an artist works bears considerable influence upon the form his work will take. Most artists by temperament take pleasure in savoring media. Drawing media divide themselves into the dry media (charcoal, pencil, silverpoint, chalk and scratchboard) which are essentially graphic and the wet media (pen and ink, wash and mixed media) which are painterly in character.

Charcoal, one of the oldest media used for drawing, is extremely friable, hence easy to manipulate and well adapted to freely executed, large scale drawings. Charcoal is now manufactured in various forms and degrees of hardness and because it can be used either for linear or value studies, erases easily, and can be used on inexpensive papers, it is recommended for students. Millet and Degas have left many refreshingly simple, direct charcoal studies while Prud'hon's "Head of a Woman" reveals the smooth and refined techniques for handling charcoal that prevailed in nineteenth-century French academic practice.

The modern graphite pencil evolved from the medieval metal stylus. Silverpoint was the type of metal stylus most used for drawing. It was well adapted to small scale drawings with precise delicate detail. Modern pencils come in a wide range of shapes and types of lead. Pencil is frequently used in making preparatory drawings or in conjunction with other media. While pencil is well adapted to the precise renderings of visual perceptions such as can be seen in the portrait drawings of Ingres, it can also be used for free sketching, for small value studies and for rather formally patterned semiabstracted studies.

The term *chalk* covers a wide range of manufactured drawing media which include the coarse, dry blackboard chalks, the soft, multicolored pastels, the hard wax crayons and the fine soft, conté crayons. Because chalk provides for variety of color and permits sustained effort it is frequently used for fully developed studies in which a more refined execution is desired than is ordinarily obtained in charcoal. Colored chalk was the medium preferred by Rubens as well as other Baroque masters and the fine-grained, slightly greasy conté is much used today.

Scratchboard is essentially an engraving process in which lines are engraved on a dark ground to expose an underlying white surface. Scratchboard drawings resemble wood or metal engravings and are most frequently used today in advertising and illustrations where a resemblance to the print processes is desired.

FIGURE 16–20

George-Pierre Seurat (1859–1891; French).
"Seated Boy with Straw Hat."
Conté crayon, 9½″ x 12¼″.
Yale University Art Gallery,
New Haven, Conn.

17

THE WET MEDIA

Ink

Inks, applied with pen or brush, were used for writing and drawing in Egypt, China, and elsewhere long before the beginning of the Christian era. Though the *Oxford Universal Dictionary* defines inks as "the colored fluid ordinarily employed in writing with a pen on paper, parchment, etc., or the viscous paste used in printing," the solid stick material used by Oriental calligraphers known as *sumi* is also referred to as an ink. Thus, contrary to general impression, inks can be fluid, paste or solid, although the quality that most generally differentiates ink from paint is fluidity. Inks are identified by their purpose (lithographic, printing, writing, and so on), by special qualities (indelible, soluble, transparent), by color, and also according to their original place of origin (India, China, and so on). Most are adapted to some particular kind of artistic use, although the commonest types of writing ink tend to be too thin and pale to be highly prized as artistic media.

The inks traditionally used for artistic purposes have varied compositions. One of the commonest ancient sources of ink were oak galls, which were treated with iron salts (usually vitriol) in solution, and then exposed to atmospheric action to produce the dark liquid. During the Renaissance and the two subsequent centuries bistre became the most popular type of ink. Bistre, of a rich reddish brown color, was made from the tarry soot produced by burning resinous woods, and could be used with either pen or brush. In the eighteenth century sepia ink made from the rich brown-black excretion of the cuttlefish became popular. Its fine grain, strength, and ready solubility produced a wide range of tones, from deepest brown-black darks to pale tan tints. India (or Chinese) inks became part of the artist's repertoire in the nineteenth century. India ink is prepared from lamp-black, that is, soot with a slightly oily character which is miscible with water. It is heavy and opaque, and produces rich, velvety blacks. It is preferred by many artists for drawing because of its uniform darkness and slightly viscous character. Modern technology has contributed a wide variety of new inks: colored inks, both opaque and transparent, in a wide range of colors, gold, silver, and white inks, acetate inks for use on either paper or acetate grounds, and an equally wide range of opaque and transparent black, white, and colored printer's inks, most of which are adaptable for use by either pen or brush.

The requirements of a pen are that it be tubular and pointed, with sufficient capacity in the tubular body to hold a fair amount of liquid which can flow from the body of the pen through the point to the paper. Two types of pen, quill and reed, have been used for both drawing and writing from very ancient times up to the modern era. Quill pens were cut from the pinion feathers of large birds, for it was only the heavy feathers growing from the leading edge of the wings and the tail of domestic fowl and large birds that have the requisite size and strength to make satisfactory pens. The point of the quill could be cut with a sharp or angular point, coarse or fine, depending upon the taste of the user. Because the quills were soft, they lost their point after some use and had to be recut from time to time. Unlike the reed pen, quill pens were light and pliable, responded readily to variations of touch and pressure, and consequently, made a responsive, smooth, and flexible line. Quill pens are not in general use today, having been replaced by the more serviceable steel pen.

Reed pens were made from tubular reeds or the hollow wooden stems of certain shrubs. Reed pens were also cut to suit the user's taste. In general reed pens are stiff, and the nib (point) is thick and fibrous. Its lack of supple responsiveness results in a harsh, almost angular line which has much character and creates bold effects. Because the reed pen does not slide easily across the surface of the paper, it contributes to a deliberate or even awkward strength of handling which tends to challenge the artist, engage his ingenuity, and these qualities inhibit overfacility and technical display. Today bamboo pens, a type of reed pen, are still imported in numbers from the Orient and are used by many contemporary artists because of the characterful quailty they impart to drawings.

The metal pen point as we know it today appeared at the end of the eighteenth century, and in the early nineteenth century almost supplanted the earlier types of pen. The steel pen, used on very smooth, partially absorbent paper, can be more completely controlled than either of its precursors and can be handled with almost infallible accuracy by a sufficiently skilled craftsman. Steel pens are manufactured with points of varying sharpness, pointedness and angularity so that lines of almost any desired character can be produced when the artist finds the steel pen suited to his particular needs. The use of the steel pen for making finished drawings came to its height in the nineteenth century when certain artists and illustrators carried their skill to astonishing levels of virtuosity (Figure 17–1).

FIGURE 17–1
Dante Gabriel Rossetti
(1828–1882; English).
"Portrait of Elizabeth Sidall."
Pen and ink, 8¾″ x 3⅞″.
Victoria and Albert Museum, London.

FIGURE 17–2

Ferdinand Victor Eugène Delacroix
(1798–1863; French).
"The Sultan on Horseback."
Pen and ink, 8⅛″ x 6″.
Musée du Louvre, Paris.

A wide variety of steel pens is now available to artists for sketching, many of which were developed for other purposes. Lettering pens come with round, straight, or angular nibs which range from a tenth of a millimeter to more than a quarter of an inch in width, and certain of the straight or angular nibbed lettering pens produce a line that in its stiff angularity is similar to that made by the reed pen. In recent years the cheap, popular ballpoint pen, a special adaptation of the stylus pen, has been adopted for sketching purposes because of its ready flow of ink, and its inexpensive availability. Felt pens, nylon tip pens, and various types of commercial marking pens such as laundry pens contribute additional resources for the artist. Many kinds of fountain pens have been specially manufactured for sketching and drawing; quill-style pens which will dispense India ink for an extended period of time without clogging or dripping and stylus-type pens with a smooth central point which enables the user to move the pen in all directions without varying the width of the lines (Figure 15–4). Fountain pens are preferred for use with a sketchbook since once filled it is not necessary to have frequent recourse to a bottle of ink, and the ink lines do not smear or smudge in the notebook format as do pencil and various other dry media.

Since the various pens and inks are used in combination with a wide variety of other wet and dry media the contemporary artist draws upon an inexhaustible variety of resources. This wide choice of tools and materials has its drawbacks, in as much as such variety demands choices, choices in turn demand experimentation and exploration, all of which can be distracting and time-consuming.

Pen and Ink   A black-ink line done with pen on a white page carries with incisive brilliance and clarity and for this reason the simple pen and ink outline drawing has an unequalled elegance and energy. Hard, pure, abbreviated, it creates a kind of shorthand impression of reality by recording only what the artist considers absolutely essential, eliminating all distracting details.

Delacroix has left us a brilliant pen and ink drawing of "The Sultan on Horseback" (Figure 17–2), in which one is only aware of the flourishing gesture by which the drawing was created. The drawing was probably done from imagination; the lines reveal the artist's spirit—the energy and enthusiasm of his mind and the abandon with which he threw himself into the act of drawing. As Delacroix conceived of the proud rider and spirited horse his bounding hand translated the mental image into an energized vortex of lines which can best be described as a gesture drawing. Pen and ink seems a logical medium for this lively performance: the smooth metal pen point and the fluid medium both contribute to ease and speed of execution. The thin sharp lines, intensely black against the brilliant white paper, seem particularly well adapted to projecting this dynamic image into graphic form.

Jean Cocteau's portrait of "Jean Desbordes" (Figure 17–3) provides us with a simple contour drawing of the sitter's profile smudged lightly with a bit of wash in a few isolated areas where the artist was conscious of the softening effects of a shadow. The line moves slowly down the carefully observed profile, losing its impetus and wavering at the moments when the artist hesitated or

FIGURE 17–3

Jean Cocteau (1892–1964; French).
"Jean Desbordes." Pen and ink, 16¾" x 13⅜".
Courtesy of The Art Institute of Chicago
(Gift of Mrs. Gilbert W. Chapman
in memory of Charles B. Goodspeed).

FIGURE 17–4

George Grosz (1893-1959; German-American).
"The Hiker."
Pen and ink, 17" x 12".
Achenbach Foundation
for Graphic Arts,
California Palace
of the Legion of Honor,
San Francisco.

FIGURE 17–5
Pietro Testa (1611–1650; Italian).
Detail of "Compositional Study."
Pen, brown ink.
*Achenbach Foundation
for Graphic Arts,
California Palace
of the Legion of Honor,
San Francisco.*
(See Figure 4–3.)

changed line direction. Subsequently it meanders around the rumpled collar of the jacket and open shirt and moves in and out over the wavy masses of hair. The direct uncomplicated response of the pen to the movements of the eye creates a very legible record, and in studying the portrait one sees through the eyes of the artist as they move along the edges of the forms being observed. The drawing reflects the genuine sophistication of the artist's tastes through its complete absence of any display of technical prowess or of irrelevant details. The indication of the pattern of the shirt, which might appear irrelevant, reflects the sitter's concern with appearances thereby adding a characterizing touch at variance with the introspective pose and casually rumpled clothes and hair.

By contrast "Dei Lichtlilie mit Schwebended Genein" by Phillip Otto Runge (Figure 7–5) projects neither the gesture of the hand nor the movement of the eye. Instead the beautiful design and the lucid rendering reveal disciplined craftsmanship at the command of a most refined and exacting intelligence. Every stroke of the pen functions in a carefully predetermined manner. For instance the outline used on the left cherub topping the page is just enough more emphatic than the neighboring figure to reinforce the space relationships established by the overlapping forms. The infinitely delicate clusters of lines used to describe the muscles suggest the tenderly rounded soft flesh of infants in a manner that seems beyond the capacity of hard pen and ink lines. Though exquisite and fragile the drawing radiates the firm certainty that comes from knowing ones goals and having command of the means of achieving them.

"The Hiker" (Figure 17–4) is another drawing that projects neither the movement of the eye nor the gesture of the hand but instead the dry wit of the critical mind. George Grosz drew with short, terse pen strokes that evoke a mood of ironic amusement very different from the tragic biting lines seen in "Workmen and Cripples" (Figure 11–7). Journalistic and casual, the precise clarity of the patterns seems exactly right for the intent.

We have just seen that the pen line can be equally successful as the vehicle for sharp observation, for romantic vehemence, or for cryptic amusement. It can also come closer to making a pure objective statement of fact than any other medium. In addition, pen and ink provides the least expensive means for reproducing drawings for illustrative purposes, as it can be reproduced without any loss of quality by a simple line cut. This has made it a popular medium with illustrators, who appreciate its efficiency. Illustrators, cartoonists, caricaturists, commercial artists, and a host of related workers use pen and ink in a great variety of ways, sometimes in pure outline, sometimes in conjunction with rather mechanically applied dots, sets of parallel lines, cross-hatchings, or with

FIGURE 17–6

Sir David Wilkie (1758–1841; English).
"Arrival of the Rich Relation." Ink on paper, 9¾" x 12⅜".
Achenbach Foundation for Graphic Arts,
California Palace of the Legion of Honor,
San Francisco (*Collis P. Huntington Collection*).

FIGURE 17–7
Édouard Manet (1832–1883; French).
"Portrait of George Moore."
Oil sketch on canvas, 25¾" x 32".
Courtesy of The Metropolitan Museum of Art
(*Gift of Mrs. Ralph J. Hines, 1955*).

contrasting masses of solid black. Among the most amazing technical performances to be executed in pen and ink are the scientific drawings made by artists
for illustrating scientific books and articles. "Prionotus Ruscarius" by Chloe
Lesley Starks (Figure 15–6) was done upon smooth Bristol board with a very
fine quill pen and India ink. Each part of the fish was carefully observed, the
spines, bony plates and scales counted, measured and carefully laid in, in hard
pencil. Then the tones and patterns were built up, dot by dot, and line by line,
in ink, eventually to describe the form without any element of ambiguity. Even
the sharpest photograph would not reveal the facts of the form with the clarity
of such a drawing, for in a photograph reflected lights, shadows, and imperfec-
tions of surface occasioned by handling the specimen could provide distracting

or irrelevant elements. Though the purpose of such a drawing is not basically artistic, the almost compulsive discipline necessary for the production of such a drawing characterizes a certain type of artist-craftsman.

In the Renaissance, pen and ink techniques were derived from two sources, from silverpoint with its precise, unblurred and isolated lines, and from the engraving techniques that developed in Northern Europe. In each instance, values of dark and light were built through sets of parallel lines placed at various angles to one another, which both by value and by direction of line created a sense of form. During the High Renaissance pen and ink was used with increasing freedom. We have already seen an example of Michelangelo's forceful yet free use of the medium in his "Head of a Satyr" (Figure 3–15). In the Baroque period a number of artists used the medium with breathtaking brilliance. Pietro Testa, an artist from Lucca who worked in Rome in the middle of the seventeenth century, is credited with a striking "Compositional Study" (Figure 17–5) in which cross-hatch is handled with unusual force and freedom. Large areas of clear white are alternated with various middle values, and a very few solid black accents establish the deepest shadows. The clear sets of line cross one another; at times, as in the deep shadowy folds of the curtain as many as four sets of overlapping lines can be identified, yet the tones never become blotched nor the form confused. It is obvious that Pietro Testa was not a great artist; many of the figures appear wooden and the gestures rhetorical, but it is equally evident that he was a brilliant technician.

"The Flight into Egypt" (Figure 4–9) by the eighteenth-century Venetian, Gaspare Diziani, provides a striking contrast to the technique of drawing employed by Pietro Testa. The preliminary lines were laid in black pencil and the pencil lines have been incorporated into the richly colored sepia ink sketch to provide an enriching contrast of color. While Pietro Testa cross-hatched in a bold, brilliant fashion, his method is essentially graphic. The sets of lines remain separately defined in direction, and thereby establish the separate planes of form with great clarity. Diziani's sketch, in contrast, is essentially painterly in its richly fluid interlacings of forms and tangled lines. The freely applied clusters of diagonal lines seldom remain within the confines of the suggested contours, but extend beyond them to create an illusion of floating tones. While at times, as in the shadow on the ground cast by Joseph, Mary, and the ass, the groups of lines, by their direction help firm up a plane, the direction of lines for the most part appears to be dictated by the easy movements of the wrist and fingers as they manipulate the pen and reflect the exuberance with which the hand responds to the spirited imagination of the artist. Directly above the head of Joseph is a delightful group of scribbles that suggest butterflies, birds, clouds, winged heads of putti, or pure effervescence of feeling. The entire drawing conveys a felicitous combination of exuberant spirits and a certainty of technique carried beyond the constraints of system.

In the seventeenth and eighteenth centuries, most major artists made studies with pen and ink, often combined with wash, chalk or charcoal. During these centuries the reed pen was particularly admired because of the vigorous quality of line it produced. In the nineteenth century the steel pen gradually replaced the reed pen in popularity. Sir David Wilkie used the steel pen with

FIGURE 17–8

Diego Rivera (1886–1957; Mexican).
"Mother and Child." Ink drawing, 12" x 9¼".
San Francisco Museum of Art
(Albert M. Bender Collection).

unusual freedom and vigor. His small pen and ink sketches were much admired during his day, and they subsequently influenced the style of a number of magazine illustrators. His "Arrival of the Rich Relation" (Figure 17–6) builds its rich value contrasts with freedom and assurance. There is no attempt on the part of Wilkie to formalize his method of drawing. Instead, the lines seem to flow freely, according to the impulse of the moment, in all directions and combinations. Outlines, sets of curved lines, blots of darks, almost scribbled passages, work together to create a sketch of admirable vitality. The lower right-hand corner in particular, with its delightful shift from almost pure contour line to fully developed tonal passages, reveals the remarkable flexibility of pen and ink in the hands of this versatile draftsman.

In the late nineteenth and early twentieth century, a number of illustrators developed very slick and facile methods of using pen and ink to produce popular book and magazine illustrations. As these popular techniques proliferated, many serious artists ceased to use the medium. Van Gogh remained one of the few painters of the period who retained a preference for pen and ink, and although it is difficult to be certain of the type of pen he used, his drawing of the "Bridge at L'Anglois" (Figure 15–2) suggests a reed pen. The pen strokes are short and jagged, frequently revealing the grainy texture characteristic of the fibrous and rough wooden nib. The long flowing lines which swell gracefully from thin to thick, so typical of the flexible metal point and which contribute the stylish look of facility desired by popular illustrators, was purposely eschewed by Van Gogh in favor of the blunt, earnest style we see here, with its bristling energetic surface. The angular character of the lines and the fact that they do not interweave but for the most part remain separate from one another, creates a staccato surface by which he was able to convey in a drawing the same sense of surface vigor that he conveyed in painting through the use of bold color laid on in thick viscous masses with brush or palette knife. The drawing of the upraised portcullis has a particular distinction because of the way in which variations of line width suggest both the structure of the forms and the play of overhead light.

Brush and Ink

In the Orient the use of brush with ink is as traditional as the use of pen in Western cultures. There has always been a close connection between the art of writing and drawing in the Orient since the techniques involved in manipulating the brush are the same, and in both the ornamental character of the lines produced through the skillful manipulation of the brush have always been highly prized. In Oriental brush drawing, sumi, the dry ink-stick, is rubbed against stone with water to produce the ink which is picked up in the brush. The brushes, made of various animal hairs such as wolf, goat, badger, or rabbit have a much longer head than European watercolor brushes; consequently, they hold more ink and the drawing process is less frequently interrupted. The brushes are made in a variety of sizes. The sharply pointed brush is most frequently used, although wide flat brushes are also employed. The brushes are held vertically above the paper and the wrist must not rest on the table. Since the papers or silk fabrics used as grounds are very absorbent, lines cannot be altered or deleted, and a skilled craftsman never repeats a line. The thickness of lines is determined by varying the pressure on the brush, and through the skillful use of a variety of brushes a very extensive range of lines, tones and textures can be produced.

All kinds of brushes, from the pointed Oriental brushes of China and Japan to the flat bristle brush employed in oil painting and the sable or oxhair brushes used in watercolor, can be used with ink, and each brush imparts its particular character to a drawing. In general, brush and ink provides greater variety of line than pen and ink, for the brush line can be varied from wide to narrow at the artist's will. Brush also provides for the rapid laying in of broad areas of dark, and when a brush is only partially dampened with ink, dry brush effects of a granular or textured nature can be produced. Dry brush is frequently combined with wash and this combination creates textures varying from fluid washed tones through rich strong lines to granular textures and so provides for an unusual range of effects. A variety of papers can be used with brush and ink, smooth papers giving clean cut lines with sharp edges, and rough papers tending to contribute granular dry-brush effects. Certain very absorbent papers such as Japanese rice papers and blotters, because they absorb the ink immediately and record all the fluctuations of brush width produced by the varying pressures of the hand, create lines of unusual character. Striking effects have been achieved by drawing with brush on wet paper. The ink creeps over the wet surface to

FIGURE 17–9

School of Sesshu or Eitoka
(c. 1590; Japanese).
Panel of a Six-fold Screen.
Sumi on rice paper, 63″ x 21″.
Stanford University Museum
(Ikeda Collection).

create curious veined effects, or unusual blobs, and the very fact that the movements of the ink on the surface cannot be predicted forces the artist to be inventive in relation to what appears on the paper in the course of carrying out a drawing, thus preventing stereotyped effects.

Brush drawings can be done with media other than ink. Black watercolor, tempera (or poster paints), and oils can all be used with a wide variety of brushes for drawing purposes. Here the viscosity or fluidity of the medium and the character of the brush influence the distinguishing characteristics of the drawings (Figure 17–7). Many experienced painters like to draw with the same tools and materials with which they paint, as it is then easy to develop a drawing into a painting; in such cases it is almost impossible to tell when the drawing ceases and becomes painting.

Master Drawings in Brush and Ink

The narrowness of line produced by a pen point gives it its bite and energy and at the same time limits the degree of linear flexibility and painterliness. When artists wish to expand the scope of line they pick up a brush, as did Diego Rivera when he drew his "Mother and Child" (Figure 17–8). The brush permits, even encourages, the expansion of line width and thereby provides an element of richness, strength, and linear eloquence which the more incisive pen line lacks. Because a pointed brush fully loaded with a not too viscous fluid was used on a fairly smooth paper, the lines are clean-edged and where the artist so desired, swell from a fine point to a full wide line and back to fine.

Though the Rivera drawing provides a bold and dramatic statement, its deliberate and controlled character suggests no sense of inner agitation or emotional turmoil. By contrast Emil Nolde's "Landscape with Windmill" (Figure 11–2) conveys an almost frenzied vehemence, as though the somber landscape of Schleswig aroused such powerfully depressing emotions that the artist could barely control his expression. A stiff, fairly broad bristle brush and heavy black printer's ink produced the grainy textures and the harsh awkward shapes that so effectively express the grim mood. Probably neither Rivera nor Nolde consciously planned their use of tools and materials to create an effect. Instead, each artist finds that he is responsive to certain ways of working, and it is this intuitive response to subject matter, tools, and materials that eventually determines style, technique, and, above all, the individual artist's uniqueness.

A discussion of brush-and-ink technique can well conclude with a study of Chinese and Japanese brush painting, since more than one thousand years of familarity with the conventions and esthetics of brush and ink technique has produced an art of great refinement, distinction, and beauty. While in the work of such masters as Li Ch'eng (Figure 9–1) and Hokusai (Figures 9–9, 13–13) technical skill remained in the service of expression, more frequently one is aware of the pure virtuosity of technique and the decorative charm of the works of the Oriental masters. The training of artists emphasized the handling of brushes and the learning of particular sequences of brush strokes for representing birds, fish, bamboo, peonies, and the other elements of their artistic vocabulary. The chief basis for determining excellence was expertness of technique and taste in the decorative disposition of compositional elements.

One panel from a six-panel screen from the late sixteenth-century school of Sesshu, Japan, portraying a Buddhist temple in a mountainous landscape, illustrates the expert and imaginative manipulations of the brush that make Oriental drawing and painting so fascinating. (Figure 17–9) In the foreground a heavy and irregular brush line moves with an angular broken rhythm to describe the trunk and heavy branches of a pair of cypress trees, and these heavy lines are supplemented by an irregular stippled texture to suggest rough bark. Two kinds of patterns: first, sets of radiating fine lines and second, hanging clusters of lines grouped to make triangular patterns, describe the foliage of the foreground cypresses. In the middle distance a brilliant pattern of rather straight lines and dots placed in an angular relation to one another establishes the character of the cypress foliage seen from above (from which position the branch pattern is not visible), and provides a subtle contrast to the foreground rendering. A few vertical brush strokes below the distant cypresses suggest the steep cliffs, and in the distance the temple is rendered with lines of astonishing precision which

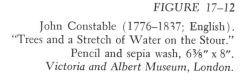

FIGURE 17–12

John Constable (1776–1837; English).
"Trees and a Stretch of Water on the Stour."
Pencil and sepia wash, 6⅜" x 8".
Victoria and Albert Museum, London.

FIGURE 17–13

August Rodin (1840–1917; French). "Nude." Pencil and water color, 17⅝" x 12½". *Courtesy of The Art Institute of Chicago (The Alfred Stieglitz Collection).*

appear almost ruled in their verticality, horizontality, and evenness of width. Still another contrast of pattern is supplied by the distant tall pines, and, beyond them, the airy distance is suggested by a soft wash. Here, in one panel a succession of brilliantly differentiated linear patterns creates a visual poem of great refinement and charm. There are no happy accidents in the work. Each brush stroke drawn from a storehouse of established patterns is carefully calculated and deftly executed.

Very different in the particular skill and taste involved but essentially the same in regard to the attitude toward tradition is a brush painting of a bird in ink on paper from an album of flowers, birds, insects, and fish, by Chu Ta, a seventeenth-century Chinese painter (Figure 9–7). This school of artists loaded different parts of the brush with different amounts of ink, and by using either the broad side of the brush or the tip, created very contrasting tones, shapes, and textures. The loaded brush was pressed against the paper so as to deposit a heavy dark in the middle of the bird's head and this, grading out toward lighter edges, gives it form. In the same way a graduated wash is laid on the body so that the black lines that describe the feather patterns stand out in great richness against the grays of the body and make a singing accent of the white spot retained so deftly in the center of the area. The sharp lines of legs and feet, the roughly textured branch created by drawing a dry brush quickly across the absorbent rice paper, and the animated calligraphy combine to create a modest work of great charm.

Since the ink used in Oriental brush drawing is dissolved from the solid block of sumi and thinned with varying amounts of water the line between brush and ink drawing and wash drawing is arbitrary and relatively meaningless. However, because the range of grays seems to outweigh the linear component in Hokusai's "The Woodcutter" it is discussed in the section on wash drawing.

Wash Drawing

Unlike brush and ink drawing, which depends for its effectiveness upon the use of solid black, in wash drawing the medium if freely diluted with water to provide a wide range of grays.

On first impression the term *wash drawing* seems a contradiction, for wash implies a painting technique rather than a drawing technique, and in truth, a wash drawing is a painted drawing. However, if we refer back to our original definition of a drawing as ". . . all those representations in which an image is obtained by marking . . . upon a surface which constitutes a background," wash drawing, because it marks with a brush, pigment and water falls as logically within the category of drawing as any other type of brush drawing. Wash drawing is usually done with black ink or watercolor which is thinned with water to provide gradation of value from dark to light. Wash drawing can, of course, be done with water and tempera, gouache, or the new acrylic polymer paints, although those media tend to be less fine-grained than ink or watercolor. Wash drawing can also be done with oil paints thinned with turpentine or paint-thinner. Wash is frequently used to reinforce line drawing with an easily applied tone, and so pencil and wash, pen and wash, charcoal, crayon and chalk and wash, are all familiar combinations. Many artists commence with line and then proceed to reinforce the line drawing with wash, others commence with the wash and then firm up edges and accent the forms by the addition of line.

An early example of wash drawing from the later fifteenth century can be seen in Mantegna's "Mars, Venus, and Diana" (Figure 3–10), executed in pen, brown ink, and blue wash with touches of white. Mantegna was inspired by the fragments of antique sculpture which were being unearthed, and he was particularly interested in the effect of classic bas-relief. By a careful application of wash, the smooth surface of marble could be evoked, and the illusion of the shiny stone was heightened by the sharp reflected lights he used to illuminate the shadow areas, thereby suggesting a marble background reflecting light into

FIGURE 17–14

Georg Kolbe (1877–1947; German).
"Nude Study." Brush and gray wash
on white paper, 19⅜″ x 14½″. *The
Cleveland Museum of Art, Ohio.*

shallow relief carving. Mantegna did not use the wash in a free painterly way
but, instead, applied it in very smooth gradations which are without any linear
texture. His choice of wash was undoubtedly influenced by a desire to avoid the
cross-hatched effects most commonly used in his day, for such effects would not
suggest the smooth surface of antique marble as effectively as wash.

In the seventeenth century a taste for free renderings, painterly manipulations of pigment and extended areas of dark and bold contrasts of value, turned
artists away from the dry media toward the more easily manipulated fluid media.
Sepia, bistre, and a variety of earth colors provided a painterly element of color.
Attractive effects were also achieved by combining a warm and cool color, black
and bistre, sepia and gray, and so on. In modern times wash has again become
popular as a medium for commercial illustration, fashion drawing, and caricature, as well as for fine arts purposes. The choice of brush used in wash drawing
varies according to the preference of the artist, but the pointed watercolor brush
is most frequently used.

A group of drawings from the seventeenth, eighteenth, and early nineteenth
centuries illustrate the versatility of wash in the hands of the great masters of the
medium.

Claude Lorrain used bistre for "The Tiber Above Rome" (Figure 17–10), thereby adding the richness of intense brown to the bold tonalities of this handsome study. Done without any reinforcing or restricting pen or pencil line, one feels the uninhibited freedom with which the study was executed and the artist's direct response to the spreading shadows of late afternoon. No other medium would enable the artist to record extended areas of dark so rapidly, retain brilliant areas of light, and cover the surface of the paper without any linear element obtruding itself. The execution of such a drawing probably did not take more than a half hour, thus enabling the painter to catch the momentary effects of late day. Particularly handsome are the areas where black-brown and dark values merge because a brushload of concentrated dark was placed into an already wet medium dark value. Such painterly effects could not be achieved with any of the dry media.

The previously discussed study attributed to Caravaggio (Figure 4–1) has as a foundation a very sketchy pen drawing which was given weight, dramatic intensity and compositional coherence as a value study by the addition of broadly washed tones of bistre. The animated but fragmentary pen lines work beautifully with the very flat broad areas of wash to reduce to its fundamentals what might later be developed into a fairly complex composition. As in the Lorrain landscape, one can almost visualize the act of applying the wash, so direct and unlabored is the mode of application, and this direct rendering adds force and energy to the sketch. The technique of wash drawing used here has a popular contemporary counterpart in the humorous illustrations of artists like Peter Arno and Dedini.

An unknown Venetian executed this magnificent drawing of a "Triumphant General Crowned by a Flying Figure" (Figure 4–6) in brown wash and pen on white paper. Unlike the two preceding wash drawings, this one achieves its effectiveness through the exciting scramble of lines, the rich blurred spots of ink in the wash and the roughly textured character of some of the washes. The ink lines were scribbled in impetuous strokes, the paper seemingly scratched and stabbed with the point of the pen, so that areas like the head of the General lose most of their linear character. This rough surface was then covered with wash, probably applied with a rough bristle brush, as many of the edges of the wash have a granular character. It is the variety and vitality of the textures achieved by wash and pen in conjunction with the great swirling movements of the composition that energize this exciting drawing.

A completely contrasting mood and technique is provided by Canaletto's "An Island in the Lagoon" (Figure 4–16). This lovely drawing was first sketched in lightly applied pencil lines to insure accurate perspective. Subsequently the architectural forms were established in brown ink lines, which waver and frequently end in curly arabesques to keep them from seeming rigid and mechanical. Thin washes of carbon ink were then added to provide a pleasant cool bluish contrast to the warm brown ink lines and to suggest the watery atmospheric envelope so characteristic of Venice. The washes are flat, relatively pale, and remain within the confines of the pen lines. The finished drawing is calm and controlled in mood, orderly but not in any way dull.

Tiepolo is probably the undisputed master of the European technique of wash drawing. No one seems to have better understood the role of untouched white paper, of the accenting blurred dark laid into the fresh wash with loaded pen and certainly no one has ever used pale translucent washes with greater effectiveness. The dexterity with which he handles wash and the charm of his gracious manner is beautifully displayed in his "The Rest on the Flight into Egypt" (Figure 17–11). A light pen line that moves with the abandon of a butterfly's flight and barely seems to touch the paper defines, or one might better say, suggests the forms. Over this sketchy framework was laid a pale wash, and into this luminous shadow tone sharp accenting darks were applied. The darks have been distributed all through the drawing to unite and relate the sketchily indicated parts. The broken texture of these dark accents intensifies the pale blonde tones of the wash so they appear even more transparent than they are, and the entire drawing appears to shimmer in a brilliant glow of reflected light. The drawing is a miracle of suggestion in which a kind of shorthand of line, wash, and accenting dark evokes both a specific image and a lyric mood.

A very different kind of shorthand can be seen in Constable's wash drawing of "Trees and a Stretch of Water on the Stour" (Figure 17–12). Small though it is (6⅜″ x 8″), this rapid notation of the effect of dark trees against shining water has the strength and magnitude of a large painting. The fluid medium and the experience of a lifetime enabled Constable to capture the essence of the subject in a few powerful strokes.

Another, but certainly no less expert handling of wash, is revealed in Hokusai's "The Old Woodcutter" (Figure 13–4). Unlike the tradition of wash drawing dominant in Europe, Hokusai does not supplement the outline drawing with wash to create the illusion of three-dimensional forms under illumination. Instead, a brilliant variety of lines and textures are given visual unity through the use of broadly applied washes, which relate and solidify into a coherent pattern what might otherwise become a fragmented scatter of lines and spots. Starting at the upper right the tones of wash move down and to the left to create a continuous dark shape, broken only when Hokusai purposely accented an area by leaving it light. No particular kind of illumination, in fact not even a consistent source of illumination, is suggested here. Rather, a concern with visual unity and pictorial coherence and a love for the rich combination of black lines on dark gray appears to have determined the distribution of the wash.

A group of modern drawings suggests some of the ways wash is used today. Rodin has washed in an almost flat tone of gray to separate a dancing figure from the penciled drapery masses and the background (Figure 17–13). There is little evidence of any systematic attempt on Rodin's part to vary the value of the wash to give form to the figure, but the seemingly accidental changes of tone within the wash inevitably suggest the volumes of the body, partly because they were reinforced by such firm contour lines. The casual nature of the wash seems right for the almost scribbled indication of the draperies and suggests that Rodin made the drawing as a note with no other thought in mind than to record the graceful gesture of the dancer. Another dancing figure, this one by George Kolbe (Figure 17–14), has been sketched with pen and then deftly modeled with a few bold washes to achieve a painterly quality. Unlike the Rodin, the wash here has been used very systematically to establish strong darks, which divide the illuminated right-hand planes of the figure from the broad shadowed area. The dark wash which established the core of the shadow shades rapidly into light on the illuminated sides of the body and only gradually turns light in the shadows, thereby creating through the effective suggestion of reflected light, an illusion of brilliant illumination.

The Japanese-French Foujita has left us a very subtle pen and wash drawing of a "Mexican General" (Figure 12–15). The clear pen lines provide a firm structure against which the delicate washes of gray play a sensuous obligato. The almost shimmering tones of the wash are in delightful contrast to the ferocious and sullen countenance of the subject. This contrast between the grotesque and the exquisite seems to be an element of his Japanese artistic heritage which Foujita brings to the Western art world in a very personal way.

Some artists are purists by temperament and take the limitations of a medium as a challenge. Such men delight in bending the medium to their esthetic will and making it do what seems impossible. We have seen Dürer do this with brush and ink, and Ingres with pencil, Sheeler with conté crayon. Other artists care only to achieve a certain effect and they freely combine media to realize their goals. A drawing might be started in charcoal. After a certain level of development the desire for richer darks might lead to the introduction of ink accents. If the ink accents stand out too much, a wash of gray may be used to relate the black ink lines and the areas of charcoal. Further study might

Mixed Media and Contemporary Experiments

FIGURE 17–15

Mac Zimmerman (1912–   ; German).
"Head." 1958. Palette knife and ink, 25½" x 19¾".
*Collection, The Museum of Modern Art,
New York (Gertrud A. Mellon Fund).*

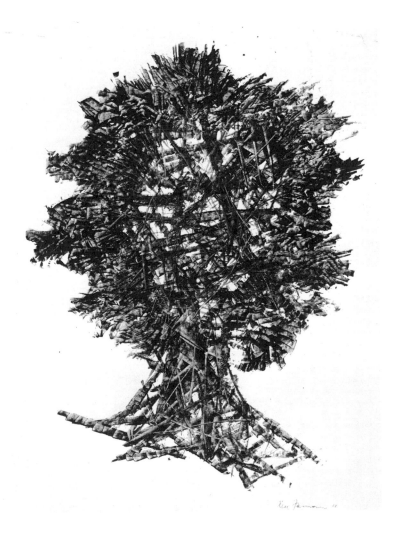

indicate the desirability of some brilliant lights. Areas of white tempera could then be added, and if the whites seem to separate from the rest of the drawing, charcoal could again be applied to provide a very pale gray which would fuse some of the disturbing whites into the rest of the drawing. Such an improvised procedure might well have occurred when Bernardino Gatti made his "Study of an Apostle Standing" (Figure 4–5) in preparation for one of the apostles in an "Ascension" at St. Sigismondo, Cremona, in the early sixteenth century. The drawing is described as follows: "Brush and pen over black chalk, heightened with body color (opaque tempera) with a little gray wash, and touches of yellow and pink pigment." The result is a beautifully fused whole in which broadly brushed areas of opaque light stand in contrast to the wiry darks. Studying any group of master drawings, particularly from the seventeenth century, reveals that this kind of impromptu combining of media and materials was standard procedure: drawings grew as it were, each step improvised by the artist to carry the work toward his goal.

Today many media are used in unorthodox ways and are combined freely to produce varied effects. From one recent exhibition of drawings the author compiled the following list of media: charcoal, pencil, graphite, carbon pencil, pen and ink, crayon and turpentine, colored pencil, charcoal and watercolor wash, ink wash, charcoal and ink, pencil and mixed media, conte, ink and pastel, ink, wash, and collage, lithographic crayon and ink, pencil and oil wash, gouache, pencil and ink, wax pencil, chalk and ink, ink and gesso, pastel and ink, crayon and pencil, lamp black and wax, ink and graphite, lithographic pencil, lacquer resist, conté and charcoal, wax crayon, wash and graphite, dry pigment and rhoplex, ink and gouache, and colored ink and oil. Undoubtedly if the grounds had been indicated the list would have been equally extensive.

One of the distinguishing characteristics of the art of our era is the desire on the part of artists to break through the restrictive barriers of convention and explore new paths. The academic conventions of the nineteenth century turned men away from the free combinations of media and materials that were accepted in the preceding centuries. Discipline was exalted beyond sensible limits, so that the kind of tedious perfection of technique was stressed, often at the cost of expressive power, spontaneity, and freshness. Charcoal, pencil, pen and ink, and conté were forced to display the artists' skill and in place of a rich creative fervor, works of art were frequently executed with mechanical industriousness. Today exploration and invention are key words; technical discipline for its own sake is frowned upon. Conventions concerning the "proper" use of media are now considered narrow and restrictive: they fail to exploit the full potentialities of the material and overlook the rich effects that are achieved by combining media.

Another contemporary tendency that has contributed to an experimental attitude toward materials grows from a deep concern with the nature of art as a social process and as a psychological manifestation. The Bauhaus in Germany tried to separate artistic production from sentimental preconceptions; thus the artist's tools and materials, the process of creation and an interest in the work of art as a purely physical entity stimulated an intense examination of the esthetic

potentialities of every material and method. Paul Klee, Kandinsky, and other artists explored new ways of using the traditional media as well as original and exciting new materials and methods, and this impulse is still alive and vital. A few pages from a catalogue of Klee's works reveal the following unorthodox items: batiked paper with watercolor, pen and ink on wet paper, vaporized watercolor and brush on cardboard, watercolor and oil on paper, chalk and ink on blotter, watercolor and wax on linen, watercolor on chalk, watercolor on paper applied with knife, and even more complex, watercolor over chalk on paper set on gauze backed with cardboard. In such works the spirit of exploration was combined with exquisite sensibilities, and exciting new vistas in the realm of drawing were opened up as a result.

Artists have also been encouraged to explore new uses and combinations of materials by the great expansion of artists' media that has resulted from modern scientific and technological developments. Plastic paints, metallic paints and papers, synthetic pigments, cellophanes, new types of inks and pencils, all challenge the artist's inventive and expressive powers. The iconoclasm of the early twentieth-century Dadaists and the consequent introduction of nonartistic objects and materials into the pictorial matrix also stimulated artists to explore the potentialities of unorthodox materials, so that what started as a derisive gesture resulted in an enlarging of the artistic vocabulary. Thus collage and assemblage, where junk, discarded objects, and materials from everyday life are incorporated into and become part of a painting or piece of sculpture, has also extended and broadened the practice of drawing.

Today, artists incorporate bits of photography or typography into their drawings, they draw with twigs or match sticks dipped in ink, ink is applied with a palette knife (Figure 17–15) or by airbrush (Figure 10–11); they draw on corrugated board, if they want a ribbed texture, or on superimposed layers of transparent tracing paper or cellophane.

Exploration is a prime mover.

Master Drawings in Combined Media

In even such a relatively conservative drawing as Bellows' "Dance in a Madhouse" (Figure 12–8) one can see the added power that accompanied greater freedom in conbining media. The drawing was done in black and red crayon, pen and ink, and Chinese white. The drawing was probably started in red and black crayon; then ink lines were added to sharpen the details of gesture, as in the raised hands of the dancers or to intensify the expressions on some of the faces. This could be done without belaboring the free and unifying chalk drawing. The addition of some Chinese white produced the very intense light accents.

In "The Doorbell," by Matt Kahn (Figure 14–16), crushed charcoal has been rubbed into the paper to create soft grays which provide a change in texture and value. In contrast to the brilliant patterns which dominate the drawing, the charcoal tone appears soft and muffled against the clangorous hard-edged blacks and whites. Even with wash it would be difficult to produce grays of such smooth grainless texture, which emphasize to the maximum the clarity of the sharply defined lines, dots and patterns.

A rich and interesting example of an unconventional use of materials can be seen in one of the many drawings Henry Moore, the great contemporary English sculptor, made in preparation for his sculptures. This drawing, done as a study for a stone "Madonna and Child" for the Church of St. Matthew, Northampton, England, was executed in ink, ink wash, and pencil on white paper (Figure 17–16). The two sculptural forms that constitute the study have been isolated from the general background tone by laying a water-resistant "stop" on the white paper before applying the background wash of ink. Either rubber cement, a liquid frisket, or water-repellent wax crayon could have been used with equal satisfaction. The stop was used wherever the artist wanted to preserve the white of the paper and was probably applied after the pencil, which can be seen as a medium dark gray line. A loose wash of middle-value gray was put over the entire page. When the wash was dry the water-resistant stop was removed and then the circular lines in pen and ink were applied to reinforce the sense of sculpturally conceived form. This technique encouraged the artist to visualize the project in very broad generalized masses. A number of elements play against each other to create interest: the soft fluid wash, the grainy middle-value lines of pencil, the sharp black-pen lines, and the white areas protected by the resist. In the larger figure group, the resist was laid on in masses so that the broad, almost clumsy white linear pattern provides a bold contrast to the sharp pen lines. Neither pencil, wash, nor pen and ink alone could have produced such varied textural effects.

Experimentation

Invention and discovery can lead to delightful, surprising, and expressive new ways of using traditional materials. Two new uses of ink are worthy of note. Harry Davis himself describes the procedure he used to create "Trees" (Figure 17–17). The artist says "The main part of the drawing was done quite spontaneously, spattering brown and black India ink with ordinary Flit-guns. Immediately, I used a dampened sponge to spread the spots of ink, developing the shapes of trees and leaves in that way. Afterwards, with a brush and pen, drawing of trunks and branches were deliberately added where needed. In order to obtain the effect of a meadow in the foreground a strip of newspaper was laid over that area during a part of the spattering." Here invention has supplemented a genuine knowlege of landscape structure and tree forms to present a familiar subject in a new and fresh manner.

Equally imaginative is the manner in which Mac Zimmerman has used ink to create his fanciful "Head" (Figure 17–15). The ink was applied by scraping it against the smooth paper with a palette knife. The variations in pressure created a relief effect suggestive of intaglio and this has been sensitively exploited by the involved overlapping lines and the sculpturally dimensioned textures.

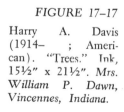

FIGURE 17–17

Harry A. Davis (1914– ; American). "Trees." Ink, 15½" x 21½". Mrs. William P. Dawn, Vincennes, Indiana.

The abundance of new materials and the inventive attitude toward techniques so characteristic of today is not an unmixed blessing. It is easy to become enamored of surfaces, materials and techniques without giving sufficient thought to the deeper levels of interpretation and meaning that constitute the major significance of works of art. It is also possible to flit from one fascinating material to the next without ever fully exploring the potential of any one. However, a period of exploration and experimentation is necessary for every artist, for only by such a process does he find the materials and media best suited to his individual temperament.

Summary   The fluid media are inks, wash, and can include mixed media. Inks can be fluid, paste, or solid and are identified according to their use, special properties, and place of origin. The ink most frequently preferred by artists is India ink because of its velvety blackness. Quill and reed pens were standard until the nineteenth century when the steel pen was perfected. Reed pens are still preferred by some artists because they produce such characterful lines. Today a multitude of pens designed for special purposes provide the artists with a rich variety of resources.

The pen and ink line is brilliant and incisive and drawings in pen and ink outline, by eliminating all but absolute essentials, constitute a kind of graphic shorthand of great power. The most systematic and controlled use of pen and ink for the objective description of forms and surface textures can be seen in scientific illustrations. Pen and ink techniques were derived from silverpoint and the print processes in the early Renaissance, became more free in the High Renaissance and assumed very free painterly qualities in the hands of the great Baroque draftsmen who also developed unparalleled virtuosity in cross-hatching and related techniques. In the nineteenth century pen and ink was used with great skill to describe surface textures and for illustrative purposes.

Brush and ink permits much greater flexibility of line than pen and ink and thus encourages a more free and expressive variation of line width and of texture than pen and ink. The most brilliant use of brush and ink is found in the Orient where such masters as Hokusai employed brush and ink with exceptional virtuosity and taste. Other media than ink are frequently used for brush drawing. In wash drawing ink or paint is thinned with water for variations of value. Wash drawing is the most painterly type of drawing. It appeared in Renaissance times and was used by such baroque painters as Tiepolo with great brilliance. It is still used with much variety and ingenuity.

Mixing media encourages improvisation and permits a wide variety of textural effects. A free combination of media was common among baroque artists, was frowned on by the academic purists of the nineteenth century but is again popular. The twentieth century has witnessed a tremendous expansion of media and materials. The contemporary interest in an inventive use of materials and techniques was stimulated by the revolt against academic restrictions, by technological progress, and by Bauhaus concepts. An undue concern with invention and new materials and techniques can mitigate against more profound expressive concerns.

part five

CONCLUSION

18

IMAGINATION

The *Oxford Universal Dictionary* defines imagination somewhat unimaginatively as "the power which the mind has of forming concepts beyond those derived from external objects." This most familiar conception of imagination is well illustrated by Piranesi's "Architectural Fantasy" (Figure 18–1). Piranesi was an architect by ambition, though he constructed no buildings until he was forty-five years old. However, he was a student of Roman architecture, and delighted in imagining vast architectural vistas that evoked visions of grandeur befitting his romantic conception of ancient Rome. His "Architectural Fantasy," exciting in its scale and magnificence, falls within the realm of the credible and possible even though it never existed nor possibly would ever exist. Were it neither credible nor possible it would be equally acceptable as an imaginative creation inasmuch as it displays some of the seemingly endless possibilities for an imaginative interplay between a lively mind, a sympathetic spirit, and the act of drawing.

Creativity and Imagination

Imagination is the precious ingredient that distinguishes the creative person; in fact, imagination and creativity are almost synonymous except that imagination can function without any concrete results, as in daydreaming, whereas creativity implies constructive action. Very simply, creative behavior might be described as the ability to create or invent. Creativity involves various capacities. First, there is the ability to react to stimuli in an unusual way, a quality which we call originality. The original person resists fixed and rigid responses, reacts in fresh and unpredictable ways to experience. Second, the creative person must be able to bring his original responses to some degree of fruition—in the case of the artist, to translate his living experience into artistic

forms. Third, the creative person is characterized by a rich inventiveness and a
certain playfulness; he retains the ability to elaborate as in daydreaming or
childhood play. These qualities of originality of response, productivity, and
inventiveness are all apparent in Theo van Doesburg's drawings of "The
Cow" (Figure 18–2).

Students of creativity have analyzed and identified the steps that seem to
occur in the course of creative activity, whether in the arts, sciences, or other
fields of endeavor. There appear to be four main phases, which can be described
as impulse, gestation, outpouring and refining. The artist "has an idea." This
may come from an assigned problem (a commission, for example) or from
seeing a potential subject (a cow) or from an artistic stimulus such as seeing
another drawing, reading a story, or hearing a piece of music. Frequently the
source of an idea remains unknown to the artist, seemingly a free-rising fantasy.
After the impulse has initiated action, the second phase occurs in the form of a
period of gestation. The gestation may be partially active (notice the way van

Doesburg played with the impulse to abstract the form of the cow into a pattern of interrelated rectangles). Or the gestation period may be one in which the impulse to all intents and purposes lies dormant, evolving and taking on form in the subconscious mind without a conscious awareness on the part of the artist of what is taking place, only to rise suddenly to the surface of the mind almost completely structured and formed. The third and most characteristic step of creative activity occurs when the imaginative projection takes concrete form. This often appears to be a spontaneous outpouring, an automatic welling up from subconscious depths. The artist seems to produce without a struggle, forms and relationships come easily; it is as though the artist were responding to some hidden voice that directs his actions without his being conscious of the source of direction. This outpouring can occur even in carrying out what appears to be an unimaginative and prosaic task such as drawing a specific object. An unexpected clairvoyance illuminates the drawing problem, the artist is suddenly aware of the relationships of shape and dark and light and he handles his materials easily and effectively. In the fourth and last step, the artist views his work with a critical eye, refines, reshapes, and makes minor changes. Here the superego takes over, and the artist views his work almost like an outsider, consciously adjusting it to his own critical standards.

It has been pointed out by the students of creativity that the creative act is not a single intuitive reaction to a situation, but a habit, a habit that grows from a sustained pattern of response to certain stimuli. Some artists, early in their careers, form the habit of drawing only in response to an immediate visual stimulus, a model, a still life, a landscape. They may draw as literally as possible, never trusting themselves to deviate from what they see, always using the same procedures and materials. Other artists always work "from their heads." They only refer to the actual objects if they cannot create a convincing image without observing the real thing.

The first approach does not deny the possibility of imagination. Monet painted certain subjects like Rouen Cathedral many times from an almost identical vantage point, but he remained imaginative in that he continuously responded to different aspects of his subject. Nor does the second course insure imagination. Many a cartoonist, though he draws without reference to actual objects, uses imagination only in that he changes the incidents depicted in his drawings. Perhaps the most valuable habit that can be formed to stimulate imagination is to follow any strong interest, idea or impulse. Independence of mind, self-direction, the ready surrender to one's own enthusiasms—all of these elements seem essential for the creation of that self-assurance which must exist if an artist is to trust his own judgment and convictions.

Certain capacities which play a prime role in effecting the heightened powers of communication characteristic of the arts are commonly grouped together under the general term of *imagination*. Imagination is multifaceted and there is no aspect of creation, even on the pure craft level, where the play of imagination is not necessary to achieve the heightened powers of communication that characterize the arts. The imaginative person avoids clichés: for him

The Elements of Imagination

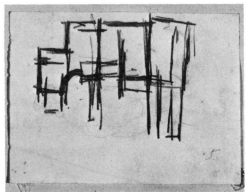
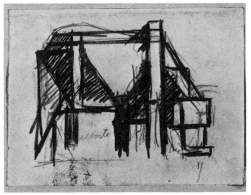
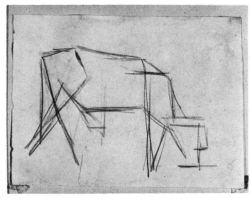

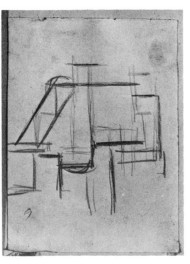

FIGURE 18–2

Theo van Doesburg (1883–1931; Dutch). "The Cow." Series of eight pencil drawings, each sheet 4⅝" x 6¼". *Collection, The Museum of Modern Art, New York.* (*Photo: Sunami.*)

what has already been said needs no repetition, and at best is only the point of departure for a more personal expression. Every person has a certain uniqueness of viewpoint because the living experience of no two persons is identical; consequently, each person has the potential for some degree of imaginative activity. However, this potential can easily lie dormant and atrophy from lack of use. We acquire habits of being or not being imaginative.

Just as the creative act can be better understood by perceiving its parts, so identifying the various components can clarify the nature of imagination. In attempting to identify the various elements of the imaginative act, four distinct abilities reveal themselves. These might be described as the ability (1) to empathize, (2) to fantasize, (3) to particularize, and (4) to generalize. The first of these, the power to empathize, is most basic to imaginative activity. It is characterized by the capacity to identify with the subject, to conceive and share feelings and experiences not readily evident in surface appearances, to perceive an emotional character even in inanimate objects and to project this sympathetic attitude through the work of art. This basic aspect of imagination might also be described as the ability to externalize feelings.

The second imaginative capacity, the ability to fantasize, involves conceiving of objects, combinations of and relationships between objects which do not occur in the external world. This is the most obvious aspect of imagination and most familiar to the layman. The third and fourth forms of imaginative activity mentioned above represent opposite facets of the ability to see relationships, similarities, and differences; it is this capacity that enables man to classify, relate, and differentiate. The capacity to individualize derives from the ability to select the characterizing detail which evokes the image of the whole. The caricaturist does this with remarkable effectiveness. The fourth, the ability to generalize, consists of seeing broad relationships and identifying the common denominator between related objects. The artist who discards individual idiosyncracies of form to create a monumental symbol, as did Michelangelo with the human figure, has this capacity. Many great works of art draw on all of these aspects of imagination; almost no work of significance depends on only one.

In analyzing the components of imagination we identified the ability to empathize as most basic. It is his ability to empathize that enables the artist to project meaning into the commonplace, to see the artistic potentialities of simple aspects of his environment. A drawing of "Baggage Carts" (Figure 18–3) by Richard Wiegmann reveals something of the nature of empathy and of imaginative activity. These awkward vehicles were probably observed lined up on the platform of a railway station. An unimaginative person would see them, think "Baggage carts" or "A train must be expected," and forthwith dismiss the matter from his mind. A more imaginative observer might be amused at their ungainly proportions and think, "Well, these are relics of an earlier era in the history of transportation," and then his mind and eyes would move elsewhere. Richard Wiegmann went further. As he observed the carts, a series of reactions occurred. He was intrigued by their shape and arrangement and saw the possibility of making an amusing drawing of them as they appeared on the

Empathy and Imagination

platform. He probably walked back and forth before them a number of times until he decided on this particular perspective grouping, evaluating various arrangements, visualizing in his mind or on paper some of the other possible groupings of carts, and finally settling on this particular view for two reasons: First, it revealed both the front and side view of the trucks and, second, by providing a long perspective it suggests almost an endless vista even though only five carts are really pictured.

At this point the artist probably commenced to sketch. There was undoubtedly a background visible behind the carts, the train station, tracks and semaphores, or the street across from the station. It was necessary to evaluate the degree to which these background elements would contribute or distract from his pictorial idea. Again, this involved the play of imagination, for the artist had to visualize the effectiveness of the unencumbered silhouettes as against the interplay of the truck forms with various backgrounds. Obviously, he decided that any additional background forms would distract the eye from these awkward vehicles, and he even went so far as to eliminate as an extraneous element the shadows which the carts cast on the ground.

In the course of drawing the trucks the imaginative element of sympathetic observation became involved. The old trucks had had a long and hard life. They had become battered, the wheels were slightly out of the round. Some of the wooden rails had sagged and lost the sharp rectangularity of new boards. An unimaginative person might note with disapproval these evidences of age and use, but a sympathetic attitude, an ability to share experience constitutes an imaginative capacity that enables the artist to empathize even with objects. The angularities of the wheels, the nonrectangularities of wooden parts were seen and stressed so that the artist communicated some of his understanding attitude even to less sympathetic eyes.

Imagination also plays its part in the technique of this simple line drawing. By varying the width of outlines, overloading the pen at times and then letting it run almost dry, variations in line widths were created that suggest the warped

FIGURE 18–3

Richard Wicgmann (1940–   ; American).
"Baggage Carts." Ink, 10½" x 16¼".
Collection of Ball State University, Muncie, Indiana.

boards, the splintered corners, and the bent iron rims of wheels. Thus an element of playful involvement with the medium, of sympathetic response to fluctuating performances of tools and materials, enabled the artist to intensify the expressive potential of his medium. The drawing under discussion is not a great masterpiece, and the imaginative play involved in executing it is not of the magnitude involved in many of the drawings we have observed, but those merits which the drawing has and which keep it from being an uninteresting factual record are the result of imagination.

Let us explore further into the role of empathy in imagination. Certain conventions exist for drawing portraits which tend to emphasize the conventional aspects of the sitter's appearance. The model is posed full face, three-quarters or in profile with the sitter's head about level with the artist's. The light comes from above and slightly to one side, thereby illuminating the planes of the head in a simple and clear way. The individual aspects of the sitter's appearance are stressed sufficiently to create a recognizable likeness but those sharply characterizing aspects of feature or expression which might make the sitter appear other than handsome, successful, happy and socially conforming are minimized (Figure 6–15). Many successful portrait artists produce from this formula likenesses which usually make the sitters happy but do nothing to reveal the unconventional aspects of form and the inner depths of personality to which the imaginative artist is uniquely sensitive.

The imaginative artist moves beyond this standardized approach. He will want to make his drawing reveal more than what the average person of his own accord sees. He may want to draw the sitter's head from far below or high above, so that the bold jaw or the massive crown of the sitter is stressed (Figure 18–4). The artist may perceive that beneath the flesh of the face there is a bony structure of unusual strength. A side view, by emphasizing this bony structure, (Figure 15–3) might stress this particular aspect of the sitter's face that made him interesting as a subject and that might remain unnoticed by the less perceptive layman, who would probably be more conscious of facial expression than structure. The artist may discover that a sharp light, by stressing the folds and wrinkles of the skin around the eyes emphasizes the texture of age and so reveals the way in which the experience of living leaves its imprint on the human countenance (Figure 18–5). A face drawn with downcast eyes may appear more sculptural simply because the open eye so frequently conveys an unsculptural vivacity by suggesting sharp and frequent changes of mood and expression (Figure 18–6). Leaving the drawing barely defined and embedded in a matrix of textured blurs might suggest a withdrawn preoccupied person, self-involved, and unaware of the external world (Figure 18–7).

At its height, imaginative insight goes beyond the external appearance of the sitter. Otto Dix has drawn an "Old Woman" (Figure 18–8) so that though such facts as feature and skin texture are explicitly set forth, one is hardly aware of them. Instead, the drawing seems to focus on the questioning eyes and on a thinness of mouth and chin that suggests timidity, world-weariness, and uncertainty. The portrait becomes a document testifying to the artist's ability to project his sensitivity to the sitter's emotional life in graphic form. A "Portrait of George Limbour" by Jean Dubuffet (Figure 18–9) departs radically from surface

appearances and from conventional representational techniques and thereby achieves a startling intensity of expression. The childlike character of the drawing at first deludes the eye; one assumes a naivete of attitude that corresponds to the naïveté of style. But closer study reveals mature and incisive observations. The sharp eyes, slightly too close together for comfort, scrutinize us sharply. The heavy bags under the eyes suggest the worldly nature of the sitter. The thin nose, the knowing smile on the mouth, all reinforce the suggestion of a sophisticated cosmopolite. The impact of the drawing is intensified by the initial illusion of a childlike scrawl and much of the effectiveness of the work results from the fact that it demands an imaginative interpretation from the observer similar to the imagination that accompanied its conception.

Such illustrations can be multiplied many times, but the essential point should be evident. The person with imagination thinks in many directions and seems free of fixed preconceptions of how things should look or be done. Given the problem of drawing a particular head, the imaginative artist is sensitive to the unique and distinguishing qualities of that head and is able to project ways of revealing and stressing his unique insights.

Imagination and Fantasy

Brueghel's "Temptation of St. Anthony" (Figure 18–10) illustrates the second and most familiar conception of imagination. The drawing does not picture a scene that does or could exist in the actual world. Instead, elements from the real world appear in unlikely combinations that suggest some dream fantasy. A great witch's head floats on an inlet of the sea. People who inhabit the head can be seen through all the apertures; a boat sailing through the head emerges from the ear. A monstrous fish crowns the head, partially resting upon a tree which appears to grow from the witch's mouth. The fish atop the witch's head has a great opening in its side which reveals many activities, including a couple throwing a man from the aperture. Every part of the drawing reveals strange and fantastic occurrences and creatures. In the lower right-hand corner kneels St. Anthony trying to dispel the flood of disturbing visions which are pictured on the page so that he can concentrate his thoughts upon godliness. Brueghel's imagination permeates the entire composition; he could not only create such unlikely combinations of form as are to be found in the human bottle at the bottom of the middle of the page, but he could imagine a wide variety of interactions between the curious creatures which make up the dramatis personnae in this imagined struggle between godliness and evil. He also imagined the compositional arrangement which permitted him to picture such a wealth of activity without confusion. The contribution of tradition to imaginative activity cannot be overlooked. Many of the ideas we find here were adapted from his predecessor, Hieronymus Bosch. Medieval legendry, theological speculation, the miniaturistic techniques of the early Flemish painters, all helped to build a substratum of resources upon which this artist drew. Tradition can be a storehouse or a prison; Brueghel drew upon this rich Flemish tradition but his imagination was not throttled by the past.

FIGURE 18–5

Hendrick Goltzius (1558–1617; Dutch). "Portrait of Giovanni da Bologna." Chalk, 14⁹⁄₁₆" x 11¹³⁄₁₆". *Teyler Museum, Harlaam.*

Salvador Dali has frequently been likened to Bosch and Brueghel for, like these earlier men, he seems able to freely invent startling combinations of forms. Dali's "Composition of Figures with Drawers" (Figure 18–11), like the Brueghel drawing, reveals many unexpected combinations of anatomical and nonorganic forms. A careful examination of the drawing provides endless surprises; it takes time to read the drawing thoroughly, to explore all of the fanciful relationships and intertwinings of form, and doing so provides a macabre kind of entertainment. The expressive nature of the drawing is, however, very different from that in the Brueghel: a sadistic intensity permeates the renderings of forms. Brueghel combines readily an astonishing variety of forms but he renders them much as they might appear to the eye. Dali's style of drawing appears to add a dimension of dreamlike intensity absent from the older master, through his ability to externalize a nightmarish element of fear and pain to an almost unbearable level of intensity.

Stimulated by psychoanalytical theory, the surrealist group, to whom Dali was indebted, was deeply concerned with utilizing as artistic material the most obscure impulses which spring from those mysterious depths of the mind identified by Freud as the subconscious. Themes and images supplied by the unconscious, memory, dream, chance, madness, hallucination, delirium, and humor, all such previously considered irrational processes or states supplied a

FIGURE 18–6

Pierre Puvis de Chavannes (1824–1898; French). "Study of a Woman's Head." Pencil, 6¾" x 5¼". *Courtesy of the Sterling and Francine Clark Art Institute, Williamstown, Massachusetts.*

new body of imagery to artists who considered the more traditional sources of inspiration as hackneyed and overworked. These men wanted to draw as directly as possible on the deep resources of the subconscious to encourage the spontaneous welling up that characterized the third, or outpouring state of the creative act. In this way the Surrealists hoped to make available to artists a fresh supply of uncensored symbols and impulses: to engender a more imaginative level of activity than had previously prevailed in the arts.

Most of Dali's symbols are easily accepted in a work of art because they are rendered in traditional techniques. Joan Miró, on the other hand, used symbols which were far removed from those by which the external world had in the past been represented. Childlike crudities of form characterize his composition, titled simply enough "Figures" (Figure 18–12). The symbols carry anatomical attributes, fingers, arms, breasts—and the fact that the elongated forms are topped by what may be heads conveys human implications. Scribbles, splotches, random marks, reinforce the impression of a childlike outpouring of forms. As a

result the viewer is projected into a world in which the imagery establishes a level of naïveté, whimsy, fantasy, humor, even a kind of naughtiness, far from what had heretofore been the domain of art. This world came into being because Miro had the conviction to follow his impulses no matter how irrational they might appear to the conventionally trained artist or to the outsider.

The same ability to fantasize in a childlike manner characterizes much of the work of Chagall, who was for a time also associated with the Surrealists. Marc Chagall drew upon his childhood memories of Vitebsk, Russia, for his gouache and ink drawing of "Old Musician" (Figure 18–13). He was not, however, satisfied with merely recapturing the factual image but evoked the entire atmosphere of childhood in the small Russian village. The sad musician, the crude houses, the general air of poverty, the lonely and fearful atmosphere of isolation in which Jews lived in rural Russia, are all vividly recreated. Much of the power of the drawing comes from the seeming naïveté of technique. The artist's imagination not only drew upon memory and embellished it with meaningful detail but also conceived of a way of drawing that would establish the evocative nostalgia of childhood memories. Like Miró, Chagall purposely avoided rendering his forms with academically skilled techniques in order to recapture the immediacy and poignancy of memory and the dream-state.

Imagination, Particularization, and Generalization

We have just been discussing imagination as it relates to fantasy, dream, and memory. Peter Blume made a study of a beggar woman (Figure 1–9) for his painting "The Eternal City" which reveals another dimension of imaginative activity, the ability to particularize. Here imagination is not made evident through the creation of fantastic creatures and objects but appears in the artist's ability to heighten the characteristic quality of each form in the drawing. The whiteness of marble, the regularity of brick, the rough texture of sandstone, the shockingly organic character of sculptured anatomical forms are all given an intensified reality through an emphasis upon characterizing qualities. This comes to its height in the drawing of the old beggar woman. Her entire head is distorted in relation to her blind eye. Her bony feet, skinny hands, and ragged bundled limbs are seen and described by the artist with sharpened awareness. In this instance there is less evidence of sympathy on the part of the artist toward his subject than of the caricaturist's almost sadistic ability to select and exaggerate characterizing aspects of appearance.

In contrast to Peter Blume's approach, when the sixteenth-century Florentine Cambiaso observed the human figure, he tended to see the forms in terms of geometrically simplified components. In his "Tumbling Men" (Figure 18–14), he proceeded to project seven figures in a variety of positions that involved as many views of the body as possible, and then to translate all of these foreshortened forms into what one might term rectangularized components. The result is most entertaining to behold. The observer in studying the drawing tends to carry on an imaginative act that is essentially the reverse of that which enabled Cambiaso to make the drawing; the viewer unconsciously reclothes the rectangular blocks in muscles, skin, hair and other surface anatomical qualities.

FIGURE 18–9

Jean Dubuffet (1901–   ; French). "Portrait of Georges Limbour." Charcoal on ivory paper, 19″ x 12½″. *The Solomon R. Guggenheim Museum (Lent by Pierre Matisse Gallery, New York).*

Whereas Blume selected and emphasized the characterizing detail, Cambiaso selected and emphasized the characterizing generality. Harold Stevenson, a contemporary artist, has responded in a very personal manner to that most familiar studio prop, the human body. Stevenson reveals, as did Cambiaso, an original capacity to generalize, however Stevenson does it through isolation and changes in scale and thereby shows the strange form of the familiar parts of our bodies. An untitled drawing of an ear (Figure 18–15) reveals its shell-like quality, its curious convolutions and depths and the luminous paleness of flesh in contrast to dark hair.

Umberto Baccioni, like the other Italian Futurists painting in the second decade of this century, was intrigued with the idea of communicating a dynamic sense of movement through another form of generalization, semiabstracted forms. In "Study for Dynamic Force of a Cyclist, II" (Figure 18–16) he created an abstraction to symbolize speed and exertion, the dynamic elements of cycling. Much as a poetic phrase can condense into a few words a complex experience that would demand lengthy prose exposition, so here through imagination a complex time and space experience is compressed into a potent abstract pattern. Analytical and inventive capacities must work together to achieve such imaginative compression.

FIGURE 18–10
Pieter Brueghel, the Elder (1525/30–1569; Flemish).
"Temptation of St. Anthony." Pen and ink, 7¹³⁄₁₆″ x 12¹³⁄₁₆″.
By courtesy of the Ashmolean Museum, Oxford.

FIGURE 18–11

Salvador Dali (1904–   ; Spanish-French). "Composition of Figures of Drawers."
Brush and ink, 21½" x 29⅞". *Courtesy of the Fogg Art Museum,*
Harvard University, Cambridge, Massachusetts (Gift of Dr. and Mrs. Allen Roos).

Imagination and the Art Elements

We have just seen a variety of drawings in which some aspect of the external world provided a point of departure for an imaginative interpretation of experience. The art elements can in themselves provide inspiration, for a line, a texture, or a pattern can also stimulate imaginative activity. Paul Klee created a charming ink drawing of "Costumed Puppets" (Figure 18–17) which appears to have been inspired by a source other than observing puppets. Close examination reveals this drawing to be made almost entirely from lines which begin and end in spirals. One can visualize Klee entertaining himself by seeing with how many such lines he could construct parts of the human anatomy or costume details, improvising playfully almost in the spirit of doodling.

As in all of Klee's works, the formal and abstract factors interplay continuously with evocative and poetic elements. Thus, though his initial inspiration may have been lines beginning and ending in spirals, and though we

FIGURE 18–12

Joan Miró (1893–   ; Spanish-French). "Figures." Watercolor, 16" x 12½". Feigen/Palmer Gallery, Inc., Los Angeles, California.

FIGURE 18–13

Marc Chagall (1887–   ; Russian-French).
"Old Musician."
Gouache and ink, 10¾″ x 8¼″.
The Solomon R. Guggenheim Museum
(Lender Mr. and Mrs. Mark A. Graubard, Minneapolis).
Robert E. Mates, Photographer.

FIGURE 18–14

Luca Cambiaso (1527–1585; Italian).
"Tumbling Men." Pen and wash,
13¾" x 9⅝". *The Uffizi Gallery,
Florence.*

may be fascinated by the ingenuity with which Klee fitted the spirals together to make the doll-like figures, the completed work evokes a sense of the whimsical and droll gaiety of puppets. The titles of his works, the works themselves and his diaries all reveal imaginative play of exhilarating variety and sensitivity. Klee saw relationships between remote and previously unrelated objects, as though the depths of his subconscious mind had the capacity to generate fanciful and unexpected affinities. The color of a faded cloth, a certain kind of line, or some unusual texture might provide the initial stimulus after which his imagination, moving in its own oblique and unpredictable trajectory, made illuminating contacts with the cityscape, the landscape, the world of music, literature, the theatre or other of his many intense areas of enthusiasm.

Imagination can, of course, operate on a purely abstract and formal level and remain there. Kandinsky has left us a small untitled ink drawing in which forms appear to have been improvised essentially in terms of contrasts of shape, texture, and value, but without any desire to relate these formal esthetic elements to the external world (Figure 18–18). Thus big sweeping curves on the right contrast with the small tight curves on the left. Curves contrast with rectangular forms, triangles balance precariously or hang. Textures appear scribbled, ruled, vertical, horizontal or directionless, and values range from solid black to sharp white.

Imagination in the Use of Tools and Materials

Imagination governs how one draws as much as what one draws. The unimaginative person confines his use of a medium to the method he has been

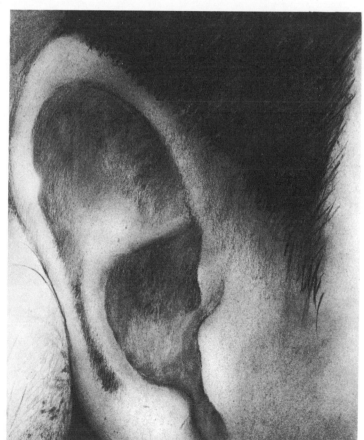

FIGURE 18–15

Harold Stevenson (1929–   ; American). Untitled. (1961) Pastel on paper, 31¾″ x 25¼″. *Feigen/Palmer Gallery, Los Angeles, California.*

FIGURE 18–16

Umberto Boccioni (1882–1916; Italian).
"Study for Dynamic Force of a Cyclist, II."
Ink, 8¼" x 12¼".
Yale University Art Gallery, New Haven,
Connecticut (Collection of the Société Anonyme).

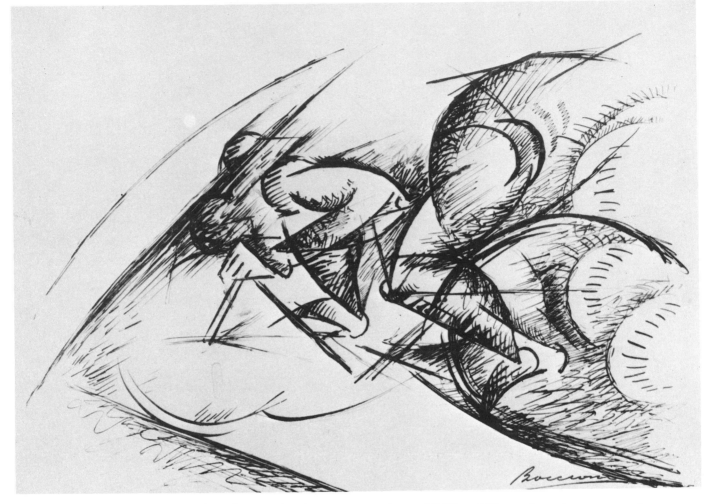

taught. The imaginative person retains a childlike ability to invent new ways of using even the most familiar material. Given a piece of chalk he might use the end, sometimes sharp, sometimes blunt, or the side, twisting it so that it alternately makes soft smears and sharp edges. He might rotate it on the paper, crumble it and then smear the crumbs to create granular and blotchy effects. Or rub the chalk with smooth cloth, with a heavily textured material, with corduroy to create striped textures. He might experiment with using the chalk on different types of paper, with various erasers, or with placing bold-textured materials under his paper so that the drawing assumes some of the textural pattern of the underlying material. Such a person will be equally imaginative about inventing situations in which he can utilize these effects for expressive purposes.

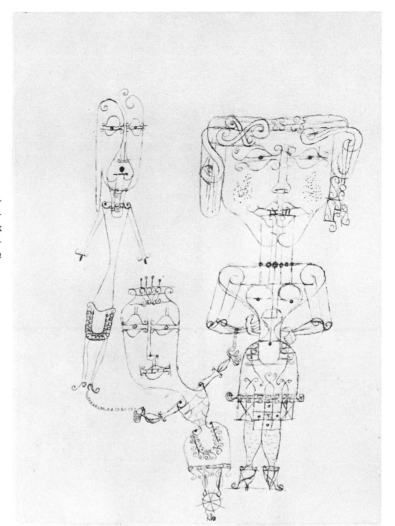

FIGURE 18–17

Paul Klee (1879–1940; Swiss-German). "Costumed Puppets." Ink, board mount, 9½" x 6¾". *The Solomon R. Guggenheim Museum Collection* (Photo: Robert E. Mates).

"The Performer" (Figure 18–19) is a tribute to the imagination with which Richard Oelze first discovered and then utilized the particular qualities displayed by white crayon on black paper. White crayon is not sufficiently opaque to cover the black paper thoroughly and so creates a gray of granular unsubstantial texture. This mysterious, foggy gray has been exploited most effectively here in conjunction with strangely disturbing forms to create an effect of miasma. The swirling textures curl like foggy wraiths and a mysterious dreamlike impression results.

A tool can also stimulate imaginative activity. The interesting texture with its suggestion of three-dimensional form created when ink is drawn across a smooth paper with a palette knife has been brilliantly explored in "Head" by Mac Zimmerman (Figure 17–15). Exploration led to discovery and discovery to imaginative projection.

Two more illustrations must suffice to round out our discussion. We have not as yet touched on humor, one of the most enjoyable manifestations of

FIGURE 18–18

Wassily Kandinsky
(1866–1944; Russian-German).
Untitled. Ink, 9″ x 8¼″.
Feigen/Palmer Gallery, Inc.,
Los Angeles, California.

imagination. Thomas Rowlandson has left us a delightful record of an eighteenth-century scene, "In the Garden of the Tuileries" (Figure 18–20). Rowlandson's drawings provided a good-humored satire upon the fashions and foibles of his day. He was able to establish a strong sense of character in each of his charming figures, no matter how sketchily they are indicated. The prosaic world took on an unexpected humor and color through the power of his insight, which by zestful exaggerations of gesture, feature, and anatomical form parodies the modes and manners of the world of fashion. This power to see and laugh at the ludicrous aspects of man's ambitions and pretensions makes humor one of the aspects of imagination that enables man to tolerate himself.

It might be interesting to end this discussion with a drawing which at first glance might seem to lack the magic ingredient. The drawings by Brueghel, Dali, or Klee are obviously imaginative creations. But "Reflections" by Charles Sheeler (Figure 18–21) at first glance reveals little imagination on the part of its creator. Let us examine it more closely. Certainly there is no fantasy evident nor does sentiment, humor, or the playful doodling with materials distinguish the drawing. Yet distinction it has, and the distinction is not inherent in the subject but rather in the artist's vision. The wooden buildings, the catwalk across the pond, the tall smokestacks and the pond itself with its reflections were in reality probably quite nondescript, neither picturesquely shabby nor a model of systematic arrangement. Many of Sheeler's works reveal that he viewed the industrial world with optimism as evidence of man's productive control over the disorder of nature. This optimistic belief in system and order represents an essentially "classic" attitude as opposed to the "romantic" delight in the heightened drama and emotional intensity that flow from conflict and disorder. Regularity, precision, clarity, and order become cardinal virtues in such a value system and as Sheeler recorded the scene before him, his belief in these virtues idealized the simple forms of the New England industrial scene into his own stylistic idiom. The dominantly vertical and horizontal composition, essentially rectangular in its basic pattern, the striking simplifications of value, the elimination of all untidy irregularites of surface, project an atmosphere of serenity almost at variance with the prosaic subject matter. Even the medium of wash, ordinarily used for loose painterly effects, is here applied in regular, small

FIGURE 18–19

Richard Oelze (1900–   ; German).
"The Performer." White crayon on black paper 19⅜" x 25½".
Collection, The Museum of Modern Art, New York
(Gertrud A. Mellon Fund). Photo: Sunami.

FIGURE 18-20

Thomas Rowlandson (1756-1827; English).
"In the Garden of the Tuileries."
Pen and watercolor, 10¾" x 15¾".
Henry E. Huntington Library and Art Gallery, San Marino, California.

strokes to produce a texture of almost mechanical regularity. Sheeler's imagination fused an abstractionist's love of geometric form, a realist's pleasure in the everyday world and a classicist's taste for order and discipline into a single work of art. The balance between these elements is so subtle that one is almost unaware of the role played by the artist in creating the work. What at first glance appears to be the product of eye and hand, is, as is every work of art, in the final analysis of product of the capacity to think and feel: imagination transmutes the dross level of daily life into the precious realm of art.

Summary

Imagination is the element through which works of art achieve their power. Four aspects of imaginative activity can be identified; the first depends upon empathy, the ability to identify with a subject; the second conceives of objects, combinations of, and relationships between objects that do not exist in the external world. The third and fourth kinds of imaginative activity involve the ability to generalize or particularize. In most works of art all of these aspects of imagination are present.

In recent years there has been much concern with the creative process and creativity depends upon imagination. There are four rather clearly defined steps in the creative act: first, the initial stimulus or impulse to action; second the period of exploration and gestation, which though initiated on a conscious level tends to develop subconsciously. Third, there is a period of seemingly spontaneous outpouring and, fourth and last, a consciously critical shaping and refining of the product. The habit of being imaginative and creative is established by activity, and imaginative potential atrophies if it is not used.

Imaginative empathy can be partly described as seeing beneath the surface of familiar experience to reveal new perceptions. For example, in a portrait the artist achieves this by providing the viewer with new insights as to the special character of the sitter's head. This can be achieved by various devices, posing the model to stress the characterizing features, emphasizing or eliminating detail, or using various levels of sophistication or naïvete in the handling of the art elements and the drawing media for their expressive effects.

Fantasy provides the most familiar form of imaginative creation. Fantasy frequently draws on the subconscious, dream-states, and memory for its irrational and unexpected combinations of objects. The Surrealists explored many modes of expression to discover fresh aspects of imaginative expression. Imagination in also involved in creating the generalized image which draws on the elements common to a category of objects and it is also present in the particularized image which differentiates sharply between similar objects. The monumental heroic image is an example of the former, the caricature of the latter. Humor is also a form of imaginative expression.

Imagination in the hands of a master like Paul Klee lifts the use of the art elements and the various drawing media to unique and original expressive effects. Imagination transmutes mundane experience into works of art.

FIGURE 18–21

Charles Sheeler (1883–1965; American). "Reflection."
Black wash, 13¾" x 16⅞". *The Currier Gallery of Art, Manchester, New Hampshire.*

A SELECTED BIBLIOGRAPHY

The bibliography presented here has been selected to provide a broad and representative introduction to the literature on drawing. Because of the nonspecialized audience for whom this book has been planned, the references have been confined to publications in English. The books listed below are grouped in three categories: (1) Books which concentrate on presenting fine quality, selected reproductions representing various collections, schools, periods, or countries; (2) a limited number of books have been listed on individual artists, determined by the importance of the master or the excellence of the reproductions, and (3) books covering technical aspects of drawing on a more analytical level than the average how-to-do-it book.

For a very complete collection of references on drawing, the reader is referred to the bibliography at the end of the article on Drawing, pages 500, 501 and 502, Vol. IV, *Encyclopedia of World Art*.

COLLECTIONS, COUNTRIES, PERIODS, AND SCHOOLS

ADHEMAR, J., *French Drawings of the XVI Century*. New York: Vanguard Press, 1955

AMES, W., *Italian Drawings*. New York: Shorewood Publishers, Inc., 1963

BENESCH, OTTO, *Venetian Drawings of the Eighteenth Century in America*. New York: H. Bittner and Company, 1947

BERGER, K., *French Drawings of the Nineteenth Century*. New York: Harper & Row, Publishers, 1950

BLUNT, ANTHONY, *The French Drawings at Windsor Castle*. London: Phaidon Press, 1945

BLUNT, A. AND COOKE, A., *Roman Drawings at Windsor Castle*. London: Phaidon Press, 1960

BLUNT, A. AND CROFT-MURRAY E. *Venetian Drawings at Windsor Castle*. London: Phaidon Press, 1957

BRADSHAW, P., *The Magic of Line*. New York: Studio Publications, The Viking Press, Inc., 1949

BROWN, P., *Indian Painting under the Mughals*. Oxford: Clarendon Press, 1924

BROWN, P., *Indian Painting*. Calcutta and London: Oxford University Press, 1927

COHN, W., *Chinese Painting*. New York: Oxford University Press, 1948

COOMARASWAMY, A. K., *Indian Drawings*. London: Royal Indian Society, 1912

D'ALBANELLA, *Venetian Drawings, XIV–XVII Centuries*. New York: The Hyperion Press, 1949

DE TOLNAY, C., *History and Technique of Old Master Drawings, a Handbook*. New York: H. Bittner & Co., 1943

DODGSON, CAMPBELL, *Modern Drawings*. London: Studio 1933

DODWELL, C. R., *The Canterbury School of Illumination*. Oxford: Oxford University, 1954

DROBNA, ZOROSLAVA, *Gothic Drawing*. Translated by Jean Layton. Prague: Artia, 195?

DUVAL, P., *Canadian Drawings and Prints*. Toronto: Burns and MacEachern, 1952

EDE, H. S., *Florentine Drawings of the Quattrocento*. London: E. Benn, Ltd., 1926

GIEDION, S., *The Eternal Present, Vol. I: The Beginnings of Art*. Bollingen Series XXXV.6.1. Pantheon Books. New York: Random House, Inc., 1962

HAVERKAMP-BEGEMANN, E., *Drawings from the Clark Institute*, 2 vols. New Haven, Conn.: Yale University Press, 1964.

HOLME, BRYAN, ed., *Master Drawings*. London: Studio, 1943

HOLMES, CHARLES, *Modern Pen Drawings: European and American*. New York: Studio Publications, The Viking Press, Inc., 1921

HUBBARD, E. H., *Some Victorian Draughtsmen*. Cambridge: Macmillan (Toronto), 1944

HUYGHE, RENE, *French Drawings of the Nineteenth Century*. New York: The Vanguard Press, Inc., 1956

ICHITARO, K., *Japanese Genre Painting*. Rutland, Vermont: Charles E. Tuttle, Co., 1961

KURZ, O., *Bolognese Drawings at Windsor Castle*. London: Phaidon Press, 1955

LECLERK, A., *Flemish Drawings, XV–XVI Centuries*. New York: The Hyperion Press, 1949

LEE, S. E., *A History of Far Eastern Art*. Englewood Cliffs, N. J., and New York, Prentice-Hall, Inc., and Harry N. Abrams, Inc., 1965

LOZOWICK, LOUIS, *A Treasury of Drawings*. New York: Lear Publishers, 1948

MARTIN, F. R., *Miniature Painting and Painters of Persia, India and Turkey*, 2 vols. London: Bernard Quaritch, 1912

Mellaart, J. H. J., *Dutch Drawings of the Seventeenth Century*. London: E. Benn, Ltd., 1926

Metropolitan Museum of Art, *European Drawings from the Collection of the Metropolitan Museum of Art*. New York: Metropolitan Museum of Art, 1943

Mongan, Agnes, *100 Master Drawings*. Cambridge, Mass.: Harvard University Press, 1949

Mongan, Agnes, and Sachs, Paul J., *Drawings in the Fogg Museum of Art*. Cambridge, Mass.: Harvard University Press, 1946

Moskowitz, I., ed., *Great Drawings of All Time*, 4 vols. New York: Sherwood Publishers, Inc., 1962

Muchall-Viebrook, T. W., *Flemish Drawings of the Seventeenth Century*. London: E. Benn, Ltd., 1926

Murrell, W., *A History of American Graphic Humor*, 2 vols. New York: Whitney Museum of American Art, 1933

Museum of Modern Art, Junior Council, *Recent Drawings, U. S. A.* New York: Museum of Modern Art, 1956

Oppe, A. E., *English Drawings at Windsor Castle*. London: Phaidon Press, 1950

Parker, K. T., *Drawings of the Early German Schools*. London: Ernest Benn, Ltd., 1926

Parker, K. T., *North Italian Drawings of the Quattrocento*. London: E. Benn, Ltd., 1927

Pataky, D., *Hungarian Drawings and Watercolors*. Budapest: Corvina, 1961

Pope, Anne Marie, *German Drawings*. Washington, D.C.: Smithsonian Institution, 1955–56

Popham, A. E., *Drawings of the Early Flemish School*. London: E. Benn, Ltd., 1926

Popham, A. E., and Wilde, J., *Italian Drawings of the XV and XVI Centuries at Windsor Castle*. London: Phaidon Press, 1949

Popham, A. E., and Pouncey, P., *Italian Drawings in the Department of Prints and Drawings in the British Museum*, 2 vols. London: The British Museum, 1950

Puyvelde, Leo van, *Flemish Drawings at Windsor Castle*. New York: Oxford University Press, 1942

Reitlinger, H. C., *Old Master Drawings*. New York: Moffat, Yard & Co., 1923

Reynolds, G., *Nineteenth Century Drawings*. London: Pleiades Books, 1949

———, *Twentieth Century Drawings*. London: Pleiades Books. 1946

Rosenberg, J., *Great Draughtsmen*. Cambridge, Mass.: Harvard University Press, 1959

Rowley, G., *Chinese Painting*. Princeton, N. J.: Princeton University Press, 1947

Sachs, Paul J., *Modern Prints and Drawings*. New York: Alfred A. Knopf, Inc., 1954

———, *The Pocket Book of Great Drawings*. New York: Washington Square Press, 1951

Scheller, R. W., *A Survey of Medieval Model Books*. Haarlem: De Erven F. Bohn N. V., 1963

Schneiwind, Carl, *Drawings from 12 Countries, 1945–1952*. Chicago: The Art Institute of Chicago, 1952

Schuler, J. E., *Great Drawings of the Masters*. New York: G. P. Putnam's Sons, 1963

Seckel, D., *Emakimono, the Art of the Japanese Painted Hand-Scroll*. New York: Pantheon Books, Inc., 1959

Sicre, J., *Spanish Drawings XV–XIX Centuries*. New York: The Hyperion Press, 1949

Slatkin, C. E. and Shoolman, R., *A Treasury of American Drawings*. New York: Oxford University Press, 1947

Sutton, D., *French Drawings of the Eighteenth Century*. London: Pleiades Books, 1949

Tietze, H., *European Master Drawings in the United States*. Toronto: Clarke, Irwin, 1947

———, and Tietze-Conrat, E., *The Drawings of the Venetian Painters*. New York: Augustin, 1944

Toney, Anthony, *150 Masterpieces of Drawing*. New York: Dover Publications, Inc., 1963

Ueberwasser, Walter, *Drawings by European Masters from the Albertina*. New York: Iris Books, Oxford University Press, 1948

University of Minnesota Gallery, *The Nineteenth Century: One Hundred Twenty-five Master Drawings*. Minneapolis: University of Minnesota, 1962

Van Schaak, E., *Master Drawings in Private Collections*. New York: Lambert-Spector, Inc., 1962

Wheeler, Monroe and Rewald, John, *Modern Drawings*. New York: The Museum of Modern Art and Simon and Schuster, Inc., 1947

Wormald, F., *English Drawings of the Tenth and Eleventh Centuries*. London: Faber & Faber, 1952

BERGER, K., *Gericault, Drawings and Watercolors*. New York: H. Bittner & Co., 1946

BENESCH, O., *Rembrandt, Selected Drawings*. New York: Oxford University Press, 1947

BENESCH, O., *The Drawings of Rembrandt*, 6 vols. London: The Phaidon Press, Ltd., 1954–57

BLUNT, A., *The Art of William Blake*. New York: Columbia University Press, 1959

BOWIE, T., *The Drawings of Hokusai*. Bloomington, Ind.: Indiana University Press, 1964

CLARK, K., *Leonardo Drawings at Windsor Palace*, 2 vols. New York: The Macmillan Company, 1935

CORDIER, DANIEL, *The Drawings of Jean Dubuffet*. New York: George Braziller, Inc., 1960

EITNER, L., *Gericault, an Album of Drawings in the Art Institute of Chicago*. Chicago: University of Chicago Press, 1960

FRIEDLAENDER, W., *The Drawings of Nicolas Poussin*, 4 vols. London: The Warburg Institute, 1949

GROHMANN, W., *The Drawings of Paul Klee*. New York: Curt Valentin, 1944

GEORGE GROSZ, *Drawings*. New York: H. Bittner and Co., 1944

HELD, J. S., *Rubens: Selected Drawings*, 2 vols. London: Phaidon Press, 1959

KLEE, P., *Pedagogical Sketchbook*. New York: Neirendorf Gallery, 1944

MACFALL, H., *Aubrey Beardsley*. New York: Simon and Schuster, Inc., 1927

MAISON, K., *Daumier Drawings*. New York: Sagamore Press, 1960

MIDDELDORF, U., *Raphael's Drawings*. New York: H. Bittner and Co., 1945

MUNZ, L., *Bruegel, the Drawings*. London: Phaidon Press, 1961

OPPE, A., *The Drawings of William Hogarth*. New York: Oxford University Press, 1948

PARKER, K. T., *The Drawings of Holbein at Windsor Castle*. London: Phaidon Press, 1945

PARKER, K. T., *Canaletto Drawings at Windsor Castle*. London: Phaidon Press, 1948

POPE-HENNESSY, J., *Domenichino Drawings at Windsor Castle*. London: Phaidon Press, 1948

POPHAM, A. E., *Selected Drawings from Windsor Castle, Raphael and Michelangelo*. London: Phaidon Press, 1954

REARICK, J., *The Drawings of Pontormo*, 2 vols. Cambridge, Mass.: Harvard University Press, 1964

REWALD, J., ed., *Renoir's Drawings*. New York: H. Bittner, 1946

RICHARDSON, J., *Manet: Paintings and Drawings*. London: 1958

SELIGMAN, GERMAIN, *The Drawings of Georges Seurat*. New York: Curt Valentin, 1947?

SHAW, J. B., *The Drawings of Francesco Guardi*. Boston: Boston Book, 1955.

THOMAS, H., *The Drawings of Piranesi*. London: Faber & Faber, 1942

VON HADELYN, D. B., *The Drawings of Tiepolo*, 2 vols. New York: Harcourt Brace & World, Inc., 1929

WALKER, R. A., (collected and edited by), *The Best of Beardsley*. London: The Bodley Head Ltd., 1948

WITTKOWER, R., *Carracci Drawings at Windsor Castle*. London: Phaidon Press, 1952

YALE UNIVERSITY PRESS, *The Drawings of Edwin Dickinson*, New Haven, Conn.: Yale University Press, 1963

TECHNICAL ASPECTS OF DRAWING

ALBERT, C. AND SECKLER, D., *Figure Drawing Comes to Life*. New York: Reinhold Publishing Corp., 1957

BARCSAY, J., *Anatomy for the Artist*. Budapest: Corvina, 1955

BRIDGMAN, GEORGE, *Life Drawing*. New York: Sterling Publishing Co., Inc., 1961

FRANK, ARTHUR J., *Drawing for Everyone*. New York: A. S. Barnes and Co., Inc., 1962

GUPTIL, A., *Pencil Drawing Step by Step*. New York: Reinhold Publishing Corp., 1949

HALE, ROBERT BEVERLY, *Drawing Lessons from the Great Masters*. New York: Watson-Guptil, Pubns, Inc., 1964

HAVINDEN, A., *Line Drawing for Reproduction*. New York: Studio Publications, The Viking Press, Inc., 1941

HERBERTS, K., *The Complete Book of Artists' Techniques*. New York: Frederick A. Praeger, Inc., 1958

LAWSON, P., *Practical Perspective Drawing.* New York: McGraw-Hill Book Company, 1943

MARSH, REGINALD, *Anatomy for Artists.* New York: American Artists Group, 1945

MAYER, R., *The Artist's Handbook of Materials and Techniques,* Rev. Ed. New York: The Viking Press, Inc., 1957

NICOLAIDES, KIMON, *The Natural Way to Draw.* Boston: Houghton Mifflin Company, 1941

NORLING, E., *Perspective Made Easy.* New York: The Macmillan Company, 1946

PECK, S. R., *Atlas of Human Anatomy for the Artist.* New York: Oxford University Press, 1951

PITZ, H., *Pen, Brush and Ink.* New York: Watson-Guptil Pubns, Inc., 1949

POPE, ARTHUR, *The Language of Drawing and Painting.* Cambridge, Mass.: Harvard University Press, 1921, 1931, 1949

WATROUS, JAMES, *The Craft of Old Master Drawings.* Madison, Wisc.: The University of Wisconsin Press, 1957

WATSON, ERNEST W., *How to Use Creative Perspective.* New York: Reinhold Publishing Co., 1955

INDEX

Numbers in italic type denote pages on which illustrations appear.
The letter c following a number indicates a color plate on the facing page.

"Figures of Drawers, Composition of," 20, 262, 432, 437
"First Presbyterian Church, Stamford, Connecticut" (Ferriss), 16, 17; (Harrison and Abramovitz), 18
"Five Grotesque Heads," 63, 65, 67
Fixatifs, 365, 368–369
Flemish drawing, Baroque, 126–136, 148; Renaissance, 100–110, 125, 126; Rococo, 136
"Flight into Egypt, The," 81, 86, 87, 403
Flit-guns, experimentation with, 419
"Floor Plan, First Presbyterian Church, Stamford, Connecticut," 18, 22, 288
Flowing line, 309
Fluid media, 395–420
Forain, Jean Louis, 163; "Riot and Sketch of a Man," 12, 163
"Forest of Compèigne, Study in," 166, 168
Form, 24, 26–27, 314–321; chiaroscuro and, 321–322, 337; pattern and, 326–327, 337; schematic, 322–324, 337; space and, 26–27, 315–316; three-dimensional, 26–27, 314–315, 321–322
Foujita, Tsugouharu, "Mexican General," 282, 284, 415
"Four Studies of Italian Actors, 137, 142, 209c
Fragmented line, 304–305
France, drawing in, Baroque, 136–140, 148–149; expressionism, 225–226, 229–230, 245, 249, 260, 307; medieval book illumination, 47–50; mid-nineteenth-century realism, 161–165, 176–177, 197; Paleolithic cave painting, 33–35, 34, 50; Renaissance, 136–140; Rococo, 140–143, 150; Romanticism, 157–159, 176; surrealism, 225–226, 229, 245, 262–266, 281, 284, 432–433, 447
"Frederick Ashton, Portrait of," 262, 265, 374, 378–379
French Revolution, 140, 151
Freud, Sigmund, 262
Friedrich, Caspar David, 159, 161; "Rock Quarry," 161, 373, 377
"Fright," 163, 165
"Fritzi, 1919," 250, 251, 295, 297
Futurism, 226
Gaddi, Taddeo, "Visitation, The," 53, 53, 55
Gainsborough, Thomas, 146
Gandolfo, Gaetano, "Figures and Animals in Deep Architectural View," 316, 317
Gatti, Bernardino, "Study of an Apostle Standing," 82, 416
Gauguin, Paul, 188, 193; "Standing Tahitian Nude," 192, 193
"Genealogical Tree of Jesus, The," 108, 113
Generalization, 226, 434–436, 447
"Gentleman and a Courtesan," 212, 213
"Gentleman Rider, A," 183, 301–302, 376, 380
Geometric patterning, 277, 280
George IV, 146
"George Moore, Portrait of," 180, 402, 406
"Georges Limbour, Portrait of," 256, 429–430, 435
Géricault, Théodore, 157, 159; "Studies of a Cat," 155, 377, 380; Study for "The Bull Market," 15, 156, 157
Germany, drawing in, abstraction, 239, 245; expressionism, 226, 245, 249, 260; Renaissance, 110–118, 125; Romanticism, 159–161, 176
Gerome, Jean-Leon, "Two Soldiers Playing Checkers," 323–324, 327

Giorgione, 75; "Landscape," 72, 73
Giotto, 51–52, 55
"Giovanni da Bologna, Portrait of," 429, 431
Gleizes, Albert, "Port," 380, 381
Golden, Michael, "Orthogenic Device," 19, 20
"Golden Age, The," Study for, 152, 155
Golden Ages, 103
Goltzius, Hendrick, "Portrait of Giovanni da Bologna," 429, 431
Gombrich, E. H., 6
Gorky, Arshile, Study for "The Plough and the Song," 240–241, 242, 299
Gothic style, 47, 100, 103, 204; International, 55
Göttigen Manuscript, "Apostles Sitting in Stocks," 47, 317, 320
Gouache, 411, 416
Goya, Francisco, 148, 150, 251, 265–266, 322; "Easy Victory," 148, 149; "Sainted Culottes," 148, 336, 337
Graphic expression, 27–29
Graphic satire, 161–163, 251, 284
Graphite pencils, 375–376, 379, 393
"Great Piece of Turf, The," 111, 113, 118, 208c
Greco, El, 148, 246
Gris, Juan, 226, 233; "Seated Harlequin," 237, 288, 289, 380
Gropper, William, "Farmer's Revolt," 266, 268, 268, 271, 353, 357
Grosz, George, 251, 256, 260, 268, 311; "Hiker, The," 399, 401; "Survivor, The," 354, 357; "Workmen and Cripple," 255, 311, 401
"Group of Vultures Waiting for the Storm to 'Blow Over'—'Let Us Prey'," 267
"Groupe de Danseuses Vues en Buste," 183, 367, 369
Guardi, Francesco, 79, 86, 96, 97; "Venetian Scene," 95, 96; "Visit, The," 96, 96–97
Guatemala, 217–218
Guercino, Giovanni, 86, 97; "Landscape," 81, 83; "Mars and Cupid," 84, 86, 88
"Guernica," Composition Study for, 233, 235
Haftmann, Werner, 251
"Hagar and Ishmael in the Wilderness," 90, 91, 93, 145c
Hals, Franz, 79, 121
"Hands and Drapery, Study of," 138, 142
Hanson, Hardy, "Landscape of the Ancients," 323, 326, 343
Haptics, 27, 28
Harrison and Abramovitz, "First Presbyterian Church, Stamford, Connecticut," 18; "Floor Plan, First Presbyterian Church, Stamford, Connecticut," 18, 22, 288
Hartung, Hans, "D. 42.2.," 25, 26, 27, 239–240, 319
"Head" (Picasso), 230, 232, 302
"Head" (Weber), 429, 433
"Head" (Zimmerman), 415, 419, 443
"Head of a Boy" (Botticelli), 59, 60
"Head of a Man" (Clouet), 133, 134
"Head of a Man" (Legros), 338, 341
"Head of St. Andrew," 429, 430
"Head of a Satyr," 69, 71, 403
"Head of a Woman" (Kollwitz), 251, 338, 339, 341
"Head of a Woman" (Prud'hon), 371, 372, 393
"Heads, Six Studies of" (Watteau), 135, 142
Hellenistic sculpture, 155

Ribera, Jusepe de, 148
Rigaud, Hyacinthe, 142; "Study of Hands and Drapery," *138, 142*
"Riot and Sketch of a Man," *12, 163*
"Ritual," *238, 239,* 353; Detail of, *353, 353*
Ritual Petroglyphs, Anasazi Culture, *36, 37*
"River Scene with Cows," *122, 124*
Rivera, Diego, 273; "Mother and Child," *273,* 309, *404, 407*
Riza-i'Abbasi, "Youth Kneeling and Holding Out a Wine Cup, A," 212–213, *214*
Robert, Hubert, 137, 140
"Robin, Portrait of Docteur," *375, 379*
Rock paintings, African, *37,* 219, 326; Anasazi Culture, *36, 37;* Australian—aboriginal, 222
"Rock Quarry," *161, 373, 377*
"Rocky Landscape, Death Valley," *338, 342*
"Rocky Mountain Landscape, A," *120, 124*
Rococo drawing, 95, 153; Flemish, 136; French, 140–143, 150
Rodin, August, "Nude," *410, 414*
Rogier van der Weyden, *104,* 105, 108; "Devils in Hell," *104, 104, 378*
Roman Empire, fall of, 44, 50
"Roman Ruins," *123, 356, 358–359*
Romanticism, 146, 153; in England, 159, 176; in France, 157–159, 176; in Germany, 159–161, 176
Rossetti, Dante Gabriel, 159; "Portrait of Elizabeth Sidall," *159, 397*
Rousseau, Théodore, 166; "Hunt, The," *166, 170*
Rowlandson, Thomas, 144, 146, 150; "At a Cottage Door," *141,* 144, *240c;* "In the Tuilleries," 144, *444, 446*
Rubens, Peter Paul, 118, 119, 123, 128, 131, 132, 140–142, 312, 322, 384; "Abraham and Melchisedeck," *127,* 128; "Raising of the Cross, The," Study of the Figure of Christ for, *131,* 298, 302; "Study of a Bullock," *128, 132*
Runge, Phillip Otto; "Die Lichtlile mit Schwebenden Genein," 159, *160, 400*
"Rural Landscape with Milkmaid," 123, *131, 132,* 136
Rysselberghe, Théophile van, "Maria van der Velde at the Piano," 346–348, *347*
"Sacrifice, Drawing for," 230, *231, 368*
"St. Barbara," *102,* 103, *177c*
"St. Bernard before Christ Crucified," *13,* 15, 81, 86
"Sainted Culottes," 148, *336, 337*
"Sawtelle Series," *241, 243*
"Scene in an Inn," *116, 121*
"Scene in a Tavern," *117, 121*
Schematic form, 322–324, 337
Scratchboard, *391, 393*
Sculpture, African, 219; Greek, 153, 155; Hellenistic, 155; Roman, 153
"Seated Boy with Straw Hat," *195, 346, 391, 394*
"Seated Clown," 284, *305, 306*
"Seated Figure" (Bischoff), 281, *353, 368, 370*
"Seated Figure" (Picasso), *230, 294, 299*
"Seated Harlequin," *237, 288, 289, 380*
"Seated Woman" (Bison), *89, 90*
"Self-Portrait" (Courbet), 171, *172, 331*
"Self-Portrait" (Dolci), *84, 84*
Sepia, 412
Sesshu, School of, Panel of a Six-fold Screen, 210,

406, 409–410
Seurat, Georges, 188, 193, 195, 197; "Cafe Concert, The," *194,* 195, 346; "Seated Boy with Straw Hat," *195, 346, 391, 394*
Shahn, Ben, 268, 284; "Dr. J. Robert Oppenheimer," 256, *268, 269, 271*
Sheeler, Charles, 276, 277, 280, 284, 415, 444–445, 447; "Feline Felicity," 7–8, *7,* 26, 280, 387, *390;* "Reflection," 280, *444–445, 448*
Signorelli, Luca, 56, 59, 63, 70; "Two Figures," 56, 58–59, *58*
Silverpoint, 373, 377–379, 393, 420
Social criticism, contemporary realism and, 266, 268, 271, 273, 284; Expressionist, 251–252, 256, 260
"Source, La," *154,* 155, *241c*
South Sea Island primitive cultures, 193, 215, 219–222, 224
Space, 24; definition of, 315, 336; form and, 26–27, 315–316; perspective and, 315–319; pictorial, 319; tiered, 316–317, 319, 337
Spanish drawing, 79, 146–150; cave paintings, 33–35, 50; cubism, 226, 230, 232–235, 239; *see also* Picasso
Spontaneous line, 293
"Standing Figure" (Thiebaud), *279, 281, 284*
"Standing Nude" (Lachaise), *292, 297, 299*
"Standing Tahitian Nude," *192, 193*
Starks, Chloe Lesley, "Prionatus Ruscarius," 343, *344, 344, 402–403*
Stevenson, Harold, 436; Untitled, *441*
"Street in Quebec," *237, 239, 323, 325*
"Stryge, Le," *163, 323, 325*
"Study" (Caravaggio), *77,* 79, *334, 413*
Stylization, 225
"Sultan on Horseback, The," *159, 397, 398*
Sumi, 395, 405, 411
Sung Dynasty, 205
Surrealism, 225–226, 229, 245, 262–266, 281, 284, 432–433, 447
"Survivor, The," *354, 357*
Swabian Master, "Genealogical Tree of Jesus, The," *108, 113*
Symbolic drawing, 22–24; African, 219, 224; Neolithic, 36, 50; Paleolithic, 33–35; Pre-Columbian-American, 215–216, 224; South Sea Island, 219–221, 224
T'ang Dynasty, 204, 205
Tanguy, Yves, 265; Untitled, *265, 295, 299*
Tchelitchew, Pavel, 161, 265; "Portrait of Frederick Ashton," 262, *265, 374, 378–379*
Tempera, 406, 411, 416
"Temptation of St. Anthony," *430–431, 436*
Testa, Pietro, "Compositional Study," *80,* 81, 83; Detail of "Compositional Study," *400, 403*
Texture, 24, 26, 338–360; determinants of, 338, 340–341, 360; disciplined, *344–346,* 360; freely rendered, 347–348; as gesture of rendering, 351–352, 360; media and, 340–341, 344, 352–360; perception of multiple units as, 342–343, 360; uniform, 346, 360
Thiebaud, Wayne, 281, 284; "Standing Figure," *279, 281, 284*
"Three Graces," Study for "The Wedding Feast of Cupid and Psyche," *70, 71–72*
"Tiber Above Rome, The," *140, 305c, 407, 413*
Tiepolo, Giovanni Battista, 79, 86, 89–93, 97, 322, 420; "Hagar and Ishmael in the Wilderness," *90,*